STRATEGIC FIXED-INCOME INVESTMENT

Thomas S. Y. Ho

DOW JONES-IRWIN
Homewood, Illinois 60430

© RICHARD D. IRWIN, INC., 1990

Dow Jones-Irwin is a trademark of Dow Jones & Company, Inc.

Project editor: Karen Murphy
Production manager: Ann Cassady
Compositor: Publication Services, Inc.
Typeface: 11/13 Times Roman
Printer: R. R. Donnelley & Sons Company

Library of Congress Cataloging-in-Publication Data

Ho, Thomas S. Y.
    Strategic fixed income investment / Thomas S. Y. Ho.
      p.   cm.
    ISBN 1-55623-120-2
    1. Bonds—United States.   2. Government securities—United States.
  I. Title.
  HG4910.H58   1990
  332.63'23'0973—dc20   89–23387
                                       CIP

Printed in the United States of America
1 2 3 4 5 6 7 8 9 0 DO 6 5 4 3 2 1 0 9

PREFACE

This book is intended for both practitioners and researchers in the fixed-income profession. The purpose of the book is to provide a foundation of bond analytics and to show the applications of bond analytics to portfolio management.

Strategic Fixed-Income Investment grew from the course I have taught the last four years at the Stern School of Business, New York University. The course is a second-year MBA course devoted solely to fixed-income securities. The warm reception to the course and the lack of teaching material for an MBA class prompted this endeavor to transform my lecture notes into this book.

Most books on fixed income focus on describing the markets, instruments, bond strategies, and models. But I find the students' desire to learn about fixed-income securities goes beyond "What are bonds?" They want to gain a deeper understanding of the securities: How to analyze them; how to interpret the valuation of bonds; how to determine the validity of bond models and theories. The challenge for me in writing this book was to answer these questions in a coherent way.

The purpose of this book is to present a progressive discussion of the interrelationship between bond valuation models and their applications in the fixed-income securities industry. The beginning chapters recap fundamental valuation principles as they apply to a stream of future cash flow. In other words, this first part addresses the often-heard question from my students, "What is a bond?"

The next few chapters continue with the concepts introduced earlier, but extend into the formalization of models that represent the time value of a dollar in a quantifiable manner. These models, derived from the observed prices of various market securities, are then used for evaluating the fair value of new and existing issues. This part of the book has topics covering such things as the estimation of an implied spot curve, the development of risk measures such as duration and convexity, and the evolution of valuation models for fixed-income securities with embedded options or with different creditworthiness and liquidity characteristics.

This second part also entails the introduction of some recent developments. Specifically, we introduce such new concepts as

- the call-adjusted spot yield curve estimation procedure
- a constant mortality model for corporate issues

The presentation of all this material is goal directed. The goal is to enhance the practitioner's understanding of the usefulness and limitations of valuation models.

The last part of the book addresses how one applies valuation models in the real world. That is, once one has identified the elements of risk in an issue, how does one manage the risks? We suggest a process for ensuring the proper identification of the various risks and the thoughtful analysis that an investor should apply concerning the probabalistic nature of any risk exposure. These explanations, as well as the examples provided, draw upon such new concepts as

- implementing cross-sector analysis via modeling
- factorization
- key rate durations
- return attribution

I hope that these new ideas will further stimulate research in fixed-income securities, particularly in the area of applications of pricing models in portfolio management. I regret that I do not include the research results in mortgage-backed securities, high-yield bonds, and bonds on foreign currencies. They are omitted not because they are less important, but rather because there was a lack of time. I hope to publish discussions of these topics in the near future.

Thomas S. Y. Ho

ACKNOWLEDGMENTS

First, I want to thank my teachers at University of Pennsylvania: Eugenio Calabi, who taught me mathematics, and Erwin Friend, who taught me finance.

I also wish to thank many of my colleagues at New York University, who have given me invaluable intellectual stimulation. I thank Ronald Singer, who first coauthored with me in bond research, and Edwin Elton, Stephen Brown, Marti Gruber, Edward Block, Anthony Saunders, and Kose John, who have all helped me so much in my research over the years at New York University. I am particularly grateful to Hans Stoll, who at Vanderbilt University encouraged me to teach the fixed-income course the first time, and to Ingo Walter, who first let me teach the fixed-income course at New York University.

Thanks are also due to the following colleagues at Global Advanced Technology Corporation for helping me complete this book: William Allen, Arnold Chu, Scot Cooper, Darryl Dagen, and Rhoda Woo. Special thanks are reserved for the following four individuals: Mark Wainger, Allen Abrahamson, Susan Marek-Kasso, and Katherine McNally.

Mark has worked closely with me since the inception of this project. His relentless development of the appropriate software for integrating mathematical formulas and financial modeling applications has been unequaled. Allen's diligence in scrutinizing specific AR model applications and unearthing formula specification errors has enabled us to ensure consistent and verifiable results. In addition, Allen was the coauthor of Chapter 11 and was instrumental in the development of Chapter 15.

I cannot thank Susan enough. Susan, who is a member of the research staff, became my internal editor and thoroughly monitored all production details associated with this book. Her insightful advice and her numerous drafts of suggested paragraphs in various chapters led to the presentation of this material in a more digestible term for students just becoming familiar with construction of some of the book's numerical examples, but also worked with Allen on the development and testing of the material covered in Chapter 16.

Last, but not least, I wish to thank Katherine McNally. Her research and careful work in compiling my lecture notes helped me tremendously in getting the project going. I appreciated her patience and support in this early stage of the project.

Of course, all this work would not have been possible without the patience and support of my family during those uncountable hours spent on the book; I am indebted to my wife, Mabel Chan, and my daughter, Xian.

CONTENTS

PUBLISHER'S PAGE

Dow Jones-Irwin would like to express a special thanks to the graciously persistent Susan Marek-Kasso and the very able professionals at Publications Services, Inc.

CHAPTER 1

BOND ANALYSIS: AN INTEGRATIVE APPROACH

OVERVIEW

What is a fixed-income security? As the market for fixed-income securities becomes more complex, the answer to this question becomes increasingly broad in scope. Fixed-income securities once were considered strictly bonds. The word *bond* is used here in the context of the following broad, generic definition: a contractual obligation for the repayment of loaned funds. Historically, bonds could be defined by their repayment date and their stipulated, constant interest rate. Ignoring credit risk for the moment, this format provided investors with a series of predictable cash flows.

However, the definition of a fixed-income security has grown to include a variety of bond-related instruments that do not have a set stream of cash flows. As these instruments have become more varied, the use of the instruments in a portfolio and their pricing have become more complicated.

This chapter, as an introduction to the following chapters, will present an overview of fixed-income markets. Fixed-income instruments will be presented in the context of the following aspects:

- The markets in which they trade.
- The types of institutions that issue and trade them.
- How portfolio managers use the instruments.

Fixed-income securities are developed in diverse sectors and are traded primarily over the counter. There is no standardization among instruments. They vary as to coupon, maturity, credit risks, and refunding options to name just a few. This chapter will first discuss the influence of the three listed aspects and then introduce the basic principles governing the evaluation of fixed-income issues. The following chapters will expand on these principles.

Instruments

The markets in which fixed-income securities trade range from highly liquid (active) markets, in which standardization is greatest and pricing is subsequently easiest, to illiquid markets, in which only a few instruments are traded on an irregular basis and according to specific terms. Figure 1–1 highlights the four general categories of fixed-income markets.

Major Market

The U.S. major market, the backbone of the entire fixed-income market in this country, consists of four primary sectors:

- Treasuries (government securities)
- Corporates
- Mortgages
- Municipals

Treasuries are debt instruments that represent the borrowing of the federal government. Treasury securities are unique in that they are fully backed by the U.S. government and consequently have no credit risk. This market is the most active fixed-income market in the world, with over 2 trillion dollars outstanding. Treasury notes and bonds, which are treasury instruments with a maturity range greater than one year, are relatively simple. Basically, they pay coupons of a predetermined rate and have a stated principal, which is repaid at a specified maturity. Chapter 8 covers Treasury issues in detail.

Corporate issues are fixed-income securities issued by both public and private corporations. They have varying maturities, coupon rates, and provisions, and may be issued publicly or privately. These debt instruments are usually backed by the assets or earnings of the issuing corporations, and their default risk is therefore determined by the solvency of the issuer. The variation among corporate bonds necessitates analysis of these bonds on an individual basis. Chapter 12 discusses two types of corporate bonds: investment grade and high-yield (junk) bonds.

FIGURE 1–1
Structure of the Bond Market

Derivative	futures	options	asset-backed	STRIPS
International	yen	deutsche marks	euro	
Minor (less liquid markets)	GIC	private placements	convertibles	agencies
Major	treasuries	corporates	mortgages	municipal

Mortgages are the borrowings of real estate owners from commercial banks, savings and loans, or thrift institutions. Typically these loans are secured by the property purchased. Mortgages represent the largest fixed-income borrowings in the market, even larger than Treasury issues in amount outstanding. In contrast with the Treasury securities, however, mortgages themselves are not traded actively, partly because of the lack of standardization and unique variety of risk associated with these agreements. Mortgages are clearly different from Treasuries in several ways and, as such, have very different risk and return profiles.

Municipal bonds are issued by local (city and state) agencies for the purpose of raising funds for specific or ongoing projects. The dominant feature of these bonds is their tax-exempt status. Consequently, these bonds are attractive to high-marginal-tax-rate individuals. Similar to corporate bonds, municipal bonds are subject to credit (default) risk. The risk involved in purchasing municipal bonds depends on the riskiness of either the project or the agency that has backed the bonds. The call and sinking-fund provisions for municipal bonds differ from those of corporate bonds.

This book will not cover mortgages or municipal bonds. The contents will focus on the Treasury and corporate bond markets and the different types of options trading in these markets. Once one understands the characteristics of any instrument in these two markets, one will be able to grasp quickly the additional complexities inherent in the mortgage and municipal markets. The concepts and examples provided in this book can be extended for the analysis of mortgages and municipal bonds.

Minor Market

The second group of fixed-income securities consists of instruments such as private placements, government agency issues, guaranteed investment contracts (GICs), and convertible bonds. The instruments in this group are smaller in outstanding dollar value and are often traded in illiquid markets. Private placements represent direct lending from one corporation to another. Because they are directly negotiated agreements, private placements, in principle, have no market.

Private placements, agency issues, GICs, and convertible bonds can be considered a subset of the corporate bond market. They all embody a degree of credit risk and hence would not be classified with Treasuries as risk-free securities. Therefore, most of the information in

Chapter 12 can be applied in the evaluation of these securities. GICs, private placements, and agency issues will not appear as separate topics in this book. However, convertible bonds, which uniquely embody equity and fixed-income characteristics, are covered in Chapter 13.

International Market
In addition to the bonds mentioned above that originate in the domestic U.S. market, there is a spectrum of bonds issued in foreign markets that are often traded in the United States as well. Although the United States is by far the largest bond-trading arena in the world, with the most active and varied markets, other markets are experiencing considerable growth. Japan and Germany, respectively, are the second- and third-largest bond markets in the world. In addition, the Eurobond market is becoming a major international market. Each of these markets offers a range of bonds with varying degrees of liquidity.

These three market groups—the major, minor, and international—provide a foundation on which to build a framework for analyzing fixed-income securities. This framework can be used to develop a methodology for identifying similarities among instruments in order to assess relative values. Once the analytic methodology is constructed, it can be a useful tool for evaluating derivative products.

Derivative Products
The successors of basic bonds are derivative products. They can be described as falling into one of two groups: (1) instruments that are basically side bets among market participants on the underlying security's return and (2) instruments created under an asset securitization process.

Examples of instruments in the first group are interest rate futures and options. These instruments are essentially used by market participants to place bets on either the direction or magnitude of interest rate movements. The products in the second group, asset-backed securities, have returns directly related to the underlying instruments. These asset-backed securities differ from their predecessors in that their underlying assets would not normally be traded. For example, a Government National Mortgage Association (GNMA) pool consists of securities backed by mortgages. Individual mortgages are difficult to trade, but in the form of a GNMA pool they gain liqudity. Further, securities are created from these derivative securities. Notable are collateralized mortgage obligations (CMOs) created from the GNMA pools. The generational process of securitization can theoretically continue indefinitely. Derivative products are discussed in various chapters of this book.

Financial Institutions

The U.S. bond market is institutional. That is to say, the market is dominated by institutions that buy and sell. This is an important point because institutional trading involves professionals making decisions. Their analyses and strategies affect the instruments' prices and return behaviors. These statements are not intended to minimize the role of the retail, or the individual client, market; the retail component of the financial market is sizable. However, individuals generally invest through institutions, given the resources and size of the latter.

Financial institutions are often classified by practitioners as either sell-side or buy-side. More specifically, given the recent market trends, some institutions have divisions that can be categorized as handling either buy-side or sell-side transactions. However, for purposes of clarity, we will focus on the traditional usage of the terms sell-side and buy-side. Sell-side firms are brokerage houses or securities firms, which issue securities and trade them in secondary markets. The sales persons of these firms are in close contact with their clients to generate trades. Once a sale or purchase order is agreed upon, the sales person relates the order to the trading desks. The traders then take positions, buying and selling as principals. The sales group generates the order flow while the traders establish the market. Such activities are important to the other aspect of a sell-side firm. Active trading leads to better knowledge of the supply and demand for securities. This knowledge is essential for corporate finance activities such as underwriting and structuring mergers and acquisitions.

The investment bank is the quintessential sell-side firm. In addition to performing sales and trading services for corporate and individual customers, these banks serve as intermediaries in public and private stock sales. They often assume all risks (as underwriters) involved with the acquisition and subsequent sale of stock. Corporate finance divisions also serve as financial consultants to firms and facilitate mergers and acquisitions through stock issues or sales. Research departments of investment banks gather and analyze information pertaining to market mechanisms, prices, and trends. Customers of the investment firm are provided with summaries of the studies. In short, investment banks specialize in information regarding financial (stock and bond) markets.

Buy-side firms include banks, insurance companies, mutual funds, and pension funds, among others. These firms originate most of the order flow to the securities firms. As clients of sell-side firms, buy-side firms rely on the sell-side firms' knowledge of the market and ability to execute trades. Essentially, buy-side firms manage funds for themselves and their clients. They may engage in active asset/liability management by investing funds received in connection with contractual agreements to provide monetary payments (liabilities). Another function they serve is repackaging products purchased from sell-side firms and selling them, in turn, to their clients. One example of a repackaged product is a mutual fund. The advantage of the buy-side firm in fund management is the use of economies of scale in the purchase and sale of securities. Buy-side firms are large, relative even to many corporate clients. These firms have access to large pools of investable funds as well as knowledge of their clients' investment objectives. Like their sell-side counterparts, buy-side firms generate revenue by charging fees for their services.

In general, buy-side firms do not perform the same functions for clients as do sell-side firms, for two primary reasons: (1) they must adhere to government regulations that prohibit them from underwriting and issuing stock, and (2) their primary functions are as client-oriented savings or insurance intermediaries. In addition, unlike their sell-side counterparts, buy-side firms are highly diverse and can be broken down into individual industries.

Institutions that are commonly referred to as "banks" are commercial banks, savings and loans (S&Ls), mutual savings banks, and credit unions. Commercial banks accept deposits in the form of, demand deposit accounts (checking and savings accounts) and issue certificates of deposit (CDs), bonds, and stock. Since the liabilities of commercial banks represent a broad spectrum of maturities, so must their assets. Assets of commercial banks include short-term assets such as Treasury bills, medium-term assets such as installment loans (consumer car loans), and long-term assets including mortgages and long (30-year) government bonds. The liabilities of S&Ls are passbook savings accounts (which now resemble demand deposit accounts). Their assets are primarily residential mortgages. Some of the mismatch in longevity between assets and liabilities has been corrected by the offering of relatively short-term consumer loans and by the ability of S&Ls to sell their mortgages. Mutual savings banks, predominantly located in the northeastern United States, are owned mutually by depositers. Mutual savings banks have deposit liabilities and assets consisting primarily of mortgages on multiple family dwellings, as well as corporate bonds. Credit unions are "owned" (in the same sense as are mutual funds) by depositers who work for a certain company or live in a specific neighborhood or housing organization. The liabilities of credit unions are demand deposits, and the assets generally consist of consumer loans but also include government securities.

Insurance companies offer their clients, both corporate and individual, services ranging from health insurance plans to pension funds. Like banks, insurance companies serve as intermediaries between those clients with funds to invest or save and clients interested in borrowing. Clients save through insurance companies by purchasing insurance policies. For example, a customer may purchase a life insurance plan whose premiums remain level over his lifetime. Should the purchaser of this type of plan, called a "whole life policy," decide to cash in on the plan, he will be able to receive a prestated amount. In essence, the policy can be used as a savings account, assuming the client realizes a return on the amount paid in premiums. With the cash flow generated from such policies, insurance companies can invest in securities. In general, the companies will want to match their assets and liabilities in terms of cash flow. Since insurance companies primarily have long-term assets, they tend to invest in longer-term instruments.

Mutual funds are strictly managers (account keepers) of stockholder assets according to prespecified fund objectives. The actual assets are retained by an investment bank, which makes sales and purchases according to the instructions of fund managers.

The functions and products of these financial institutions provide the object of study for this text.

BOND STRATEGIES

Fixed-income securities, as distinct from equities, tend to have stipulated payments at specified dates. Since bonds and equities have different characteristics, they also have different investment applications. For example, the purchase of a 10-year default free zero-coupon bond could be used simply as a buy-and-hold investment that will provide a known return if held until maturity. However, if the bond is held for less than 10 years, the return on the bond would be uncertain. The uncertainty is attributable to the unknown future level of interest rates that will govern the bond's resale value. For coupon issues, in addition to the bond's resale value, there is also uncertainty relating to the amount of income earned from the reinvestment of coupon payments.

Horizon returns involving fixed-income instruments are directly affected by market interest rates. For instance, if the investment horizon (the period of time the investor plans to hold the security) is greater than the term to maturity, then the total return for the period will also be uncertain. Upon maturity, the bond principal would have to be reinvested at an uncertain market rate. In this case, the uncertainty of the total return for a period using bonds is similar to that of using stocks. The only case in which the total return will be certain is when the investor's horizon equals the bond's maturity and the bond is held to maturity. In this case, the investor is able, in purchasing the bond, to lock in a specific return.

Bonds can be passively or actively managed. The nature of the management strategy chosen is often related to the bonds' characteristics. There are two types of passive management. The first type involves holding an asset and forgetting about it. For example, an investor buys and holds bonds that generate a desired cash flow and return; there is no need for any further action. Another type of passive management technique is the buying and selling of bonds according to certain preset rules for replicating an index. A bond index is a hypothetical bond portfolio representing a cross section of a market sector. This portfolio is monitored on a regular basis and provides an objective return measure attributable to holding a diversified portfolio of the sector's bonds. Investment firms use this return as a benchmark for evaluating a portfolio manager's investment performance in a given market sector.

Active management, in contrast, seeks to exploit market (price) inefficiencies. Managers continuously attempt to sell overpriced bonds and buy underpriced bonds while satisfying some management objectives (e.g., risk minimization). In this sense, active management of bonds is similar to equity fund management that seeks a high return for a given level of risk exposure.

Although the objectives of active managers in both the equity and fixed-income markets may be the same, there are a couple of fundamental differences between the instruments, which limit the development of similar risk/return strategies. First, because bonds have a known maturity and cash flow, there are portfolio strategies that are more easily performed with bonds. For example, asset liability managers depend on the known cash flow patterns of bonds to structure portfolios whose funds can be used to meet liability payments. Second, the sources of risks for bonds are more well-defined. Bond funds can be constructed such that the only risk in holding a fund is interest rate risk. Since the risk exposure can be limited to a certain type, the theory of diversification that applies to stock management is not necessarily useful in bond portfolio management.

Bond investment strategies evolve in response to bond return uncertainty or inefficiency in the marketplace. Uncertainty refers specifically to the breadth of possible returns on bonds, also termed "return risk." Among the various bond strategies considered in this book, two—hedging and arbitrage—deal specifically with this return risk. The objective of hedging is to minimize return risk for a portfolio of bonds. Hedging may involve using futures and options on bonds to maximize return and minimize loss in light of changes in interest rates. Arbitrage is a profit-maximization strategy that exists due to the inefficiencies in the bond market. As the liquidity of the bond market varies, so does the availability of accurate price information on bonds. Bonds that trade in less liquid markets provide more opportunities for large arbitrage profits. In less liquid markets, the prices of the bonds may significantly differ from a calculated value. Arbitrage takes place as a result of the price uncertainty.

SECURITIZATION AND NEW PRODUCT DEVELOPMENT

Securitization, which has been mentioned briefly in this chapter is the process by which a diverse body of agreements (i.e., loans) is transformed into a standardized instrument. GNMA pools were used above as an example of securitization. However, any agreement can be securitized as long as it is based on an underlying asset. As implied above, the importance of securitization is that it guarantees the continued growth of the bond market.

The need for securitization arises when a financial institution (e.g., a bank) seeks to raise cash for future loans. There are a variety of ways for the bank to obtain cash, including the purchase of overnight federal funds. Banks can also sell their current loans individually or in part (participations) to other institutions. The most recent and efficient means of selling loans is through securitization. Loans are securitized by bundling existing loans with similar characteristics and selling the package, or pieces of the package, to third-party investors. The advantage of this process is that it provides an avenue for diversifying loan portfolios within a relatively liquid market. The liquidity arises from the fact that raising funds in this manner minimizes the use of resources for handling loan transactions. The standardization of characteristics in each package facilitates analysis and trading.

Although virtually any type of loan may be collateralized, most securitized loans are mortgages that were the original liability of savings and loan, thrift, or commercial banking institutions. As mentioned above, S&Ls and thrifts, in particular, commonly have long-term assets (the mortgages) and short-term liabilities (demand deposit accounts). The securitization and sale of their long-term assets permits savings institutions to make liquid their long-term assets while achieving a greater balance in terms of maturity between their assets and liabilities. Other securitized loan products, which receive only brief mention here, include packaged automobile loans or Certificates of Automobile Receivables (CARs), which were devised by Salomon Brothers in 1985. In addition, receivables, primarily credit card receivables, are also commonly bundled and sold as securities.

The increasingly popular process of securitization of long-term loans, enhancing their liquidity, has hastened the process of disintermediation. Securitization has provided a means by which individuals may invest in securities created from bank assets. The bank assets, in their liquid form, are now able to be sold and traded in secondary markets such that the bank no longer plays the integral role in the transferal of funds from savers to borrowers. In short, banks are no longer necessary intermediators, as investors and savers can directly place excess funds with borrowers.

Up to this point we have covered the different aspects of the general environment for fixed-income securities. We will now focus on those factors that directly impact security prices.

BASIC PRINCIPLES

Four basic concepts concerning the valuation of bonds are these:

1. The term structure of interest rates
2. Interest rate risk
3. Credit risk
4. Marketability

Term structure refers to the time value of money. At any point in time the financial market determines the price of a zero-coupon bond with a certain face value and specified maturity (Treasury bonds are used as the benchmark). The relationship between the price and this maturity is called the "term structure" of interest rates. All bonds are priced according to the term structure. The term structure of interest rates is described in detail in Chapter 3.

Interest rate risk refers to unanticipated or stochastic movements of the term structure. When market interest rates change, the value of a bond changes as well. For example, zero-coupon bonds exhibit an inverse relationship between interest rates and bond prices. A new bond issue's price is relatively close to par, if not par. If the bond is sold prior to maturity, and interest rates are higher than they were on the date of issuance, the bond's price will be lower than its initial price. Because a bond's value is determined by the term structure, uncertainty about future interest rates will result in uncertainty about the bond's future price at any point prior to maturity. At any instant in time, the magnitude of uncertainty, as perceived by market participants, is reflected in the price of bonds with embedded options. This characteristic of bonds with embedded options derives from the fact that the value of the option component is directly affected by interest rate uncertainty, otherwise known as interest rate risk, existing in the market. Options are covered in Chapter 11.

Credit risk for bonds refers to the probability of default that negatively affects a bond's anticipated return; the issuer may be unable to repay interest and principal to the bondholder. A company's bonds are rated on the basis of the company's credit worthiness. Bonds with considerable credit (default) risk compensate the purchaser by providing higher return than a bond with lower or no credit risk. The price of risk can be measured by comparing the differences in return between bonds with high credit risk and those with little or no credit risk.

Marketability of a bond refers to the level of the bond's trading activity in the secondary market. For example, bonds with a small issue size, which are not widely held and subsequently experience little trading in the secondary market after issuance, are said to have low marketability. Such bonds may have no quoted prices (i.e., there is no dealer activity in the markets for these bonds). If their prices are quoted, the market bid/ask spread can be very wide to reflect the infrequent trading of the bonds. Under these conditions, an investor who wants to sell this type of bond prior to maturity will have to do so at a price lower than that of a similar bond that is actively traded. Consequently, bonds with low marketability have lower prices or higher yields to compensate for the difficulty of selling the bonds prior to maturity.

For any bond strategy, these three risks associated with purchasing bonds must be identified and taken into account for estimating returns. The integrative approach, as discussed in this book, provides a procedure for identifying these and other risk components associated with various fixed-income securities.

ANALYTICAL FRAMEWORK AND INTEGRATIVE APPROACH

Bonds are defined simply as a stream of payments over time. This definition holds true in practice, with some contingencies placed on the consistency of the stream as well as on the number of payments. Bonds can be classified as straight bonds or option-embedded bonds. A *straight bond* has prespecified coupon payments plus a principal payment upon maturity. For both discount (zero-coupon) and other straight bonds, it is assumed that the initial terms of the bond's interest payments, if any, and maturity date will not change. For *option-embedded bonds*, however, this assumption does not hold. Option-embedded bonds have contractual provisions that give the bond issuer (or occasionally, the bondholder) the right to alter the initial terms of the bond. Examples of option-embedded bonds include those with call or sinking-fund provisions. The details of such provisions will be discussed in future chapters.

The analysis of option-embedded bonds can be quite complex, depending on the nature of the option. In order to simplify the task of analyzing bonds, we use zero-coupon and other straight bonds to replicate the actions of option-embedded bonds. The framework of this book provides a cumulative analysis of bonds from the simplest to the most complex. The serial introduction and discussion of the factors that affect bond prices have been purposely designed to convey the pyramidal structure of various influences. For some securities with a specific feature known as a call option, the factors affecting call values can offset the influence from broader market factors. For example, although declining interest rates normally lead to bond price increases, the call option's effect on the bond will override and curtail the expected price appreciation.

This book is structured to help the fixed-income investor properly identify all possible factors that will affect the price performance of an instrument. The cumulation of counteracting factors is represented in a security's performance profile. The most complex instrument's performance profile can be recreated with simpler instruments. For instructional clarity, the simplest bond is used as an analogy to more complicated bonds whenever possible. The next chapter is the beginning of the sequential development of fixed-income analysis.

CHAPTER 2

BOND ARITHMETICS

This chapter uses the straight bond to illustrate different methods of calculating bond return. These measures of return can be applied to all bonds in general.

DESCRIPTION OF A STRAIGHT BOND

The simplest type of bond to evaluate is the straight bond, characterized by a fixed set of cash flows distributed on specified dates. The coupon bond is the most common type of straight bond. The principal of the coupon bond is paid at maturity, and coupon payments are made on a semiannual basis. Generally the norm in the United States and Japan is semiannual coupon payments, whereas in Europe the norm is annual payments.

Bonds are commonly denominated in either $1,000 or $10,000 face value. Because it is easier to think of a bond's price in percentage terms, the par value of a bond is often said to be simply 100. One percent of par is one point. When sold at the date of issue, bonds are sold either at par (face value), at a discount (some price below par), or at a premium (some price above par). The issue price reflects the actual value of the security and is associated with an internal rate of return measure (yield to maturity).

When a bond is sold at any time prior to maturity, the value of the bond must reflect any interest accrued between coupon payments. The accrued interest is simply the interest accrued to the holder of the bond until the sale or settlement date. To illustrate how accrued interest is calculated, assume the number of days between payments equals N and a bond is sold at time T such that n days have passed since the last coupon payment (or issuance date, if the bond is sold prior to the first coupon date). The accrued interest will be

$$\text{accrued} = (n/N \times \text{coupon payment}) \qquad (2\text{--}1)$$

Thus, at the trade or settlement date, the purchaser of the bond must pay the bond price stated by the seller of the bond plus accrued interest. In sum, the total value (the invoice price) of a bond sold before maturity is the price of the bond and accrued interest. Note that the term *invoice price* is not used in practice. It is important to remember that the bond price as quoted by dealers is the invoice price net of the accrued interest.

To illustrate the concept of accrued interest, consider the sale of a bond with a quoted price of $90.00, semiannual coupon payments of $5.00 made on January 31 and July 31, and a settlement date of March 31. The accrued interest of the bond will be $59/181 \times 5$, or $1.63, so the invoice price of the bond (the stated price plus accrued interest) is $91.63.

Table 2–1 shows the price, invoice price, and accrued interest over six months for a 12 percent semiannual coupon bond maturing January 1, 1991. The yield to maturity is assumed to be constant at 12 percent per year. The invoice price of a bond is equal to the quoted price plus the accrued interest. However, the invoice price of a bond—that is, the amount one pays for the bond—is the quantity that is financially equal to the present value of the future cash flows. Since accrued interest is independent of yield levels, it follows that the nominal price is itself an artifact of the bond-pricing process; it is simply the difference between the present value of the bond's Table 2–1 cash flows and the accrued interest.

Bond price behavior patterns are different from those of stock prices. The difference in patterns is attributable to their distinct trading characteristics. Bond prices are quoted net of accrued interest. Stocks

TABLE 2–1
Invoice Price, Accrued Interest, and Nominal Price

	2/1/88	3/1/88	4/1/88	5/1/88	6/1/88	7/1/88
Invoice	100.997	101.940	102.956	103.950	104.987	100.00
Accrued	1.022	1.978	3.000	3.989	5.010	0.00
Price	99.975	99.962	99.956	99.961	99.977	100.00

are traded with a provision called the *ex-dividend date*. The ex-dividend date, which is a few days prior to the dividend payment date, is the start of a brief period that precludes purchasers of the stock from receiving the upcoming dividend. On the ex-dividend date, whoever has ownership of the stock is deemed to be the recipient of the dividend. If the stock is sold any time after the ex-dividend date and before the nearby dividend payment date, the seller receives the full amount of the dividend. The purchaser becomes eligible to receive all the subsequent dividend payments.

Because the quoted price of the bond is net accrued interest, it follows a steady pattern over time. Immediately prior to and until the coupon date, the quoted price of the bond remains consistent. The total price changes as it reflects accrued interest. At a coupon payment, however, the bond has no accrued interest, and the total cost once again equals the quoted price. This pattern is in contrast to that of stock prices. When one buys stock prior to the ex-dividend date, one is paying for the forthcoming dividend. At the ex-dividend date, the stock price drops to reflect the value of the stock, which is now "less" one dividend payment. This is not the case for bonds, for which the quoted price does not reflect the upcoming coupon payment. The accrued interest is included in the total price, not the quoted price, of the bond.

One final precursor to the introduction of pricing a straight bond is the concept of *present value*. An investor who purchases a bond is concerned not with its future value but with the present value of its future cash flow. For example, if a bond is purchased at time T, the investor will be concerned only with the present value of payments beginning at time T, including accrued interest. Present value calculations ignore a bond's history. The future cash flow may be the remaining payments of a bond issued several years in the past. In other words, if two bonds have the same cash flow, even if they were issued at different times with different maturities, their present market prices should be the same. Therefore, the bond price represents the present value of the future cash flow of the bond.

A bond's present value, equal to its future value discounted according to the bond's stated rate of interest, is calculated as follows:

$$\text{Present value} = \text{Future Value}/(1 + r)^n$$

where r is the bond's stated interest rate and n is the number of payment periods (which for present purposes are generally years).

MEASURES OF RETURN

Bond returns are commonly calculated according to the formula for the yield to maturity of the bond (YTM). The YTM represents the internal rate of return of buying the bond and holding it until maturity while receiving its cash flow in the interim. As such, the YTM may be used to compare the returns of bonds that differ in coupon rates and maturities. In other words, the YTM is the constant discount rate at which the present value of the bond cash flows becomes equal to the bond price, and which can be determined if the bond cash flow and price are known.

For example, consider an annual coupon paying bond with coupon rate C and maturity in T years. Let P equal the price of a \$100 par value bond. Then, the price P and the YTM are related by

$$P = C/(1 + YTM) + C/(1 + YTM)^2 + \cdots + \$(100 + C)/(1 + YTM)^T$$

To illustrate the use of the YTM formula, suppose now that the price of the bond $P = \$81.00$, the coupon rate $C = 8$ percent, and the time to maturity $T = 3$ years. The YTM may be derived using the previous equation such that

$$\$81.00 = \$8.00/(1 + YTM) + \$8.00/(1 + YTM)^2 + \$108.00/(1 + YTM)^3$$

The YTM for this bond to satisfy the preceding equation is determined to be 8.4 percent. The bond can be represented schematically, as illustrated in Figure 2–1.

For straight bonds that pay fixed coupons at regular intervals, the relationship between the bond price and the YTM has two interesting properties. First, the bond price and the YTM are negatively related— an increase in the yield signals a drop in the bond price, and a decrease in the yield signals a rise in the bond price. Second, it is clear that a bond sells at premium if and only if the coupon rate is above the YTM. This observation makes sense because if the bond is paying a rate higher than the market discount rate, then investors would pay more than the par value for the bond. Similarly, the bond sells at discount if and only if the coupon rate is below the YTM.

There are other means of computing the return on a bond that also permit comparison of return among bonds. Before a discussion of these means, the concept of *compounding* must be presented. Recall that the YTM assumes the reinvestment of coupons at the internal rate of return of the bond. Compounding is based on the same idea: that coupons

FIGURE 2–1
Schematic Diagram of a Straight Bond. The horizontal line represents the time to the cash flows. The length of the vertical lines represents the size of the payments. The vertical lines above the horizontal line represent the cash *inflow* to the bondholders. The line below the horizontal line represents the cash outflow. In the example, $81 is the price paid today to receive the three annual payments of $8, $8, and $108.

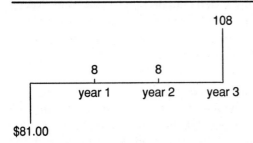

are reinvested. The formula for calculating the future value of a one-year bond purchased today at price P with interest compounded n times during the year is

$$FV = P(1 + r)^n$$

For example, consider an 8 percent semiannual interest-paying bond with a face value of $100.00 (a bond trading at par). The YTM of the bond if the coupons were paid annually would be 8 percent. However, since we are dealing with semiannual payments, each payment represents 4 percent of the bond's face value, or $4.00. If the bond specifically pays semiannual interest, then the first interest payment is assumed to be reinvested at a rate of 4 percent, and the total rate of return (or bond yield) is $1.04^2 - 1 = 8.02\%$. Compounding can occur many times a year over the life of a bond. The equation to compute the future value of a bond with a coupon rate of r, compounded n times a year over a period of X years is

$$FV = P\left(1 + \frac{r}{n}\right)^{Xn}$$

Compounding can be continuous, meaning there are no discrete intervals between compounding periods. In this case, the future price of a bond, compounded continuously over X years, is calculated as

$$FV = Pe^{rX}$$

The concept of compounding illustrates differences between the YTM and other means of computing the actual yield of a semiannual coupon-paying bond. The YTM calculates the yield based on a stated annual coupon rate. As seen above, the stated coupon rate is not the actual yield of a bond that has semiannual compounded coupon payments. A (par) bond's actual yield is calculated based on the number of coupon payments per year as well as the stated coupon rate on the bond. Recall that the semiannual coupon bond is the standard or benchmark bond in the United States. Consequently, it is useful to have a means by which to compare the bond yield of a bond with x coupon payments per year with the bond yield of the semiannual coupon-paying bond. This is done by calculating the bond equivalent yield (BEY).

In sum, the BEY is a standardized measure used for making cross-comparisons among instruments that have different coupon-paying intervals. The following formula shows the relationship between YTM and BEY:

$$\left(1 + \frac{BEY}{2}\right)^2 = 1 + YTM$$

Based on knowledge of the bond's price P and its stated coupon rate, the semiannual coupon-paying benchmark bond's yield can be calculated according to

$$P = C/\left(1 + \frac{BEY}{2}\right) + C/\left(1 + \frac{BEY}{2}\right)^2 + \cdots + (\$100 + C)/\left(1 + \frac{BEY}{2}\right)^N$$

(Note that C remains the dollar amount received per coupon payment. If the stated yield is 8 percent, then each coupon payment for a semiannual, $100.00 par value bond is $4.00.)

This formula provides the BEY for a semiannual coupon-paying bond. As will be illustrated shortly, the yield on any bond can be transformed into a BEY measure in order to provide consistency for bond yield comparisons.

Clearly, the BEY (semiannual compounding) and the YTM (annual compounding) are different measures of bond return. As seen earlier, an 8 percent semiannual coupon-paying bond selling at par has a bond yield of 8 percent. But on an annual effective basis, the bond yield should be more than 8 percent. The midyear coupon can be reinvested, and therefore the total interest earned will be greater than $8.00 by year end. Accordingly, an 8 percent semiannual coupon-paying bond should be worth more than an 8 percent annual coupon-paying bond. Both issues have an 8 percent coupon, but the former's true yield is greater than the latter's.

The above example illustrates the effect of different reinvestment rate assumptions governing the calculations of the YTM and the BEY. Given these assumptions, one can see why BEY is more convenient as a rate-of-return measure for a coupon-paying bond than the annual compound rate of return (YTM).

For any bond, the yield will be lower if the yield is stated in terms of the BEY and higher if stated as YTM (if the assumption of annual compounding is made). For example, a one-year zero-coupon bond priced at $90.00 can be evaluated as follows:

$$\text{Yield to Maturity} \quad \$90.00 = 100/(1 + \text{YTM}) = 11.11\%$$

$$\text{Bond Equivalent Yield} \quad \$90.00 = 100/\left(1 + \frac{\text{BEY}}{2}\right)^2 = 10.82\%$$

Here, the bond equivalent yield transforms the zero-coupon bond such that its yield can be directly compared with the yield of a semiannual coupon-paying bond.

An intuitive means of comparing different yield measures for a bond is that the less frequently a bond's interest payments are subject to compounding, the higher the calculated yield will be for a bond with a specific cash flow and market price. The YTM will be the highest yield, and the continuous compounding will be the lowest. In fact, if Y_n is the n-period compounding yield of a bond, then the bond equivalent yield is

$$\left(1 + \frac{Y_n}{n}\right)^{n/2} = 1 + \frac{\text{BEY}}{2}$$

The BEY transforms the yield measure for a bond whose payments are compounded any number of times per year such that it can be compared in terms of yield with a benchmark (semiannual compounded coupon). For example, the quarterly compounding yield on a two-year bond with a 16 percent (annual) coupon rate, whose quarterly interest payments are compounded, can be calculated as follows:

$$P = 4/\left(1 + \frac{Y}{4}\right) + 4/\left(1 + \frac{Y}{4}\right)^2 + \cdots + 104/\left(1 + \frac{Y}{4}\right)^8$$

(Note: Each coupon payment, and there are four each year, is $4.00. There is a total of eight coupons paid.) The bond equivalent yield for this bond is

$$\left(1 + \frac{Y}{4}\right)^2 = 1 + \frac{BEY}{2}$$

For zero-coupon or discount bonds (e.g., Treasury bills) the time value of money is often expressed as the discount rate. The discount rate is not a yield; rather, it is the percentage by which the bond price differs from the bond's face value adjusted to the annual basis. Treasury bill discount rates are quoted on the basis of a 360-day year. The formula for converting this rate into a BEY incorporates a transformation to a 365-day basis yield measure. The following is an example using the results of a Treasury bill auction as published in the July 5, 1989 issue of *The Wall Street Journal*.

Here are details of Monday's auction of new short-term Treasury bills: Rates are determined by the difference between the purchase price and face value. Thus, higher bidding narrows the investor's return while lower bidding widens it. The percentage rates are calculated on a 360-day year, while the coupon equivalent yield is based on a 365-day year.

	13-Week	26-Week
Applications	$25,592,815,000	$22,551,770,000
Accepted bids	$6,602,020,000	$6,610,110,000
Accepted at low price	17%	57%
Accepted noncompet'ly	$1,296,960,000	$1,105,540,000
Average price (Rate)	97.988 (7.96%)	96.143 (7.63%)
High price (Rate)	98.003 (7.90%)	96.168 (7.58%)
Low price (Rate)	97.985 (7.97%)	96.138 (7.64%)
Coupon equivalent	8.24%	8.05%

Both issues are dated July 6, 1989. The 13-week bills mature Oct. 5, 1989, and the 26-week bills mature Jan. 4, 1990.

Source: The Wall Street Journal, July 5, 1989.

For the 26-week issue, or 182-day term, the average price was $96.143 and the discount rate, d, was 7.63 percent. The discount value, dv, was computed as follows:

$$dv = .0763 \times (\$100) \times (182/360) = \$3.857$$

The quoted discount rate, d, can be transformed into the BEY in the following manner. For a bond with a $100 face value and maturity T^* (in 360-day years):

$$\frac{1}{\left(1 + \frac{BEY}{2}\right)^{2T}} = 1 - dT^*$$

As reported in the preceding table, the bond equivalent yield for the 26-week issue was 8.05 percent, determined as follows:

$$d(\text{quoted discount rate}) = .0763$$

$$T = \frac{182\text{-day maturity}}{365\text{-day year}} = .498630 \text{ year}$$

$$T^* = \frac{182}{360\text{-day year used in quoted discount rate}} = .5055 \text{ year}$$

$$\frac{1}{\left[1 + \left(\frac{BEY}{2}\right)\right]^{2T}} = 1 - .0763T^*$$

$$\frac{1}{\left[1 + \left(\frac{BEY}{2}\right)\right]^{2(.498630)}} = 1 - .03857389$$

$$\frac{1}{\left[1 + \left(\frac{BEY}{2}\right)\right]^{.997}} = .96143$$

$$BEY = .080459 \text{ or } 8.05\%$$

YIELD SPREAD AND YIELD DIAGRAMS

Bond yield measures (assuming only one yield measure is used) permit comparison between (1) different types of bonds with the same maturity and (2) similar bonds with different maturities. The frequency with which a bond is traded is positively related to the accuracy of its market value. Treasury bonds are highly liquid, and they often serve as benchmarks against which to price infrequently traded bonds. When comparing, for example, a corporate bond against a Treasury bond, it is important to compare the two at issue. Comparison between the two provides information about the time value of money. If the two are not compared at issue, the time value of money will be distorted.

Comparison between two bonds on the basis of yield elicits a *yield spread*. The yield spread between two bonds can be tracked over time, and changes in the spread can be used as a basis for repricing a bond. Examination of a yield spread over time is a form of relative pricing. Relative pricing is a simple means of pricing a bond with a minimum of quantitative analysis.

A *yield diagram* is a graphic representation of a yield spread between two bonds. The graph plots the yield to maturity of one bond against another over time. By convention, the bond that is more actively traded and simpler (closer to a straight bond) is the *underlying bond*. The second bond is the *corresponding bond*. The yield diagram depicts how the corresponding bond behaves relative to the underlying bond. First, the yields to maturity of the two bonds are calculated at regular intervals (e.g., daily and weekly) to facilitate comparison. Second, the points of the yields to maturity are plotted, with the underlying bond on the x-axis and the corresponding bond on the y-axis. Two bonds with identical yields and other characteristics will form a single 45-degree line from the origin. Statistically speaking, these bonds have perfectly correlated yields and are substitutes for each other. Bonds with divergent yields have varying degrees of correlation. An extreme case would be two bonds with no correlation, whose yield diagram exhibits no pattern whatsoever. The scatter plot for two bonds with a consistent spread between their yields will also consist of a straight line, but in this case the line will start at some point above the origin to indicate the presence of a spread. A scatter plot of bond yields is given in Figure 2–2.

A scatter plot is used to depict the yield relationship (or lack thereof) between two bonds. For example, the yield diagram should make clear that there is no close correlation in yield either between short- and long-term bonds or between junk bonds and Treasuries. Conversely, given a yield diagram, the identities of the underlying and corresponding bonds can be determined. The yield diagram is not based on economic modeling. Rather, it depicts the historical statistical relationship, which must be analyzed and interpreted.

The yield diagram of a callable corporate bond against a Treasury bond with similar maturity can provide valuable information about the callable corporate bond's price sensitivity to interest rates, relative to a

FIGURE 2–2
Scatter Plot of Yield to Maturity (YTM) Bond B versus Bond A

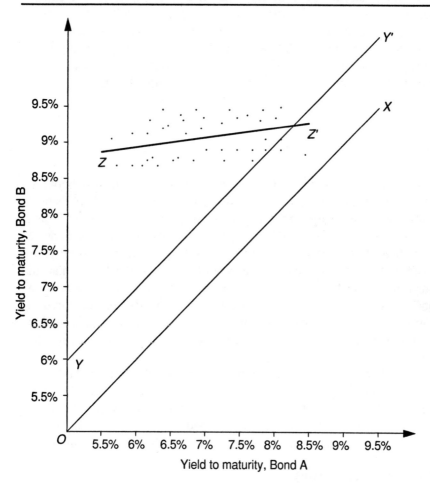

1. If the plotted points lie on a line *OX,* the YTMs
   of Bond B and Bond A vary in step over time.

2. If the plotted points lie on line *YY',* then the
   YTMs of Bond B and Bond A also vary in step,
   but at a constant 100 bp spread relationship;
   Bond B's YTM is always higher.

3. If the plotted points lie on line *ZZ',* then the
   YTM of Bond B changes less than Bond A's. If
   Bond A and B have the same maturity, then
   Bond B is often a callable bond.

Treasury bond's. When a corporate bond has a call schedule, a change in the yield to maturity of a Treasury bond often leads to a lower percentage change in the yield to maturity of the corporate bond. This happens because if a bond is callable, its market price cannot exceed the call price. So, if the market interest rate drops, the corporate bond price is capped. Therefore, the price movement is much less than that of a Treasury bond with similar maturity. In other words, the change of yield of the corporate bond is less than that of the Treasury bond.

CANONICAL EXAMPLE

This section will appear at the end of some chapters in this book. It will provide a progressive comparison of a group of three hypothetical bonds and, eventually, three actual bonds, for which historical data is used. One purpose of this section is to provide a comprehensive illustration of the practical use of concepts presented in each chapter. Another purpose is to reinforce a central theme of the book: that all bonds, no matter how complex, can be decomposed to replicate straight bonds with options added. This view of how bonds are structured is central to the book's approach to bond pricing. To this end, this section introduces three hypothetical straight bonds in order to illustrate the concepts presented in each chapter. Although the bonds may change form in future chapters, they will retain their fundamental characteristics (i.e., bond type, maturity, and yield). Three actual bonds will be included in later versions of this section. Actual bonds are not initially introduced, to permit the reader time to become accustomed to the basics of bond theory without being distracted by more complicated mathematical calculations.

Yields on Coupon Bonds
The three fictitious bonds that will be used in this section and the proceeding sections are all straight bonds. These bonds are named according to their maturities:

1. A short-term bond (ST)
2. A medium-term bond (MT)
3. A long-term bond (LT)

For the present, these bonds can be considered risk free (they face no default or credit risk). The bond statistics of interest are summarized in tabular form:

Bonds	ST	MT	LT
Market value	101	98	100
Coupon rate (in %)	13	9	8
Maturity in years	1	2	3

The yield to maturity on each of the three bonds is calculated as follows:
Bond ST:

$$101 = \frac{113}{(1 + \text{YTM}_{ST})}$$

$$\text{YTM}_{ST} = 11.8812\%$$

Bond MT:

$$98 = \frac{9}{(1 + \text{YTM}_{MT})} + \frac{109}{(1 + \text{YTM}_{MT})^2}$$

$$\text{YTM}_{MT} = 10.15478\%$$

Bond LT:

$$100 = \frac{8}{(1 + \text{YTM}_{LT})} + \frac{8}{(1 + \text{YTM}_{LT})^2} + \frac{108}{(1 + \text{YTM}_{LT})^3}$$

$$\text{YTM}_{LT} = 8\%$$

To calculate the BEY on these bonds, in order to compare them to semiannual coupon bonds:

Bond	ST	MT	LT
Annual yield (YTM)	11.8812	10.1548	8.0
BEY	11.5478	9.90931	7.846097

The YTM is translated to the BEY using the formula $[1 + (\text{BEY}/2)]^2 = (1 + \text{YTM})$.

SUMMARY

The basic characteristics of straight bonds were discussed in this chapter. The first few sections of the chapter reviewed bond pricing basics. Prices incorporate present values of future cash flows. The subsequent sections built upon the concepts of pricing to introduce the procedures for converting prices to return measures. Numerical examples accompanied the explanations of yield to maturity (YTM) and bond equivalent yield (BEY).

APPENDIX TO CHAPTER 2: PRICE-YIELD RELATIONSHIPS: ZERO AND PERPETUAL BONDS

Zero-Coupon Bonds

$$P = \text{Price} \qquad T = \text{Time to maturity in years}$$

Annual Compounding Yield:

$$P = \frac{100}{(1 + \text{YTM})^T}$$

Semiannual Compounding Yield (BEY):

$$P = \frac{100}{(1 + \frac{\text{BEY}}{2})^{2T}}$$

Continuously Compounding Yield (r):

$$P = 100 \times e^{-rT}$$

Perpetual Bonds (No Maturity)
Bond pays annual coupons (c):

$$P = \frac{c}{1 + \text{YTM}}$$

If one could lend a fixed amount today that would accrue interest continuously and indefinitely, this type of instrument could be deemed to be a bond that pays coupons continuously with the coupons continuously reinvested. The price today of such a bond could be represented as follows:

Bonds with continuous coupons, reinvested at rate r:

$$P = \frac{c}{r}$$

CHAPTER 3

THE TERM STRUCTURE OF INTEREST RATES

This chapter introduces the premises underlying different bond-return measures. It begins with a review of both cash-flow structures and periodic returns and then discusses comparative yield analysis. The conclusion of the chapter provides a comprehensive illustration of these concepts.

PURE DISCOUNT BONDS AND THE DISCOUNT FACTOR

The most basic straight bond is the pure discount bond. A pure discount bond is a bond that pays the par value of $100 at maturity, with no other payment in the interim. The time to maturity, T, can be any real number, and the price of the bond is denoted by $P(T)$, indicating that the price of the bond is a function of time to maturity. We assume that there is no default risk involved and that the market is liquid.

The pure discount bond, for the time being, is a theoretical construct. The instruments that closely resemble these hypothetical bonds are U.S. Treasury bills. Treasury bills have single payments and trade in relatively liquid markets. As noted in the previous chapter, there is a one-to-one correspondence between the price of the bond and its yield. For a given maturity, if we know the yield (whether stated as YTM or BEY), we can determine the price. Conversely, if we know the price, the yield can be determined. The main point is that each defines the other; they are not separately determined according to different sets of economic parameters—a bond's price and yield contain the same information, presented in different ways.

Among discount bonds another unique relationship exists. This is the relationship between the discount factor, F, and the bond's time to maturity, or $F(T)$. The discount factor of a discount bond is that percentage of the future (par) value of a bond represented by the current price.

$$F = \text{Current price/par value}$$

If price, $P(T) = \$90$, then $F = .90$. Note that $P(T)$ for a discount bond equals $100 \times F(T)$. It is essentially the reverse of the formula for future value.

$$PV = F \times FV$$

Also,

$$F = \frac{1}{(1 + r)^n}$$

where, given F, one can solve for r, the periodic discounting rate.

THE TERM STRUCTURE

The discount factor as described above is a numerical representation of the relationship between a zero-coupon bond's current price and its price at maturity (or par value). The realm of discount bonds constitutes a unique group or portfolio of bonds with different maturities and, subsequently, with discrete $F(T)$ relationships. From this family of bonds subject to the constraints of $F(T)$, where $(T > 0)$, a function can be defined. This function provides the discount factor for a pure discount bond, of any maturity, such that $F(T) > 0$.

The graph of the discount function can be sketched. $F(T)$ should be a monotonic, decreasing function (downward-sloping) because the present value of 1 decreases with time. At time 0 (today), the pure discount bond matures instantaneously (i.e., its price is par), so its discount factor must be 1, and the graph of the function starts from 1 on the y-axis. In addition, if the bond is not going to mature for a long time, its present value must be negligibly small, and the graph of the function will approach zero. In sum, the discount function 'decays' from 1 toward 0. Its general shape is depicted in Figure 3–1. The shape of this curve changes somewhat within the constraints outlined above as the underlying economic parameters that determine the time value of money

FIGURE 3–1
The Discount Function

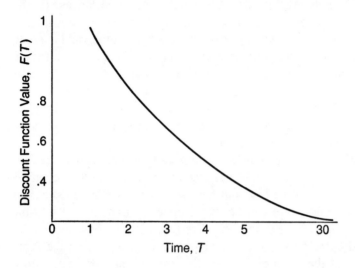

Where $F(t)=\dfrac{1}{(1+r)^T}$, where T = time, and r = the discount rate.

For this example is , r = 8%.

For instance :

F(T)	T
.92593	1
.85734	2
.79383	3
.58349	7
.39711	12
.09938	30

change from day to day. But this change is too subtle to be descriptive on this graph. Thus, another graphic representation is used to depict the market scenario.

Each discount factor can be translated into a percentage yield. Assume a maturity of one year for a $90 bond with a discount factor of 0.9. Its yield can be stated as 11 percent. This bond can then be depicted as a point on the graph of the yield curve. The yield of each bond can be graphed against the maturity, T, to depict the value of money over time in a way other than the discount function: in terms of the yield against the time to maturity.

Unlike the discount function, the yield curve has few constraints on its configuration (i.e., it need not be a decaying function). In principle, the yields of the individual bonds represented in the curve can take on any positive value. Therefore, the curve can be upward-sloping, downward-sloping, or even bumpy. One may expect the points on the yield curve to be continuous; they reflect our time substitution of funds, which should be quite continuous. Yield curves necessarily change their shapes over time, given changes in market conditions. Figure 3–2 illustrates some of the shapes of the yield curve. Factors affecting the slope of the yield curve are discussed later in this chapter. For now, we are interested in knowing how to use the yield curve.

Much information on the market forces can be captured and depicted by the yield curve, but this does not mean that the yield curve captures more information than the discount function. As was mentioned earlier in this chapter, one curve can be mathematically transformed into the other (the discount function can be determined from the yield curve, and the yield curve from the discount function); they contain the same information, but the yield curve visually presents the information in a more concise manner.

In sum, both the yield curve and the discount function represent the time value of money of all zero-coupon bonds. They depict the term structure of interest rates (meaning the monetary value of all zero-coupon bonds) at any instant in time. In practice, the term structure may be constructed by zero-coupon Treasury bonds. The yield curve of these Treasury bonds serves as the benchmark against which any bond can be priced, depending on its maturity and other characteristics.

A clear way of contrasting the yield curve with the discount function is by postulating a flat yield curve. Assume a flat yield curve that is constant at 8 percent across all maturities. This curve implies that all bonds of all maturities yield 8 percent. The discount curve corresponding to this flat yield curve, however, will be downward-sloping according to the equation $F(T) = 1/(1.08)^T$ over time T.

PRICING STRAIGHT BONDS AND THE ARBITRAGE CONDITIONS

The yield curve provides what is known as the "fair value" of a bond. Central to the concept of the fair value of a bond is *the law of one price*. The law which really is a reasonable hypothesis, states:

FIGURE 3–2
Types of Yield Curves

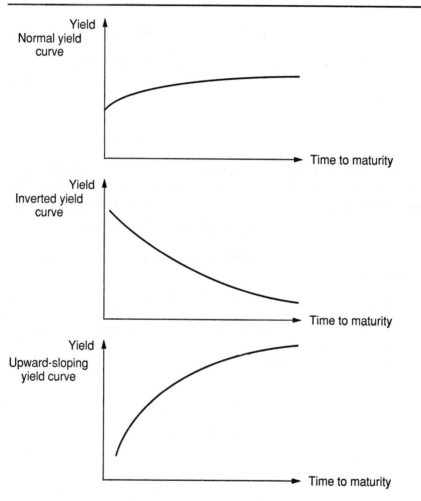

The yield curve represents the time value of money.
In principle, it can take on any shape.

If two straight bonds have identical cash flows (we ignore credit risk for the time being), then they should have the same price. This simple assertion allows us to price any cash flow, as long as we know its discount function. Suppose a bond pays X_1 at time T_1, X_2 at time T_2, and so on until X_n at time T_n. Instead of looking at the bond as one instrument, with separate coupon payments, we can think of the bond as a portfolio of discount bonds with maturities $T_1 \ldots T_n$. The portfolio value is

$$P = X_1 F(T_1) + \cdots + X_n F(T_n) \qquad (3\text{--}1)$$

As an example of a bond as a portfolio of bonds, consider a three-year annual coupon-paying bond, with a coupon rate of 8 percent. The cash flow is represented by

$$\begin{array}{ccc} 8 & 8 & 108 \end{array}$$
$$|\text{-------}|\text{------}|\text{------}|$$

But this bond is a portfolio of pure discount bonds: an 8-dollar par value one-year bond, an 8-dollar par value two-year bond, and a 108-dollar par value three-year bond. The price of the bond is computed as follows:

$$\text{Price } P = 8 \times F(1) + 8 \times F(2) + 108 \times F(3)$$

Given that the discount function of a bond is related to its yield to maturity by

$$F(T) = 1/(1 + \text{YTM}_T)^T \qquad (3\text{--}2)$$

and assuming that the discount factor for each bond, $F(1)$, $F(2)$, and $F(3)$, is known to be 0.90, 0.82, and 0.75, respectively, the price for each bond can be calculated. For example, the price on the one-year bond is

$$\text{Price } P(1) = 8 \times .90$$

The remaining prices can be similarly computed.

$$P(1) = \$7.20 \text{ \rule{4cm}{0.4pt} } 8$$
$$P(2) = \$6.56 \text{ \rule{5cm}{0.4pt} } 8$$
$$P(3) = \$81.00 \text{ \rule{6cm}{0.4pt} } 108$$

Therefore, the price of this bond would be $94.76.

By calculating the prices on the individual discount bonds and adding them up, the fair price of the original coupon bond is determined. Note that there is no reinvestment assumption involved. We are simply interested in demonstrating how one bond can be seen and priced as three individual bonds.

Therefore by the law of one price, P is the price for all bonds with identical cash flows and features. Given all pure discount bond prices of all maturities and all bond prices determined by Equation 3–1, there is no arbitrage possibility. That is, it is not possible to realize a profit by buying a bond portfolio and simultaneously selling another bond portfolio with the same cash flow. (Arbitrage possibilities would exist only, for example, if one could purchase a bond at a set price, decompose it into zero-coupon bonds, and sell the individual coupon bonds at a profit.) Therefore, Equation 3–1 can be thought of as an arbitrage-free condition; it is known as the "pricing model" for straight bonds.

THE YIELD CURVE AND REINVESTMENT RATE: DEFECTS OF YIELD MEASURES

If one were pricing a security using the existing yield curve, the derived yield to maturity or bond equivalent yield measures would not reflect the true structure of the underlying curve that generated the measures. The nature of the mathematical procedures used in the computation—that is, the internal rate of return formula—inhibit reflection of the true yield curve environment.

Therefore, it is possible to draw conclusions about the yield measures discussed in the previous chapter. Both the YTM and the BEY assume that a bond's coupons are reinvested over time at the one rate: the YTM. In other words, the yield measures assume a flat yield curve.

FACTORS AFFECTING THE SHAPE OF THE YIELD CURVE

Thus far the discussion assumes the existence of the yield curve without specifying the factors that determine its shape. In order to examine these factors, real interest rates, nominal interest rates, and term structure must first be defined.

Real Rates

An important component of interest rates comes from the tradeoff between the investment and consumption of each individual. Imagine an economy in which there is one consumption good—wheat, for example. Everyone in the economy consumes only wheat, and what is not consumed is invested immediately to produce more wheat in the future. Suppose a citizen of this economy has 10 bushels of wheat. He will have to decide how much to consume now and how much (the rest) to use as seeds for the next harvest. The expected return should be higher than the investment; that is the individual should be able to harvest more than he plants, or he would be better off just storing under his bed the portion of wheat that is not consumed. From this analogy, it can be inferred that there is an optimal level of consumption and investment for each individual.

Suppose a second citizen wants to borrow one bushel of wheat from the first. If so, the first will not just want one bushel back next year, but will want more since he can produce more himself through planting the bushel. Therefore, the first citizen will demand "interest" to the principal. When all individuals trade in a central market, borrowing and lending wheat, a clearing rate on interest, or the return of investment from lending wheat, is determined. This rate is *the real rate of interest* (or *real rate*), and it represents the value of extra wheat to individuals in general.

The real rate of interest has nothing to do with the inflation of money, since it arises from trading real goods. Also, it is not related to the riskiness of borrowing or lending wheat. We see that the real rate is positive, even in a world of uncertainty.

This example is simplistic, but the idea it illustrates is important. In essence, it shows that even in a complex economy there will be a real rate of interest for a bundle of goods. The level of this rate depends on the individual's propensity to save and the productivity of the economy.

When the propensity to save is low, and individuals seek to consume more, the real rate rises. When individuals prefer to invest, then the rate drops. Both of these rate changes occur as a function of supply and demand. Also, if the real sector is producing a high rate of return (i.e., if harvests are abundant), the economy will increase its investment into the economy, further raising the real rate. However, if the return of the real sector is risky, then the individual will prefer lending the real good rather than investing in the production. This change in preference lowers the rate.

Nominal Rate of Interest

The economy consists of many goods for which "money" is used as a medium of exchange for all goods. Suppose again that an individual consumes and invests only in wheat, which now takes the form of money. When she puts her money in the bank, inflation must come into the calculation. How? For simplicity, assume a world of certainty.

At time $T = 0$, the price of 1 bushel of wheat is \$1. At the end of the period, the price of 1 bushel of wheat goes to \$2. During this period, the individual can grow 1.5 bushels at harvest. This is because, without lending to the bank, she can buy 1 bushel of wheat for \$1 and produce 1.5 bushels at harvest. In selling the crop, she realizes \$3. The bank, therefore, must pay her back \$3 for the \$1 she deposited. The argument can be represented in this diagram:

1 bushel	—————— \$1
1.5 bushel	—————— \$3

The diagram must commute. That is, starting off with \$1, the individual can either invest her money at the nominal rate (200 percent, which is the real rate plus the rate of inflation) or she can buy 1 bushel of wheat and realize 1.5 bushels at harvest. By either investing or selling the wheat for cash, she ultimately receives \$3. Formally:

$$I = \text{investment in dollars}$$
$$P_0 = \text{price level at time } t = 0$$
$$P_1 = \text{price level at time } t = 1$$

Then, at $t = 0$, she can buy I/P_0 bushels. By growing the crop and selling it, she realizes:

$$\text{Profit} = I/P_0(1 + \text{real rate})P_1$$

But this profit is equivalent to banking her investment and realizing the nominal return. Therefore,

$$(1 + \text{real rate})P_1 = (1 + \text{nominal})P_0$$

If

$$(\text{nominal rate}) = (\text{real rate}) + (\text{inflation rate})$$

This Fisher equation portrays the nominal rate of interest as the sum of its component parts. Hereafter, *interest rate* refers to the nominal rate of interest, unless otherwise stated.

So far, our arguments hinge on only one period. What if one can borrow and lend at any maturity? According to Fisher's equation, the nominal interest rate can be decomposed into two components. In addition, the equation shows that the real rate and the inflation rate depend on the time horizon. Therefore, the term structure or yield curve need not be flat, as stated earlier, and the yield of the bond must depend on the maturity. This is true even in a world of uncertainty. Yet the rates for different maturities must be related. The way they should be related is suggested by the following two hypotheses.

Expectation Hypothesis

Consider an investor who wishes to realize a return in a two-period time frame. The investor can either lock in a two-period rate (by investing now at a set rate for two periods) or roll over a one-period investment (by investing for one period at one rate and reinvesting for a second period at another rate). According to the expectation hypothesis (EH), the return for the two strategies must be the same.

Let r_{01} and r_{02} be the interest rates of the one period and two period, respectively. Also, let r_{12} be the one-period rate in the second period. Then we have

$$(1 + r_{02})^2 = (1 + r_{01})(1 + r_{12})$$

Only in a world of certainty would we know precisely r_{01} and r_{12}. As an approximation, EH replaces r_{12} by the expected rate $\bar{r}_{12}$, and EH is written as:

$$(1 + r_{02})^2 = (1 + r_{01})(1 + \bar{r}_{12})$$

Liquidity Premium Hypothesis

In the uncertain world, however, the expectation hypothesis may not hold. In fact, in a risky environment, borrowers tend to seek long-term funding to lock in at a fixed borrowing rate, while lenders prefer investing in short-term instruments to retain liquidity. For this reason, the short-term rate would generally be lower than the long-term rate. This difference is called "liquidity premium." In sum, we have

$$r_{12} = \bar{r}_{12} + \text{(liquidity premium)}$$

which is the expected return of a one-period bond, one period hence.

The expectation hypothesis says that the expected return on all bonds is the same if they are held for only one period. In other words, the yield, as determined by the term structure, for the one period during which all bonds are held, applies to every bond. In addition, according to the liquidity premium hypothesis, the expected return is higher the longer the maturity period of the bond. (As explained earlier, the premium is intended to compensate for the illiquidity of longer-term bonds.) Other reasons for this premium, which shall be called the "term premium," will be considered in a future chapter.

We have presented a summary of factors determining the general shape of the yield curve. The yield curve itself is composed of individual rates that can be characterized by a volatility measure. The following section will describe this measure.

INTEREST RATE VOLATILITIES

Interest rates are stochastic (uncertain). Their movement depends on many economic factors inherent in the real and financial sectors. Following is a list of some of these factors. They are roughly grouped into three types:

1. Inflation factors: money supply, producers price index, consumer price index, federal deficit, unemployment, discount rate.
2. Real sector and saving propensity: housing starts, GNP, unemployment level, political events.
3. Supply and demand for credit: Treasury funding, corporate borrowing.

As a result of such risks, investing in bonds (or fixed-income securities) for one holding period involves uncertain returns. Interest rate volatility, or changes in return on a bond based on changes in underlying economic factors, can be examined statistically.

Interest Rate Volatility Defined

Having defined yields, we want some measure of uncertainty of yields. At any time, the spot yield curve can be derived. On the given spot curve, a bond is purchased with 10 years to maturity. In the next period from the date of purchase, another yield curve emerges with a new 10-year yield. There is no way of knowing beforehand what the next period's curve will be; each particular yield is stochastic. We need to derive a measure that represents the volatility of a particular yield.

The common practice in measuring yield volatility is to assume that the proportional change in the yield follows a normal distribution and that the process is symmetrically, independently distributed:

$$\frac{\Delta(r)}{r} \approx \text{normal distribution}$$

Therefore, given a time series of yields (e.g., 10-year yields), we can compute the standard deviation of a proportional change in yield. The standard deviation is a measure of the volatility of the 10-year bond yield over one time period (for example, one month). This volatility of course, should be smaller than if we use a two-month time period. To make the two volatilities comparable, we have to annualize the volatility measure. This is achieved by multiplying the standard deviation by the square root of T (in the one-month case, $T = 1/12$).

Note that these measures are commonly used in practice to represent market interest rate uncertainty. The implicit assumption—that yields follow a random walk—is very strong. An alternative to this assumption would have to precisely specify the stochastic process of the yields and estimate that process, which is a complicated procedure. Up to this point we have discussed the underlying concepts of the term structure of interest rates. The following section will show the application of these concepts for deriving the "fair value" of a straight bond.

CANONICAL EXAMPLE

The Discount Function

The discount function calculates the rate at which the face value of a bond is discounted to the present value (market price). Using the three bonds introduced in Chapter 2, the discount factors, F, can be derived for each of the three periods as follows:

$$\text{Bond ST:} \quad F_1 = 1/1.1188$$
$$= 0.8938$$

The present value of bond ST, with a one-period yield of 11.8812 percent, is $101 \times 0.8938 = \$90.27$. The annual yield (YTM) of this bond is the true yield, as it is assumed that interest rates do not change over the one-period life of the bond (YTM = 11.88 percent).

The discount factor for the second period is implied. Although the true rate of interest for the bond's second period is unknown, it can be derived. The formula to calculate the second period's spot rate and subsequently the second period's discount factor is

$$98 = \frac{9}{1.118812} + \frac{109}{(1 + Y_2)^2}$$

$$\text{Bond MT:}\quad F_2 = 1/(1 + Y_2)^2$$

$$= 0.825284405$$

Note that the first-period yield is known, from bond ST, to be 11.8812 percent. The spot yield for the second period implied by the formula is 10.0774045 percent. The second-period discount factor is $1/(1 + 0.100774045)^2$, or 0.82528. This factor represents the present value of one dollar, two periods in the future, when the bond's yield for that period is 10.0774 percent.

Similarly, we can derive the third-period discount factor.

$$\text{Bond LT:}\quad F_3 = 1/(1 + Y_3)^3$$

$$= 0.79858595$$

The discount function of this bond is implied by the formula

$$100 = 8/(1.118812) + 8/(1.100774)^2 + 108/(1 + Y_3)^3$$

The actual yield for the bond in the third period is found to be 7.7853 percent. The discount factor, which represents the present value of one dollar three periods in the future, is computed as $1/(1 + 0.07785278)^3$ or, as above, 0.798586 (rounded).

By plotting the discount factors for each of the three periods, 0.8938, 0.82528, and 0.798586, the discount (factor) function can be determined. The yield curve can be drawn in a similar manner by plotting the yields for each individual period: 11.8812, 10.0774045, and 7.7853, respectively. This example shows how a bond's internal rate of return for one specific period can be calculated based on knowledge of the bond's price, coupon payments, and the YTM for a one-period bond. To summarize the statistics above:

Bond	ST	MT	LT
Maturity	1	2	3
Discount value	0.8938	0.82528	0.798586
Spot Yield%	11.8812	10.0774	7.7853

Using the knowledge of discount factors derived above, a straight bond with, for example, a maturity of three years and 12 percent coupon rate we can price as follows:

$$P = 12 \times 0.8938 + 12 \times 0.82528 + 112 \times 0.798586$$
$$= 10.7256 + 9.90336 + 89.4416$$
$$= \$110.07$$

In sum, once information about the yield curve is known, the discount factor of any bond can be determined.

SUMMARY

This chapter introduced the concept of condensing price information on straight bonds into relative yield measures. The process started with using a series of discount bonds to deduce the yield curve and was concluded with the computation of periodic discount factors. The description of the process was supported with a discussion of arbitrage-free conditions and the relevance of the yield curve. Topical content included a synopsis of market factors affecting the yield curve and of current theories relating to the term structure of interest rates. The emphasis throughout the chapter was on the pricing of a straight bond. Numerical examples accompanied each phase of the progression from pricing a discount bond to developing comparative yields and discount functions.

CHAPTER 4

THE FORWARD YIELD CURVE

This chapter builds upon the concepts of the nominal and spot rates introduced in the previous chapter. Forward rates encompass a time-value measurement that is inherent in valuing all types of contingent claims. This chapter will provide the groundwork for the forthcoming chapters dealing with options and relative pricing methodologies.

ARITHMETICS OF FORWARD RATES

Thus far we have considered the yield curve for spot (current) rates only. Future rates are implied on the basis of the expectation and liquidity premium hypotheses. Note that the law of one price, or the arbitrage-free condition, does not impose any constraint on the shape of the yield curve. The term structure of interest rates reflects the demand for bonds across maturities. Once the supply and demand equilibrates and a configuration of the yield curve prevails, no one can buy any portfolio of pure discount bonds and sell another bond portfolio and realize arbitrage profits. Therefore, the yield curve in principle can take on any shape even when there is no interest rate risk.

The argument goes as follows: Suppose the initial discount function is given by $F(T) = 1/(\text{current spot})^T$. After the passage of time, t, the expected new discount function (forward spot rates factors) could be defined as $F_t = 1/(\text{then spot})^T$. Let $F(T)$ be the factor (price as a percent of par) of a pure discount bond with maturity T at the initial time. After a lapse of time t, the bond would have shorter maturity, $(T - t)$.

The new price of this bond will be determined by the discount factor for a shorter maturity. Therefore it should be $F_t(T-t)$. The bond return is·

$$R = [F_t(T-t) - F(T)]/F(T) \qquad (4\text{--}1)$$

Since we do not assume any interest rate risk, this is a risk-free return, and it must also be equal to the return of holding a bond such that

$$[F_t(T-t) - F(T)]/F(T) = [1 - F(t)]/F(t)$$

Simplifying, we get

$$F_t(T-t) = F(T)/F(t) \qquad (4\text{--}2)$$

Essentially, we are stating that if the passage of time were segmented into distinct time periods (i.e., 1 day, 1 month, or 1 year), the forward rate would represent the equilibrium "bridge rate" between any two nonsequential risk-free investment alternatives.

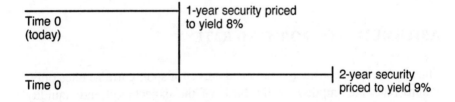

Time 0 (today) — 1-year security priced to yield 8%

Time 0 — 2-year security priced to yield 9%

For instance, if the passage of time, t, is equal to one year, then one can derive the market's implied one-year discount factor, for one year from now, $F_1(1)$, from the existing one-year and two-year factors as follows:

$$\text{Current one-period factor: } F(1) = \frac{1}{1 + r_{01}}$$

$$\text{Current two-period factor: } F(2) = \frac{1}{(1 + r_{02})^2}$$

$$\text{One-period factor, one year from now: } F_1(1) = \frac{F(2)}{F(1)} = \frac{1}{1 + r_{12}}$$

The forward factor for the next one-period rate should be equal to the ratio of *current* two-period factor divided by *current* one-period factor. All risk-free securities, in equilibrium, should exhibit the same percentage change in value over the one-year holding period. Specifically, this annual percentage change, or total return, should equal $[1 - F(1)]/F(1)$.

The left-hand side of Equation 4–2 specifies the discount function at the end of t time periods. The right-hand side of the equation is concerned only with the discount factors at the initial date. Hence, we have shown that the initial discount function can uniquely define all the discount functions in the subsequent period. These discount functions are called the "forward discount functions." When the forward discount function is converted to a yield curve, the resulting yield curve is called the "forward yield curve." The yields of the forward yield curve are called the "forward rates."

Computing Forward Rates

Suppose the initial yield curve is given by

$$(r_1, r_2, \ldots, r_n)$$

Then the discount function is also given by

$$(1/(1 + r_1), 1/(1 + r_2)^2, \quad)$$

Let $r_t(T)$ denote the forward rate of term $(T - t)$ in t periods hence Then

$$F_t(T - t) = 1/[1 + r_t(T - t)]^{T-t}$$

Substituting the above expression into Equation 4–2

$$[1 + r_t(T - t)]^{T-t} = (1 + r_T)^T/(1 + r_t)^t \qquad (4\text{–}3)$$

Assuming a flat yield curve, $r_T = r_t = r$. Thus

$$r_t(T - t) = r$$

When the yield curve is flat, forward rates equal spot rates.

Applications of the Forward Yield Curve

Suppose an individual's investment time horizon is one year, and you are hypothesizing how a yield-curve shift would impact on the portfolio value. If the yield curve shifts upward over this time period, the portfolio value need not drop. This happens because an upward-sloping yield curve means that yield curve the maturities of the bonds are now shorter and the cash flows may be discounted at a lower rate. Therefore, the price may rise. However, if the yield curve has shifted above the implied forward curve, then the bond returns would be less than the one-year rate.

Suppose the discount function that prevails at time t is the forward discount function; that is, $F_t(T-t) = F(T)/F(t)$. Then we can compute the total return of a bond with maturity T. Using Equation 4–1 we can calculate the bond return. We can show that the return is $[1-F(t)]/F(t)$, the return over the time horizon of t, independent of any maturity T. In other words, all bonds give the same return.

MEANING OF THE FORWARD RATE

Three statements sum up the concept of the forward rate. First, in an uncertain world the forward rate is the expected rate if the expectation hypothesis holds. That is, if investors' expectations about forward interest rates shape the forward yield curve, then the forward yield curve is the expected yield curve. Second, in a world of certainty, the forward yield curve is the yield curve that will prevail at the horizon date. In other words, since investors have full knowledge today of what future rates will be, their behavior today is based on certain knowledge of the future. Third, if the yield curve that will be realized in the future is the forward yield curve derived from the yield curve of today, all bonds will have a total return that will be the same as the risk-free rate. The total return will be the change in price or dollar value of the original investment plus coupon and, if any, reinvestment income.

The shape of the forward curve is determined from the current yield curve. Therefore, the shape of the forward curve can be predicted by the shape of the spot yield curve. Consider how the forward yield curve will look if the spot yield curve exhibits any of the following three shapes:

1. A steeply upward-sloping yield curve
2. A steeply downward-sloping yield curve
3. A humped yield curve

The first spot yield curve will produce a forward yield curve that is above the spot (interest rates will be higher). The second spot curve will produce a forward yield curve that is below the spot (future interest rates will be lower than the spot rates). The third curve will produce a forward yield curve that is higher than the spot rate when spot rates are rising and lower than the spot rates when spot rates are falling. The implication is that forward rates will be higher for shorter-term bonds and lower for longer-term bonds. These curves are illustrated in Figure 4–1.

FIGURE 4–1
Spot versus Implied Forward Yield Curves

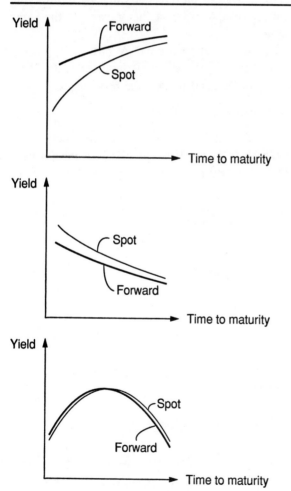

Knowledge of the forward yield curve comes into play in pricing forward contracts. How, then, does the predictability of market rates in the future influence an investor's decision regarding purchase of forward versus spot contracts?

It turns out the answer to this question is quite straightforward. For each cash flow we get, we reinvest it at the forward rate that takes the cash flow to the maturity of the bond. More precisely, let T be the maturity of the bond and t the time to the interim cashflow. Given a discount function, the forward factor is then $F(T)/F(t)$. It then can be shown that by adding all the future values of each cash flow at the maturity date and discounting back to the present value by multiplying the total future value amount by the discount factor, we get the same bond model described earlier.

Consider a simple example. Suppose bond A has an 8 percent coupon with a two-year maturity. If the discount function is $F(T) = 1/(1 + r)^T$, then, according to the bond model, the bond value is

$$P = 8F(1) + 108F(2)$$

The one-year forward discount factor for the one-year horizon is $F(2)/F(1)$. Now if we can reinvest the first cash flow at the forward rate, by the end of the second period the cash flow is

$$\frac{8}{F(2)/F(1)}$$

which is also

$$8 \times \frac{F(1)}{F(2)}$$

The total cash inflow at the end of two years is

$$8 \times \frac{F(1)}{F(2)} + 108$$

The present value is therefore

$$PV = \frac{8F(1)}{F(2)} \times F(2) + [108 \times F(2)]$$

In summary, we applied the bond model and were able to use the forward rates as the reinvestment rates for the periodic cash flows.

CANONICAL EXAMPLE

The Forward Yield Curve

This installment of the canonical example uses the three hypothetical bonds, ST, MT, and LT, to demonstrate uses of the formulas presented in this and the previous chapter.

Once the discount rate on each bond has been established, the forward discount rates can be calculated according to Equation 4–2. This equation can be used to calculate all forward discount rates except for those that are more than one period away from the spot rate. The future discount function is based on information in the table below (assuming a downward-sloping yield curve):

Maturity (in yrs)	1	2	3
Spot discount	0.8938	0.82528	0.798586
1 year	0.923338	0.893467	N/A
2 years	0.967649	N/A	N/A

Applying the concept using actual values for forward factors:

$$PV = \frac{8F(1)}{F(2)} \times F(2) + [108 \times F(2)]$$

$$= \$8(.8938/.82528)(.82528) + [\$108(.82528)]$$

$$= \$8.6642(.82528) + [108(.82528)]$$

$$= \$96.28$$

Note that $8.6642/8 = 1.0830$, an implied reinvestment (spot) rate of 8.30 percent. In the equation above, $F(1)/F(2) - 1 = 8.30$ percent. This reinvestment rate can also be obtained by solving for r in $.923338 = 1/(1 + r)$.

Applying the information provided in the previous section, we can price bond LT as follows:

Reinvesting the first coupon, the future value at time 3 is

$$8/.893467 = \$8.9537953$$

Reinvesting the second coupon, the future value at time 3 is

$$8/.96764939 = \$8.26745129$$

Therefore, at time 3, the total cash is

$$\$108 + 8.9537953 + 8.26745129 = \$125.2213368$$

The present value of this bond is

$$\$125.2213368 \times .79858595 = \$100$$

which is the same value as the price of the bond.

The spot discount factor for each bond was calculated in the canonical example of Chapter 3. According to Equation 4–2, the discount factor for a given one-year bond, one year in the future (the future discount factor) is calculated as the ratio of the factor for a two-year bond over the factor for the one-year bond. As previously mentioned, every factor can be converted into a spot rate according to Equation 3.2 in Chapter 3.

For the above table, since our examples did not include bonds with a maturity beyond three years, we could not solve for the other future discount factors. For example, the two-year future discount factor, two years in the future, is unknown because it requires knowledge of the future spot rate four years in the future.

Once the spot rates have been calculated, forward yield curves can be determined according to the same method used in the canonical example of Chapter 3.

Maturity (T)	1	2	3
Yield Curve (%)			
Spot	11.8812	10.0774	7.7853
1 year forward	8.3027	5.7939	N/A
2 years forward	3.3434	N/A	N/A

The intuitive explanation for these forward yield curves is essentially the same as that for the discount factors.

It is important to note that, given a certain forward yield curve, all three bonds will have the same yield. This is assuming the yield curve has been accurately predicted according to the expectation hypothesis and that the arbitrage-free condition applies. The return on each bond for the one-year holding period is 11.8812 percent (assuming that the implied future one-year spot rate is the one-year rate, next year).

$$\text{Bond ST:}\quad 113/101 - 1 = 11.8812\%$$

$$\text{Bond MT:}\quad [109 \times 0.923338 + 9]/98 - 1 = 11.8812\%$$

$$\text{Bond LT:}\quad [(108 \times 0.893467) + (8 \times 0.923338) + 8]/100 - 1$$

$$= 11.8812\%$$

The payments for each bond are discounted by the appropriate one-year factor. For example, bond MT, after one-year, will have its final principal and coupon payments discounted at the then one year factor, or implied spot rate. At the end of the first-year holding period, the bond's total return is the sum of the cash received from the coupon payment and the present value of the future payments divided by the initial investment.

The preceding scenario assumes a downward-sloping one-year forward yield curve. With a one-year forward horizontal yield curve, the results are different.

When the horizontal yield curve (10 percent) is compared with the downward-sloping yield curve, implicit in the current prices of our three bonds, we find that the short-term bond has the highest return.

$$\text{Bond ST:}\quad \frac{113}{101} - 1 = 11.8812\%$$

$$\text{Bond MT:}\quad \frac{109/1.1 + 9}{98} - 1 = 10.30\%$$

$$\text{Bond LT:}\quad \frac{(108/1.1^2) + (8/1.1) + 8}{100} - 1 = 4.5\%$$

SUMMARY

A discussion of the extraction of a forward rate curve from the implied spot rate curve was supported with the mathematical procedures. In addition to the basic analysis of a forward rate curve, this chapter highlighted the curve's importance for calculating holding period returns.

CHAPTER 5

PERFORMANCE PROFILES

This chapter will discuss the usefulness of graphical representations of bond price changes under changing interest rates for comparing different types of bonds.

DESCRIPTION

We have seen how the interest rate level determines the bond's price. This relationship can be demonstrated using performance profiles (PPs). A PP depicts bond price changes under changing interest rates, showing the bond's interest rate risk characteristics.

Although we can use any shape of a yield curve for constructing a PP, for simplicity we will assume a flat yield curve. The performance profile is concerned with the dollar value of the bond at different interest rate levels. In particular, we assume instantaneous shifts of the yield curve irrespective of an investment time horizon. Although the curve seldom exhibits parallel shift movements, a performance profile is useful for depicting bond price changes under rising or falling rates.

The PP is a graph of bond prices against different yield levels. The y-axis indicates bond price; the x-axis indicates the yield level (in percentage terms). The performance profile of a straight bond is given in Figure 5-1.

For straight bonds with an inverse yield/price relationship, the PP is always downward sloping like a radio dish. In addition, since the price of a bond cannot go to zero, the PP must maintain a convex shape.

EVALUATING THE RISK EXPOSURE
OF A BOND POSITION

The performance profile of a bond or portfolio of bonds is used to convey the magnitude of the interest rate risk. If the rate goes up or

FIGURE 5–1
Performance Profile

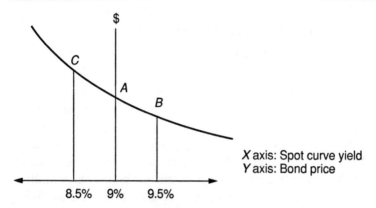

Point *A* is the prevailing bond value. Point *B*
is the bond value if the yield curve makes
a parallel move upward. Point *C* is the bond
value if the yield curve makes a parallel
move downward.

down, the PP shows how the bond value would react. If the slope of
the PP is steep, the risk is high (i.e., a slight change in interest rate
greatly affects the bond price). The curvature or convexity of the PP can
be useful for comparative purposes. If one bond's PP is more convex
than another bond's, then the higher-convexity instrument will have a
higher return performance, under any interest rate change. For example,
if rates drop, the higher-convexity instrument will have proportionally
more price appreciation. The PP takes all rate levels into account without
assigning probabilities of occurrence.

DETERMINING THE TARGET
PERFORMANCE PROFILE

The PP thus far has been used to represent the reactions of a single
straight bond, but it can also be used to represent the reactions of a
portfolio of many different types of bonds. The configuration of the PP
presents many aspects of bond yield and price relationships.

The PP generally represents the price/yield relationships of bonds
in a portfolio. If the portfolio is altered, the PP's characteristics will also
be altered. Thus, the PP can be used to determine buying and selling

decisions. Changing the PP of a portfolio of bonds involves depiction of three separate PPs:

1. The initial PP, representing the current position
2. The target profile, representing a desired position
3. The strategic profile, representing the buy/sell decisions necessary for the initial profile to replicate the target profile

The strategic profile is the difference between the initial PP and the target PP, and it incorporates expectations regarding interest rate changes. The basics of bond strategy include construction of an optimal strategy profile that will transform the original portfolio into the target portfolio. Effecting the target profile may include entirely changing the initial portfolio. Any subsequent change in interest rate levels will affect not only a bond's or a portfolio's value, but also its PP. Figure 5–2 is an example of the use of performance profiles.

For example, consider a portfolio of long-term treasury bonds. If the rates go up, the value will drop rapidly. One could say that the interest rate risk is high. If one wants to lower this risk exposure, one could implement a series of buys and sells that have a profile similar to the strategic profile. The net effect on the portfolio would be a new performance profile which would meet the objective, the target profile.

BOND STRATEGIES

Bond strategies using performance profiles include three steps:

1. Evaluate the interest rate risk exposure (construct the initial PP).
2. Establish the target PP by incorporating a subjective interest rate anticipation and/or institutional constraints (e.g., limit the interest rate increase exposure).
3. Construct the optimal portfolio by combining initial portfolio with strategic portfolio (buying and selling bonds to effect the target portfolio).

The following example will highlight the construction and use of a strategic PP in order to effect a change in an initial portfolio's sensitivities to interest rate shifts. The material will display some terminology that has not yet been discussed in this book, namely duration and convexity measures. We have included them here as additional information. They can be ignored for the purpose of this example. At this point we are

FIGURE 5–2
Use of the Performance Profile

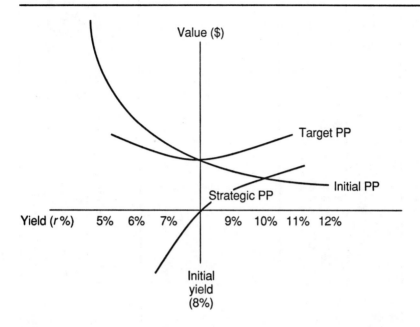

showing how performance profiles graphically depict information pertaining to changing portfolio values under changing interest rates. After reading the next two chapters, which discuss duration and convexity, the reader may wish to review this example again.

Example

The initial portfolio, as of July 21,1989, is shown in Table 5–1. The objective is to reduce the initial portfolio's downside market risk under increasing interest rates. The portfolio's effective duration should be equal to 6.5, and positive convexity should be maximized. The strategic portfolio (bond swap) in Table 5–2 is therefore constructed.

Figure 5–3 compares the performance profile of the initial portfolio to those of the strategic and target portfolios. The target portfolio is the change in the initial portfolio after the bond swaps; the duration is 6.5 and the convexity is 0.97.

This example has illustrated the usefulness of a strategic performance profile. By reviewing the initial portfolio's profile with the strategic profile, one can immediately ascertain the impact of a series of trades.

TABLE 5–1
Initial Portfolio

Size/Par	Description	Price	YTW (%)	Market Value w/Accrued	Effective Duration	Convexity
100	Treasury Note, 8%, due 7/91 (not a real note)	100.00	8	$100.28	1.78	0.00
100	Treasury Bond, 8.875%, due 2/19	108.00	8.15	$111.90	10.72	2.00
100	Treasury Bond—Callable, 13.250%, due 5/14	147.13	8.34	$149.65	8.86	1.20
300 (total portfolio)				$361.83 (total)	7.74 (avg)	1.13 (avg)

TABLE 5–2
Strategic Portfolio

Size/Par	Description	Price	YTW (%)	Market Value	Effective Duration	Convexity
49.51	Treasury Note, 8%, due 7/91	100.00	8	$49.65	1.78	0
−33.18	Treasury Bond—Callable, 13.250%, due 5/14	147.13	8.34	($49.65)	8.86	1.2
Total strategic portfolio's characteristics:					−3.51 (avg)	−0.58 (avg)

(Results: No additions to or subtractions from existing initial portfolio's market value)

FIGURE 5–3
Performance Value Profiles: (a) Initial and Strategic Portfolios; (b) Initial and Target Portfolios

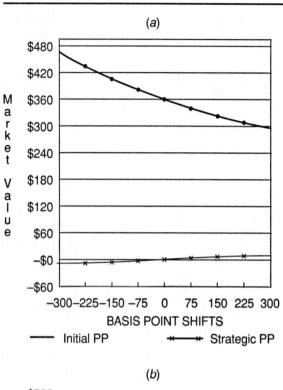

(a)

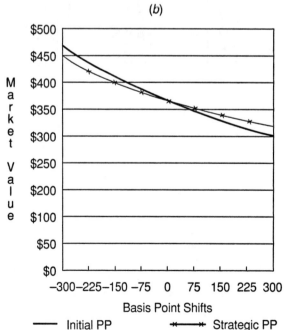

(b)

TABLE 5–3
Bond Prices

Spot Rates Derived in Canonical Example of Chapter 3

One Year	11.8812%
Two Year	10.0774%
Three Year	7.7853%

	Basis Point Shifts						
Bond Prices	*−150*	*−100*	*−50*	*0*	*50*	*100*	*150*
Zero-Coupon 1	90.60	90.19	89.78	89.38	88.98	88.59	88.20
Zero-Coupon 2	84.82	84.05	83.28	82.53	81.78	81.05	80.32
Zero-Coupon 3	83.29	82.12	80.98	79.86	78.76	77.68	76.62

ST, MT, and LT from Canonical Example of Chapter 2

	ST	MT	LT
Market Value	101	98	100
Coupon Rate	13%	9%	8%
Maturity	1	2	3

	Basis Point Shifts						
Bond Prices	*−150*	*−100*	*−50*	*0*	*50*	*100*	*150*
ST	102.37	101.91	101.45	101	100.55	100.11	99.66
MT	100.61	99.73	98.86	98	97.15	96.32	95.49
LT	103.98	102.63	101.30	100	98.72	97.46	96.23

Figure 5–3*a* shows that the strategic profile indicates the trades will only marginally reduce the initial portfolio's interest rate risk exposure. A review of the target profile in the second figure confirms this portrayal.

Minimization of interest rate risk exposure involves keeping the value of the portfolio the same (i.e., avoiding losses in bond price that accompany increases in interest rates). This implies a horizontal target PP. This horizontal target PP ensures that the value of the portfolio (price of all bonds in the portfolio) remains the same at all interest rate levels. The effective duration of the target PP would be 0.

CANONICAL EXAMPLE

Performance Profiles

This installment of the canonical example provides a tabular and graphic explanation of the performance profile of the three coupon bonds, ST,

FIGURE 5–4
Zero Coupon Bonds: Three Different Maturities.

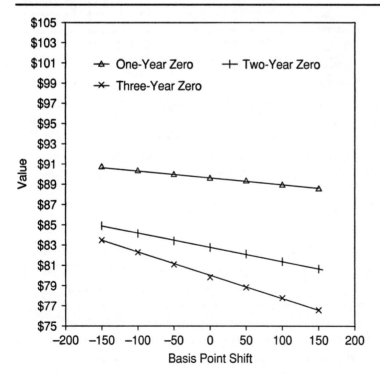

FIGURE 5–5
Coupon Bonds: Three Different Maturities

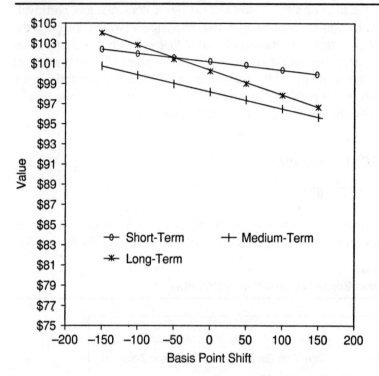

MT, and LT, as well as for three zero-coupon bonds with corresponding maturities and prices. Table 5–3 depicts changes in bond price according to parallel changes in interest rates (as measured in basis points). We are using the spot rates derived in the previous chapters.

The performance profiles of the bond(s), based on the numbers in Table 5–3, are shown in Figures 5–4 and 5–5.

SUMMARY

This chapter discussed and illustrated basic bond strategies for a straight bond with a negative-slope, positive-convexity PP. Evaluation of the performance profile of any type of bond is essential for optimal management of the bond itself or the entire portfolio of bonds. In subsequent chapters, we will see that different types of bonds have entirely different PP curves and as a result require different bond strategies.

CHAPTER 6

DURATION

Duration is used to estimate a change in bond price for a change in rate. This chapter presents effective duration as the appropriate measure for quantifying the interest rate risk for bonds. The measure is compared against the more commonly applied Macaulay and modified Macaulay duration measures.

MANAGING INTEREST RATE RISK

The Treasury bond prices enable us to estimate the yield curve, or the time value of money, at any time. However, the yield curve is not static nor is its movement predictable, because its level and shape depend on a multitude of economic factors: economic outlook, inflation expectation, and investors' demand, to name a few. As a result, the yield curve may swiftly change its configuration at any time.

Such unanticipated movement of the yield curve in general leads to unexpected change in a bond value. Take a Treasury bond, for example. If rates drop, the bond value will rise, and as rates rise, the value drops. These unanticipated changes in the yield curve shape constitute the interest rate risk. The uncertainty of the bond value, subject to the interest rate risk, is the interest rate risk exposure of the bond.

The interest rate risk exposure of a bond depends on the bond characteristics. A short term bond value is less sensitive to shifts in the yield curve than the long term bond. But there are many factors other than maturity that affect the bond interest rate risk exposure. For example, coupon level, credit risk premium, call provision, and other features are factors that may raise or lower a bond's interest rate risk exposure As a result the risk exposure varies greatly across different types of bonds. Indeed, corporate bonds, mortgage-backed securities, and interest rate options all react differently to shifts of the yield curve.

The next few sections of this chapter will explain the methodology of duration. Duration is a summary measure that characterizes the interest rate risk components of an issue or a portfolio. The subsequent sections will discuss the applications of this summary measure for managing the risk exposure of bonds and interest rate options. Managing interest rate risk refers to the procedure of quantifying the interest rate risk exposure of a position and then implementing security trades that will alter its exposure in order to meet a defined objective.

Conceptual Description

The most important and commonly used measure of interest rate risk exposure of a bond is the *duration measure*. Duration quantifies the price sensitivity of a bond to small shifts of the yield curve. It assigns a measure of the interest rate risk exposure to a bond, independent of the size of the bond holding within the portfolio. The same number is assigned whether the bond is held in long or short position, or in large or small amount.

A duration measure is also independent of any individual interest rate forecast or of any subjective views of interest rate risk. As a result, the expected yield curve shape, the interest rate volatilities, and the distribution of the future interest rates are not required for calculating duration. The bond duration, an attribute of the bond, is determined by the bond's characteristics. As mentioned earlier, not all bonds have the same characteristics, so there may be market factors that affect the cash flows, and hence the price, of one bond and not the price of another bond. Since an issue's price is a reflection of all market factors, the duration measure, which is extrapolated from the bond price movements, also embodies the unique characteristics of a particular issue. Notice that a change in price for a given change in rates can be seen as a slope of a performance profile, as discussed in Chapter 5. This characteristic of effective duration will be discussed later in this chapter.

Effective duration is a summary of the bond's price sensitivity to interest rate changes. A bond price is just the sum of the present values of a series of cash flows; each cash flow is discounted by the spot rate associated with its time to maturity. Therefore, duration is nothing more than a measure of the interest rate sensitivity of this stream of present values.

If any component affecting the present value computation changes, the duration measures will change. For instance, if changing market factors lead to a new interest rate environment, then the change in discounting rates will translate into a new duration measure for every fixed income instrument. As will be explained in this and the following chapter, the change in duration will not be consistent across securities.

The duration measure has many applications in fixed-income management. First, duration enables investors and issuers to compare the risk exposure of bonds. Bonds with higher duration have higher risk exposure than bonds with lower duration. Second, duration directly relates the price change to the rate change, and therefore it provides an indication of the bond's future value, assuming a specific level of rate shift. Finally, duration provides the means to manage the interest rate risk of a bond position or portfolio. Managers can attain the appropriate level of risk exposure by implementing trades that will either raise or lower the net duration of the combined positions.

To derive a measure of a bond risk exposure, we first need to find a representation of interest rate risk: How should we describe the movements of the yield curve over a time horizon? Unfortunately, the yield curve's historical movement offers little insight into the pattern of the unanticipated shift of the yield curve. Over the years many duration measures have been proposed, such as stochastic duration. Stochastic duration is defined by a stochastic process model of interest rate movements. Researchers have proposed that the short-term rate follows a random-walk or a mean-reverting process or a process that converges to a stochastic long-term rate. However, research has not uncovered any adequate modeling of the yield curve movements. Failing to determine a "realistic" representation of the yield curve movement, we settle on the simplest representation, though it is not necessarily realistic or theoretically correct. We assume that the yield curve shifts instantaneously in a parallel fashion, possibly up or down. This allows us to derive *effective duration*, the duration measure associated with this particular presentation of interest rate risk.

EFFECTIVE DURATION

Effective duration of a bond is relatively simple to define and yet general enough to have broad applications. For these reasons, effective duration has recently become an industry standard. Simply described, effective duration of a bond (or of any interest-rate-sensitive security) is the ratio of the *proportional **drop*** in bond price to a small parallel *upward shift* of the yield curve. For example, if we know a particular bond price would drop 0.2 percent with a rise of one basis point in market rates, then the effective duration of the bond is as follows:

Effective duration $= D = 0.002/0.0001/\text{year} = 20$ years

Notice there are two specific characteristics of duration:

1. Duration depicts the property of a negative correlation between price (discount factor) changes and interest rate changes.

   A security with positive duration indicates that its price will drop when interest rates increase.

   A security with negative duration has a price/yield performance profile that is reversed. The security's price will increase when interest rates increase. We can immediately deduce that a security with negative duration is not a simple bond. Its price is not directly determined by the spot discount factors.

2. The unit of measure for duration is years because the shift is measured in yield, which is a return per year.

The more precise definition is given below. Suppose we have estimated the time value of money from the Treasury market, and that it is represented by the "implied" spot yield curve. Each point on this curve is a yield measure depicted as $r(T)$. The yield $r(T)$ is the internal rate of return (in semiannual compounding rate) required by a single payment at a time horizon of T years by the Treasury market. Consider a bond priced at P. This bond can be any interest-rate-sensitive instrument including bond options.

Suppose the yield curve makes a parallel, infinitesimally small upward shift (Δr). Then the new yield curve is given by $r_1(T) = r(T) + \Delta r$ with T being the time to maturity. By the definition of parallel shift, Δr is a constant number, independent of the time to maturity. Suppose that under this new interest rate level the bond price is P_1. Then the change in bond price is

$$\Delta P = P_1 - P$$

The effective duration D is defined as

$$\Delta P/P = -D \cdot \Delta r$$

where Δr is infinitesimally small

Granted, it is somewhat unrealistic to believe that the yield curve moves in a parallel fashion and that fixed-income management is concerned with instantaneous time horizon. However, as mentioned earlier, these simplifying assumptions do provide us with a useful duration measure. Although the definition requires the shift to be infinitesimally small, for all practical purposes shifts as large as 10 basis points are acceptable for most bonds.

Although effective duration is defined for a rise in yield, it can be shown to be consistently defined for a drop in yield in relation to the rise in the bond price. This is true because in a well-functioning market the bond price should be smoothly related to small shifts of the interest rate, otherwise arbitrage opportunities prevail. When the price is smoothly related to the yields, (Δr) may be viewed as the change of the yields and the change may be an increase or decrease in yields.

Having formally defined effective duration, we now go through some simple examples to discuss how to derive and use these measures.

EXAMPLES OF EFFECTIVE DURATIONS

In this section, we will derive the effective durations of some bonds, from the simplest type to the more complex. Because effective duration depends on the bond price, which in turn depends on the shape of the yield curve, we first need to specify the yield curve shape. For simplicity, we shall assume that the yield curve is flat at the rate r.

Zero-Coupon Treasury Bond

Perhaps the simplest bond is the zero-coupon Treasury bond, or U.S. STRIP. Let P be the price of a U.S. STRIP with maturity T. Then we know that the bond is priced by the formula:

$$P = (1 + r/2)^{-2T} \qquad (6\text{--}1)$$

If we differentiate the equation with respect to r, we get

$$\partial P/\partial r = -T/(1 + r/2) \times P$$

By the definition of effective duration, representing a percentage change in price, we have

$$(\partial P/\partial r)/P = -D = -T/(1 + r/2) \qquad (6\text{--}2)$$

Equation 6–2 shows that the effective duration of a zero-coupon Treasury bond is the maturity adjusted downward by the factor $(1 + r/2)$. For a 30-year U.S. STRIP at 10 percent interest rate, the bond duration is

$$D = 30/(1.05) = 28.57 \text{ years} \qquad (6\text{–}3)$$

Now, what do we know about this bond that has duration 28.57 years? By the definition of duration, the proportional change in the bond price should be approximately the same as the product of the duration and the shift of the yield curve. So, for a 10-basis-point drop in the yield curve, we have

$$\Delta P/P = -28.571428 \times (-0.001)$$

That is, the bond price will rise 2.8571 percent. We can cross-check this estimation. First, before the rate drops the bond value is

$$P = 100/(1.05)^{60} = 5.3536$$

After the rate drops 10 basis points, the bond price will rise to

$$P_1 = 100/(1.0495)^{60} = 5.5088$$

The proportional change in price is given by

$$dP/P = (P_1 - P)/P = 2.899\%$$

This simple calculation shows that the duration measure quite accurately estimates the proportional change in bond price. Also, this result shows the extent of interest rate risk exposure of a 30-year zero-coupon bond. A mere 10-basis-point drop/rise can lead to 2.86 percent increase/decrease in bond value.

Indeed, Equation 6–2 says quite simply that the interest rate risk exposure of a zero-coupon bond is approximately the maturity of the bond. As a result, the maturity of a U.S. STRIP bond is approximately the price sensitivity to the shift of the yield curve. The shorter the maturity, the smaller the risk exposure.

In line with a zero's duration being defined by the zero's maturity, the zero's duration declines proportionately with the passage of time. If we assume that the yield curve remains constant at r as time passes, the duration will drop with time. Figure 6–1 depicts the duration/time relationship for the 30-year zero coupon bond. Initially, the bond duration is 28.571 years; then it drops proportionally with time and reaches zero duration in 30 years.

FIGURE 6–1
Duration/Time Relationship

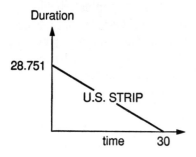

PERPETUAL BOND

Consider a semiannual coupon-paying bond with infinite maturity. Suppose the annual coupon rate is C and the next coupon date is in half a year. Then the price of the bond is given by

$$P = C/r \qquad (6\text{--}3)$$

The duration is $D = -(\partial P/\partial r)/P$, or

$$D = 1/r \qquad (6\text{--}4)$$

The effective duration measure of the perpetual bond is remarkably simple. Suppose that the market yield is 10 percent; then according to Equation 6–4 the duration is 10 years. Some interesting observations can be made here. The interest rate risk exposure of a perpetual bond is similar to that of a 10-year zero-coupon bond. They both have 10-year duration. We find the bond that has infinite maturity can have less risk exposure than a 30-year zero-coupon bond. This observation is understandable. A zero bond has only one principal payment. Therefore, the longer the bond's maturity, the more influence the compounding time component has on the present value computation of the distant principal payment. On the other hand, a perpetual bond's cash flows are evenly distributed over time. Since the earlier payments represent a larger proportion of time-weighted present value stream, there is a reduction in the influence of long compounding periods on a coupon bond's price.

Now suppose that the market rate level remains constant at r. We want to investigate how the bond duration will change over time.

Equation 6–4 is somewhat misleading. The duration expression seems to say that the bond duration remains constant as time goes on. Such is not the case. The duration is derived for the first coupon date being half a year away. As time goes on, the first coupon payment approaches, reducing the duration of the bond. As soon as the coupon is paid, the duration would go up again, but only slightly; it would not be as high as it was prior to the the the time passage of a coupon payment.

COUPON BOND

Consider a coupon bond with a very low coupon rate. The duration should be slightly less than the zero-coupon bond with the same maturity. This is because the coupons of the coupon bond represent cash flows coming in earlier, and they reduce the interest rate risk exposure of the bond. However, consider another coupon issue with the same coupon rate but with longer maturity. It will have a longer duration. For a coupon bond with very long maturity, the bond duration must be similar to that of a perpetual bond, because the principal payment is so far away that it contributes little to the bond risk exposure.

The duration of a coupon bond in relation to the bond maturity is depicted in Figure 6–2. Curve C represents the duration of a low-coupon bond. The duration of such a bond must necessarily be similar to that of a zero-coupon bond. Therefore, the curve C rises at approximately the same rate as the curve A. However, at some point the curve C must bend down, because for some sufficiently long maturity the duration of the coupon bond must be similar to that of a perpetual bond, as discussed before. Therefore, curve C must approach curve B, the duration of the perpetual bond. This results in a hump for curve C. That is, the duration of a coupon issue can exceed the perpetual bond duration. However, such is not always the case. If the coupon rate is sufficiently high, the coupon bond duration must necessarily be less than that of the perpetual bond. For this case durations of two such bonds are represented by curves D_1 and D_2.

Duration of a Portfolio of Bonds

The use of the effective duration concept can be quite simply extended to the portfolio context. Effective duration of a portfolio has broad implications to fixed-income management. The effective duration of a

FIGURE 6–2
Duration versus Maturity—Premium, Par, and Discount Bonds

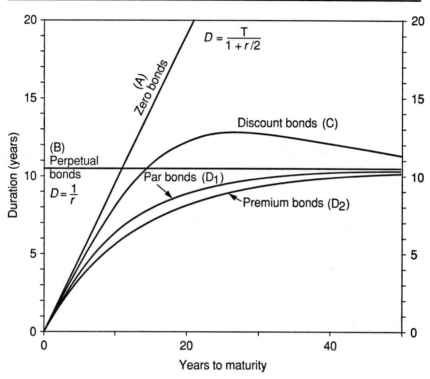

bond portfolio is defined to be the ratio of the proportional change in the portfolio value to an infinitesimal parallel shift of the spot yield curve.

The effective duration of a portfolio is closely related to the effective duration of the securities. The link is simple, and it is one of the most wonderful results in fixed-income analysis. The effective duration of a portfolio is the weighted average of the durations of each security in the portfolio, with the weights being the proportion of the security value to the total portfolio value. More precisely, let V be the portfolio value, D the duration of the portfolio, V_i the value of bond position, and D_i the duration of security i. Then, we have

$$D = (V_1/V)D_1 + \cdots + (V_n/V)D_n \qquad (6\text{–}5)$$

where n is the number of types of securities in the portfolio. Equation 6–5 can be derived quite simply. V, the value of the portfolio, is simply the sum of all the bond position values, $V = V_1 + \cdots + V_n$.

For a small parallel shift of the yield curve we have

$$\Delta V/\Delta r = \Delta V_1/\Delta r + \cdots + \Delta V_n/\Delta r$$

But we define the portfolio duration to be

$$D = -(\Delta V/\Delta r)/V$$

which in turn is given by

$$(-\Delta V/\Delta r)/V = -(V_1/V)(\Delta V_1/\Delta r)/V_1$$
$$+ \cdots + -(V_n/V)(\Delta V_n/\Delta r)/V_n$$

Let m_i be the number of bond i we hold in the portfolio and the P_i be the bond price. Then we have

$$V_i = m_i P_i$$

From above, it is straightforward to show that

$$D_i = -(\Delta V_i/\Delta r)/V_i \qquad (6\text{--}6)$$

By substituting Equation (6–6) to Equation (6–5) we get

$$D = W_i D_i + \cdots + W_n D_n \qquad (6\text{--}7)$$

where W_i are the weights given by

$$W_i = V_i/V$$

The result is intuitively appealing. Consider a bond portfolio with a large proportion of bond A and small proportion of bond B. The interest rate risk exposure of the portfolio is clearly some kind of an average of the durations of bonds A and B. But the value sensitivity of the portfolio has to be more similar to that of bond A than that of bond B. This is precisely what Equation 6–7 is expressing. What is significant about Equation 6–7 is that it shows precisely what determines the weights. They are the proportions of the values of bond positions to the total portfolio values in terms of market prices, not book values or other value measures.

The calculation of the portfolio duration, while simple, has many implications. The following examples illustrate a few. Consider the portfolio in Table 6–1 to illustrate the calculation of the effective duration of a portfolio. The portfolio has six types of bonds. The second column shows the number of bonds in each type in the portfolio. For example, the first row shows that the portfolio has 10 Treasury bonds with maturity

8/15/13. The value of each bond is the traded price plus the accrued interest. Since the par value for each bond is $1,000, the total market value of that bond position is $12,749. The percentage of the bond position in the portfolio is given by the bond value divided by the total portfolio value times 100. The effective duration of the portfolio is the weighted average of the effective durations of each bond, in the last column, weighted by the percentage in market value.

Duration with Credit-Liquidity Spreads

So far in this sequence of examples, we price the bonds by using the discount rates of the spot yield curve. Implicitly we assume that the bonds are default-free with no premium for the credit risk and have no liquidity premium. When there is a spread to compensate for the credit risk and liquidity of a bond, the effective duration will be affected. In general, the widening in the spread leads to shortening duration.

Maybe we should analyze the problem a bit more rigorously first. Take a zero-coupon bond with maturity T. Suppose the spread is sp. Then the bond is priced by

$$P = 1/[1 + (r + sp)/2]^{2T} \qquad (6\text{--}8)$$

By comparing Equation (6–8) with Equation (6–1), we see that

$$D = T/[1 + (r + sp)/2] \qquad (6\text{--}9)$$

It is clear from the above that the spread lowers the duration. But the effect of the spread on a coupon bond duration is more significant. A coupon bond is a portfolio of zero-coupon bonds with each coupon payment and the principal being a zero-coupon bond. The discussion in the previous section shows that the portfolio duration is

$$D = W_i D_1 + \cdots + W_n D_n$$

where D is the duration of a zero-coupon bond with maturity equaling the time the payment of the ith coupon. W_i is the present value of the ith payment to the coupon bond value.

If the spread widens, the weights assigned to earlier payments will increase while the weights to the later payments decrease. But the earlier payments have shorter durations, and therefore the coupon bond duration will drop. In sum, for a bond that is subject to more default risk, the interest rate risk is less relevant to its risk exposure, and it has a lower effective duration.

TABLE 6–1
Portfolio Analysis of April 21, 1988

Bond	Amount	Description	Coupon	Maturity	Type Rating	Price	Accrued Interest	Market Value	% in Value	Effective Duration
1	10	Treasury bond	12.00	8/15/13	government	125.28	2.21	12,749	21.8	8.40
2	10	Treasury bond	10.375	11/15/12	government	110.19	4.53	11,472	19.62	8.28
3	10	Treasury bond	10.375	11/15/09	government	109.47	4.53	11,400	19.49	7.75
4	10	Treasury bond	11.750	2/15/01	government	102.44	2.16	12,260	20.97	6.93
5	5	Chrysler Financial	13.250	12/15/88	BBB	103.29	4.87	5,398	9.23	0.61
6	5	General Electric Credit	13.625	9/15/91	AAA	102.35	1.40	5,188	8.87	0.15
Total Portfolio								58,467		6.49

Duration of Interest Rate Options

Effective duration is applicable to any interest-rate-sensitive instruments, not solely to bonds that pay coupons and principals. Determining the effective duration of interest rate options is central to analyzing option-embedded bonds and formulating bond portfolio strategies. Here we will discuss the effective duration of put and call options on T bonds or T bond futures. The discussion is general, and it should apply to both European and American options. Option terminology used in the following section, such as *bond equivalence* and *delta*, will be discussed in greater detail in Chapter 12. Here we are concerned with presenting the concept of duration as it applies to options and option-embedded bonds.

First we consider the call options. Consider an in-the-money option where the strike price is low relative to the market price. The option behaves much like the underlying security. In this case, the price/yield performance profiles for both the option and the underlying security are similar. The slopes of the price/yield curves are the same as depicted in Figure 6–3. If we consider the proportional changes in price, or effective duration, the duration of the option will be higher than the underlying security's. The reason is as follows. An option represents a right, but not an obligation, to purchase the underlying security at a specified (exercise or strike) price. For this right, an investor pays a small premium. Any increase in the security's value will translate into a higher proportional change on the initial option value compared to that on the underlying security's initial value.

This result can be seen as follows for a call option. A change in the option value for a given change in rates, or its slope, is the product of the underlying security's price response to change in rates and the option's hedge ratio (or delta).

$$\frac{\Delta C}{\Delta r} = \frac{\Delta B}{\Delta r} \times \frac{\Delta C}{\Delta B}$$

where C = call option value (initial)
ΔC = $ change in option value
Δr = change in interest rates (change in yield)
B = underlying bond price
ΔB = $ change in bond price
$\frac{\Delta C}{\Delta B}$ = hedge ratio, or delta

FIGURE 6–3
In-the-Money Option—Performance Profile

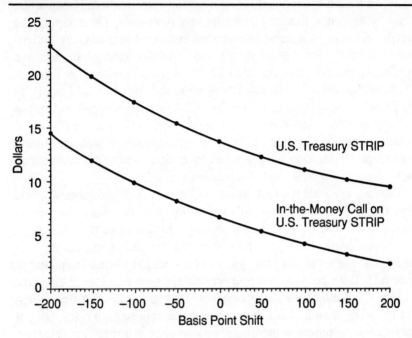

Note: For in-the-money options, delta is 1. That is, the slope of the tangent of the performance profile of an option is the same as that of a bond.

This formula can easily be extended to represent price changes in a percentage format using the duration ($D_B = \Delta B/\Delta r/B$) of the underlying instrument.

$$\frac{\Delta C/\Delta r}{C} = \frac{[(\Delta B/\Delta r)/B] \times B \times (\Delta C/\Delta B)}{C}$$

An in-the-money option has a delta, $\Delta C/\Delta B$, of 1; the option's dollar value change will be exactly the same as the underlying security's. This result is expected since an option position mimics an underlying bond equivalent position. An option holder essentially holds 100 percent of an underlying security and thus is accruing the same dollar benefit as the security holder; the cash flows of the two positions are identical.

On the other hand, when an option is out-of-the-money, the delta of the option is less than one. It is equivalent to holding less than 100 percent of the underlying bond since the bond price has not yet met or exceeded the strike price. The option has value only in the sense that before its expiration there is a probability that the security's market value may exceed the strike price. The option value, which can be quite low, represents an investor's payment for holding this right to future market appreciation over a certain time interval. The more the option is out-of-the-money, the lower is the initial value of the option (holding other factors constant).

For each $1 increase in security value, this translates into a delta × $1 increase in the option value. Since the dollar amount of the increase in value is unbounded, the option investor could realize an investment return exceeding 100 percent. For this reason, the effective duration of the option increases as the option becomes increasingly out-of-the-money. The duration number can become very high; in principle, there is no upper limit.

Now consider a put option. Much of the discussion above also applies to a put option, with one interesting exception: the put option value on a Treasury bond goes up along with the interest rates. Therefore, the option has negative duration. Suppose a put option has a duration equal to -100 years. With a shift upward of one basis point, the put option will increase in price by 1 percent.

OTHER COMMONLY USED DURATION MEASURES

Effective duration has the broadest application in fixed-income management. Thus far we have shown how the duration measure can be used. But aside from bonds with known cash flows, the effective duration in general is very difficult to calculate. The procedure to determine such a risk measure requires the mathematical modeling of an instrument's probable cash flows. Instruments such as mortgages and callable bonds fall into this category. A model of a bond or other instrument is the mathematical formulation of how the price is determined given the relevant market parameters. These parameters include the yield curve, interest rate volatilities, and other factors. If a mathematical model can relate these parameters to the price, we can simulate the price given a small parallel shift of the yield curve and can calculate the proportional change in price. In this way we can determine the effective duration.

Although effective duration is the most useful measure, there are two other commonly used duration measures: the Macaulay duration and modified Macaulay duration.

Macaulay Duration

Macaulay duration measures the average life of a bond, ignoring any options embedded in the bond. For example, a corporate bond may have call provisions. Macaulay duration measures only the average life of the coupon and principal payments. We have seen that for bonds that have simple cash flow, the effective duration or the interest rate risk exposure is somewhat related to the average life of the bond. For this reason, Macaulay duration is sometimes used for measuring the bond risk exposure.

Formally, Macaulay duration is defined as follows for a bond purchased on its coupon date. Suppose a bond pays $\$X_1$ at time 1, X_2 at time 2, and so on until the nth payment X_n at time t_n. The price of the bond is P. Given these data, we can calculate the yield to maturity of the bond. Macaulay duration is the weighted average maturity of all the payments, where the weight is the proportion of the present value of the payment to the bond value multiplied by the time period. The present value is calculated by discounting the payment by the yield to maturity.

Hence, we have

Macaulay duration $= D_{\text{mac}}$

$$= \frac{\dfrac{X_1^* t_1}{(1+\text{YTM})} + \cdots + \dfrac{X_n^* t_n}{(1+\text{YTM})^n}}{P} \tag{6-10}$$

It is instructive to discuss the behavior of the Macaulay duration using the fulcrum of a leverage system as an analogy. Consider a 9 percent coupon bond with three-year maturity. The cash flow is diagrammatically represented by

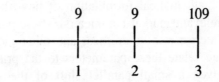

Let the YTM of the bond be 8 percent. Then the present value of each payment is 7.407, 6.85, 85.733, for the first, second, and third payments, respectively. The price of the bond is 100.00. Diagrammatically:

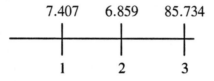

$$\text{Macaulay duration} = \frac{7.407(1) + 6.859(2) + 85.734(3)}{100.00} = 2.78 \text{ years}$$

Think of this diagram as a weightless leverage system with the horizontal line being a beam with weights placed on it at the payment dates. The weights represent the present value of each payment. This is depicted in Figure 6–4.

The Macaulay duration is the distance from the initial time to the point where the fulcrum would perfectly balance the weights on the weightless beam. Several interesting observations may be made about Macaulay duration. For any coupon bond, and for the same coupon rate, Macaulay duration increases with the bond maturity. With the lengthening of maturity, the beam stretches farther, and the fulcrum must move farther out in step. Also, for a higher given coupon rate, the bond duration shortens. This is because more weight is assigned to the earlier payment and less to the final (principal-plus-coupon) payment. Finally, when the interest rate increases, the duration shortens. This is because the increase in rate leads to a decrease in the present value of payments that are farther in the future than those up front. Therefore the interest rate decrease reduces the weight farther out by diminishing the present value of the payments farther in the future.

For a zero-coupon bond, the Macaulay duration is the maturity of the bond. This is clearly seen in the fulcrum analogy. With only one payment, the weightless beam can only balance at the payment date.

Due to the accrual of interest, the Macaulay duration changes over time. The price used to compute duration is the invoice price (i.e., the quoted price plus the accrued interest). For this reason, as the coupon date approaches, the invoice price increases, leading to a steady drop in the Macaulay duration. Immediately after the coupon payment date, the duration rises slightly as the invoice price drops as a result of the coupon payment and loss of accrued interest. The passage of time

FIGURE 6–4
Macaulay Duration

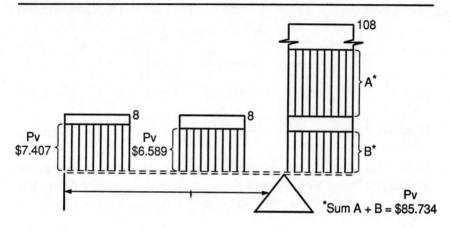

and decrease in remaining coupon payments has another effect on a bond's duration. As each coupon payment is made, and analogously, as each weight falls off the beam, the duration decreases to reflect the smaller value of remaining payments. Duration can parallel maturity as both decrease over time. However, the decrease in duration is influenced by the weight of each coupon payment and, as such, may decrease at a rate faster or slower than that of maturity, if the size of each payment in the cash flow is not uniform.

As noted before, most bonds are not straight bonds. In order to compute Macaulay duration for option-embedded bonds, practitioners often treat these bonds as if they were straight bonds. For a callable bond, one can ignore the call provision and simply consider the bond to be a coupon issue in order to calculate the Macaulay duration using the yield to maturity of the bond as the discount rate. In such cases, the Macaulay duration may not be anywhere close to the bond's actual expected life.

Modified Macaulay Duration

Modified Macaulay duration measures the price sensitivity of a bond to the change in yield to maturity. The change of the bond's yield to maturity may be the result of the shift in the yield curve, the change in the credit premium, or other reasons. In fact, the modified Macaulay duration need not measure the price risk exposure of the bond to the shift of the yield curve. It is only a relationship between the bond price sensitivity and the change of its YTM. In short, modified Macaulay duration is the relationship of the price and the YTM of a bond.

Let P be the price (and YTM the yield to maturity) of the bond. Then modified Macaulay duration is defined as

$$\text{Modified Macaulay duration} = D_{\text{mod}}$$

$$= (-\Delta P/\Delta YTM)/P \qquad (6-11)$$

As it turns out, modified Macaulay duration has a much simpler expression. By the definition of yield to maturity, we know that

$$P = \frac{x_1}{(1 + YTM/2)} + \frac{x_2}{[1 + (YTM/2)]^2} + \cdots + \frac{X_n}{[1 + (YTM/n)]^n}$$

$$(6-12)$$

Using Equation (6–11), we can calculate modified Macaulay duration directly, and we can show that

$$D_{\text{mod}} = D_{\text{mac}}/(1 + YTM/2) \qquad (6-13)$$

The above expression gives the reason for calling the measure modified Macaulay duration, since it is simply modifying the Macaulay duration by a factor of

$$\frac{1}{1 + (YTM/2)}$$

A few words about the modifier are in order. It is somewhat curious as to how the modifier is determined. The modifier changes according to the means by which the bond yield is calculated. For an annual yield, the modifier is $1/(1 + YTM)$. For a semiannual bond equivalent yield (BEY), which we have been using, the modifier is $1/[1 + (YTM/2)]$; for a quarterly yield it is $1/[1 + (YTM/4)]$, and so on. Therefore, in general the modifier is $1/[1 + (YTM/n)]$, where n is the number of periods of compounding.

The reason for changing the modifier depending on the bond yield is quite clear. A shift of one basis point of the bond YTM has different impact on the bond price depending on whether the yield is measured by semiannual or annual compounding. A yield shift of one basis point measured by semiannual rate is less of a yield change than that measured in quarterly compounding rate, but more of a change than that measured in annual compounding rate. For this reason, the price change has to depend on how the yield is measured. It is larger for the yield measured with more compounding periods for each basis point movement. The modifier makes exactly that adjustment.

Modified Macaulay duration is somewhat related to the effective duration. Consider a Treasury bond when the yield curve is flat. The bond yield to maturity must be the same as the level of the yield curve. In this case, the change of the yield to maturity must be identical to the shift of the yield curve, so the modified Macaulay duration is the same as the effective duration. Indeed, all of the following conditions must hold for a bond's modified Macaulay duration to be the same as the effective duration:

1. The bond has only cash flows with no options embedded in the bond. Credit and liquidity are constant, independent of the time of the payments.
2. The yield curve is horizontal, and yield is measured by a continuously compounding rate.

These are rather stringent conditions. In fact, the two measures often differ greatly, particularly when the bond has embedded options (i.e., call provisions).

USAGE OF THE DIFFERENT MEASURES IN THE MARKET

Effective duration, Macaulay duration, and modified Macaulay duration are similar in some ways. In particular, when applied to the Treasury market, they all relate the price sensitivity of the bond to the shift of the yield curve. However, beyond the Treasury market these measures can differ significantly, and they represent different attributes of the bond. Macaulay duration measures the average life of the cash flows. Modified Macaulay duration measures the price sensitivity to a small change in the YTM of the bond. Effective duration measures the price sensitivity to the shift in the yield curve.

Therefore, effective duration measures directly the bond price sensitivity to the changes of the market rates, while modified Macaulay duration relates the bond's YTM to the price. It is important to note that a bond's YTM does not in general move in step with the yield curve.

For a given bond, unless the investors know the relationship between the change of the YTM and the change of the yield curve, the modified Macaulay duration offers little insight into a bond's interest rate risk exposure.

There are many generalizations of the concept of effective duration. As presented so far, effective duration represents the first step in measuring interest rate risk exposure of a bond. For example, as we mentioned earlier, it is for simplicity that parallel shift of the yield curve is used. But surely the yield curve is not required to make a parallel shift, and we can still measure the price sensitivity of any change of the yield curve shape. In principle, all the analysis used for effective duration can be extended to any nonparallel shift of the yield curve. We can model the effect of a nonparallel yield curve change by constructing a new yield curve, implementing parallel shifts on this new curve, and noting the new, computed duration value of the bond. The bond's price sensitivity under a nonparallel shift is now characterized by this new duration measure. The original duration measure is no longer applicable. It was a price-sensitivity measure associated with the original yield curve environment.

This capability to derive a duration measure for different types of spot curve movements was not feasible with the modified Macaulay duration measure. As previously stated, the modified duration measure used only changes in a bond's YTM for gauging price sensitivity. There was no way to separate the influence of changes in the spot curve from other factors, such as credit or liquidity, that affected YTM. The next chapter will expand on the duration concept by introducing a second interest-rate-sensitivity measure; this measure is known as convexity.

SUMMARY

Investors in fixed-income securities are increasingly referring to effective duration measures to represent a bond's expected price performance under changing rates. This chapter presented a detailed analysis of effective duration and compared it to the more commonly understood Macaulay and modified Macaulay measures.

CHAPTER 7

CONVEXITY

Effective duration quantifies the interest rate risk exposure of a bond and measures the price sensitivity to a small parallel shift of the yield curve. Therefore effective duration can be used as an indicator of a bond's performance with a shift of the interest rates; if a bond has a high duration, then the bond return would be high with a relatively small drop in interest rates. Although effective duration is useful, it does have limitations. This chapter will begin with a discussion of these aspects and then introduce another measure that, when used with duration, more accurately quantifies the interest rate risk exposure of a fixed income security. This additional measure is commonly known as convexity.

There are many interpretations of convexity. We will limit our discussion to two of these. The most relevant is termed convexity. The less accurate description is "the change in duration." We now begin our discussion of duration and how it is associated with convexity.

As discussed in the previous chapter, implicit in the effective duration is the assumption that the dollar amount gain (loss) for a unit shift upward in the spot curve is the same as the amount loss (gain) for a unit shift downward. However, this does not accurately describe a bond's performance in most cases. For most bonds, the loss is not the same as the gain with the yield curve shifting upward or downward.

Indeed, in many cases a bond makes a substantial gain with a drop of interest rates but only a limited loss with a rise in interest rates. In such cases, we say that the bond has a "high positive convexity." On the other hand, there are bonds that can yield limited gain but substantial loss. In this case we say the bond has "negative convexity." This asymmetry of returns is an important aspect of an option-embedded bond's performance. For example, a long call option has high positive convexity because the option provides downside protection under increasing rates and unlimited upside returns under decreasing rates. However, when an instrument incorporates a short call position, the outcome is reversed. Specifically, for a bond with an embedded short call position (a callable bond), the bond cannot be traded above its call price. For this reason, when interest rates drop the bond's upside return is limited, and the loss can be substantial when interest rates rise.

Understanding convexity is important for managing bond portfolios because in many cases the duration measure alone is inadequate for depicting the bond's expected return performance. The duration and convexity measures, used together, would provide a more accurate prediction of the bond's performance.

Like the duration measure, convexity is an attribute of a bond. The convexity measure is independent of the size of the bond holding in the portfolio and whether the bond is held long or short. Nor does convexity depend on any investor's subjective view of interest rate movements. Convexity is determined by the bond's maturity, coupon level, and most important of all, the types of embedded options.

MATHEMATICAL FORMULATION

Relationship to Duration

Duration is a risk measure for bonds in the sense that the duration number relates the price sensitivity of the bond to the shift in interest rates. Suppose a bond has duration D years. Then the proportional change in price of the bond is directly related to each unit change in the shift of the yield curve by a factor of D. The higher the duration, the more sensitive the bond price to the change in yield curve.

Consider the following analogy: Suppose we travel at a constant speed v. The speed relates the distance traveled to the time-elapsed. Specifically, the distance is directly proportional to the units of time magnified by a factor v. Hence, duration is the speed of the price change relative to the yield curve shift. However, in general, bond price does not move at constant speed with the parallel shift in the yield curve but accelerates or decelerates with the rates, and that difference must be taken into account. *Convexity* is the measure of the acceleration and deceleration. Specifically, convexity is derived from *the quadratic approximation of a curve*, called "Taylor expansion."

The Taylor polynomial is essentially a series of mathematical terms that has to be solved for under the constraints that a polynomial's first and second derivatives provide the same answer as the *known function's* [$f(x)$] derivatives when $x = 0$. Of course, this type of mathematical representation of the price function assumes prices follow a smooth or continuous pattern. In reality, each price is a discrete point. We use the Taylor function to approximate where the next price of the security would be if interest rates made an instantaneous shift. The polynomial uses a known function's given (initial) value as a departure point for *estimating* the function's next value. The next value is determined in two steps; first the future value is projected using a linear path from the first value, and then the future value's deviation from the linear path, which is attributed to either a slowing down or speeding up *of the price change* that the linear estimator cannot represent, is computed. The second step provides an original-price-change correction factor that ˙s to be *added* to the first step's change of price.

It is important to note that the *initial value* is used in this second step, which provides the "curve" factor, either upward or downward. This "adjustment" to the linear path is the concept underlying the *convexity* measure. A graphical explanation is provided at the end of the Appendix to this chapter.

Below is a mathematical representation. In the Taylor expansion, each coefficient in the polynomial is estimated from a series of higher-order terms involving one function, $f(x)$. For example, if we use the polynomial $p_n(x)$ to predict the bond's next price and $f(x)$ is the equation for the current price, we can apply the mathematical concepts. A zero's existing price (discount factor), $f(x)$, would be $1/(1 + r + x)^n$. The zero's next price, $p(x)$, for a given change in rates, $\Delta r = x$, would be computed using the Taylor expansion format. We start off assuming no change in rates, $\Delta r = x = 0$, for the initial price. (For readers ˙nterested in a more thorough explanation of the Taylor expansion, any calculus book should be helpful.)

$$p_n(x) = f(0) + \frac{f'(0)}{1!}x + \frac{f''(0)}{2!}x^2 + \cdots + \frac{f^n(0)}{n!}x^n$$

Notice that the second and third sections of the above formula are the first and second derivatives divided by 1! and 2!, respectively. These two sections are used to derive the effective duration and convexity measures, respectively. This is what we were refering to when we previously stated that the convexity is derived from the quadratic approximation of a curve, or Taylor expansion.

When we apply the above polynomial for approximating the expected value of a bond for very small changes in interest rates $\Delta(r)$, we will use only the first three sections of the polynomial (up to and including the second derivative). For instance, solving for point $f(+1\text{bp or} + .0001)$, we use

$$p_2(.0001) = f(0) + \frac{f'(0)}{1!}(.0001) + \frac{f''(0)}{2!}(.0001)^2$$

The first term represents the price for a given interest rate. For each change in rates or the change in a bond's YTM, $\Delta(r)$, there is a new price. Using the Taylor expansion we start with the known price and try to estimate the new price based on a small change in rates.

The second term is the first derivative. We can obtain a measure that shows percentage price change instead of absolute dollar value change by factoring out sections of the term and dividing both sides by the initial price. This is effective duration precisely as discussed in Chapter 6. Here we are really just trying to approximate the price movement of the bond by a constant velocity.

The price movement is the new price associated with a parallel shift in interest rates; for instance,

+ 1 basis point, − 1 basis point

This duration measure, or slope, assumes constant change or a linear path of price changes. Because we are not dealing with a linear function, the duration measure will be slightly off in its price approximation. To improve the estimation, we use convexity, the acceleration/deceleration measure, to further approximate the movement.

The third term is the second derivative of the *initial equation* of $f(x)$ at $x = 0$. Again, by restructuring some sections of the term and dividing by price, we obtain a percentage of initial price measure, termed "convexity." When this measure's value estimate is added to the duration measure's estimate, it acts as a "correction factor" that ultimately provides us with a close approximation of the true change in a bond's price.

What the Taylor expansion has done is show us how to approximate price movement. Figure 7–1 is a graphical depiction of duration and convexity as they apply to straight bond prices. Notice we are assuming

FIGURE 7–1
Price/Yield Relationship of a Zero Coupon Bond

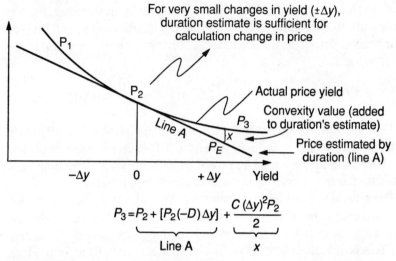

For very small changes in yield ($\pm\Delta y$),
duration estimate is sufficient for
calculation change in price

P_1

P_2

Line A

P_3

Actual price yield

Convexity value (added
to duration's estimate)

P_E

Price estimated by
duration (line A)

x

$-\Delta y$ 0 $+\Delta y$ Yield

$$P_3 = P_2 + \underbrace{[P_2(-D)\Delta y]}_{\text{Line A}} + \underbrace{\frac{C(\Delta y)^2 P_2}{2}}_{x}$$

very small changes in rates for depicting new values of P along the curve. We start at point P_2. Duration can be depicted as the slope of Line A, which is tangent to point P_2. If point P_2 is initial price, then with a given change in yields (i.e., $t\Delta y$), one would expect the new price, P_E, to fall on the same tangent line. However, the actual point of P_E is on the curve, above the tangent line. Therefore, to define the movement of P_3, we draw upon the third term of the Taylor expansion to mathematically represent that the duration term alone is not sufficient.

Note that the bond's return is different depending upon which direction the bond price moves away from P_2. We use the first derivative and second derivative of the price equation (the graph of equation is the depicted curve) at P_2 to estimate the next value of either P_1 or P_3. The change in the x *value*, or $+/- \Delta y$, is very small. The Taylor approximation is helpful for very small yield changes, that is, shifts of 1 to 10 basis points in yield.

The Appendix to this chapter provides the mathematical equations underlying the above concepts. There will be no loss in continuity of the book if the reader chooses to skip the Appendix.

The shape of a performance profile is intimately related to the convexity. For review, the following two examples represent each side of the relationship.

Examples: Interrelationship with Performance Profile

Constructing the Performance Profile from Duration
and Convexity

Assume for the moment that we have no computerized resources to plot new bond prices for given changes in yields using an available bond model. We can still construct the approximate performance profile of the bond, given its price, duration, and convexity measures. We will use a zero-coupon bond to illustrate the procedure of construction. Consider a 10-year zero-coupon bond and a flat yield curve of 10 percent. With reference to Figure 7–1, we will assume this value represents point P_2.

The fundamental price equation is

$$\text{Price} = \frac{100}{(1 + .10)^{10}}$$

So

$$\text{Price or } P_2 = \$38.55$$

By taking the first and second derivatives of above equation, we are able to derive the duration and convexity measures of 9.09 years and 45.45 years^2, respectively. The unit of measure for convexity is years squared. As mentioned in Chapter 6, a shift in rates is quoted in a return per year. Convexity is derived by implementing another instantaneous shift, or a return on a return. This leads to a measure quoted in terms of a rate in years squared.

Now we consider the following parallel shifts of the yield curve. For each shift of the curve, we calculate the value of the bond estimated by the application of the Taylor expansion, where the duration and convexity measures, combined with the change in yields, by mathematical formulation, describe the percentage price change effects. For example, for a 10-basis-point parallel shift in yield (i.e., + .001), the new expected price, $\hat{P}_3$ (referring to Figure 7–1), could be computed as follows:

$$\hat{P}_3 = \$38.55 + [-9.09 \times 38.55 \times .001] + [45.45 \times 38.35 \times .001^2]$$

$$\hat{P}_3 = \$38.55 - \$0.35 + \$0.0017 = \$38.20$$

For very small changes in rates, $\hat{P}_3$ will be very close to actual P_3.

The performance profile can then be constructed by plotting the values computed for each increase or decrease in yield value.

Computing the Duration and Convexity from the Performance Profile

Now suppose we have a bond model that enables us to simulate the bond values under different yield curve regimes. In particular, we can calculate the bond values over a range of parallel shifts of the yield curve and construct the performance profile. Then we can compute the duration and convexity measures of the bond using the numerical differentiation methodology—which uses the same mathematical concepts as the Taylor expansion.

For instance, if we were able to get the equation used to calculate the bond prices in a bond model, we would just apply the Taylor expansion; that is, we would take the first and second derivatives of the equation. However, without the equation we can still use the same concepts underlying the Taylor expansion. Essentially, the first derivative is nothing more than the slope between two points, and the convexity is just the capturing of the acceleration or deceleration of price change at that moment. This "capture" of movement is estimated by a third point in the analysis. We simply use the points on the curve to compute the slope between two points for a given change in yield and divide this value by the inital price point to obtain a percentage-change measure; to obtain the convexity measure, we just extend this same application by including a third point. We are essentially modifying the computed slope using a third point on the curve. With reference to Figure 7–1, the third point allows us to calculate two slopes: one between P_1 and P_2, and one between P_2 and P_3. Then we compute the differences between the two slopes to derive the convexity measure.

The Appendix to this chapter (see p. 103) has a complete example of this methodology using three points from a performance profile of a bond.

The interrelationship between performance profiles and duration and convexity measures consolidates our presentation into one point: that either way, one can attain the same objective—depicting a bond's values under different interest rate levels and extracting summary measures that describe the movements.

We can extend our understanding of the performance characteristics of one bond into an understanding of the attributes of a portfolio of bonds. The following summary of convexity characteristics, covering a zero-coupon bond to a portfolio of bonds, highlights the consistent usefulness of a convexity measure.

CONVEXITY'S PROPERTIES

The first case that follows describes the general attributes of convexity relative to duration. The concepts presented using the example of a zero-coupon bond are then applied to more complex investment positions.

Convexity of a Zero-Coupon Bond

If the price of a zero-coupon bond is

$$\frac{100}{(1 + r)^T}$$

then the convexity of a zero-coupon bond can be represented as

$$\frac{T^2 + T}{2(1 + r)^2}$$

Note first that the convexity is a positive number. That means that when rates drop, the price rises at an accelerated rate. When rates rise, the bond price falls at a decelerated rate. However, the convexity number is not large. In what sense is it not large? If you put the numbers into the equation of bond price change, the second order (convexity component), relative to the first order (duration component), has little impact on the bond value over a very large range of yield curve shifts. For instance, except for a relatively large increase in a bond's yield (very large shift in yield curve), the price decline represented by the duration component will exceed the price gain represented by the convexity component; the bond's price will exhibit a net decrease. We saw this effect in the preceeding example involving a 10-year zero-coupon bond in a 10 percent yield environment.

Second, the convexity impact on price grows at a rate faster than the rate of duration impact on price. This is due to the fact that the duration of a zero-coupon bond increases linearly with maturity while its convexity increases quadratically, a speed faster than linearity. This concept is depicted in Figure 7–2. We will comment on the implication of this effect when constructing barbell portfolios.

Barbell Bond Position

Consider a barbell bond position: a portfolio of two zero-coupon bonds with maturities T_1 and T_2. Suppose the portfolio has equal weights

FIGURE 7–2
Duration versus Convexity of a Zero-Coupon Bond

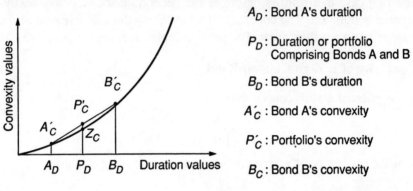

A_D : Bond A's duration

P_D : Duration or portfolio
Comprising Bonds A and B

B_D : Bond B's duration

A_C' : Bond A's convexity

P_C' : Portfolio's convexity

B_C : Bond B's convexity

Z_C (Zero Bond$_C$): Convexity of a zero issue
with a duration equal to P_D

in each bond position. The portfolio duration is the weighted average of the durations of each bond. By the same argument, the portfolio's convexity is the weighted average of the convexity of each bond.

However, if we consider a zero-coupon bond with the same maturity and duration as the portfolio, we can see in Figure 7–2 that the bond's convexity would be less than the portfolio's weighted average convexity. This bond has the same duration as the portfolio, but it has a lower convexity. In another words, a barbell portfolio of two zeros with different maturities has a higher convexity than a zero-coupon bond (given that the duration of the portfolio and zero are equal).

Convexity of a Coupon Bond

We can also apply this concept to compute the convexity of a coupon bond by viewing a coupon bond as a portfolio of zero-coupon bonds. For each payment, its convexity would be calculated as if it were a zero-coupon bond. Then we would obtain the coupon bond's convexity by summing the weighted average convexities of each payment (zero bond).

For two bonds with the same duration, the bond with a higher coupon rate has a higher convexity. This characteristic can be clearly seen by representing the two payments as two zero-coupon bonds. If we have one bond that pays $9 at the end of the year and another bond that pays $3 dollars at the end of the year, using a flat 10 percent yield curve, the present-value relative proportions would be greater for the $9 issue than for the $3 issue, as indicated below:

$9/1.10 = $8.18   PV as a proportion = .90889
$3/1.10 = $2.72   PV as a proportion = .90667

We could depict these proportions as the places the fulcrum would have to be set in order to balance the weight of the proportionate cash flows. One fulcrum would be placed at the .90889 point and the other at the .90667 point.

```
                         90.889%
0 _____
                           △    100%

                         90.667%
0 _____
                           △    100%
```

If we wanted our fulcrums to be located at the same point, or in other words, to match in present value proportions, then the only way to drop the present value of the higher coupon issue would be to extend its maturity.

If we did extend the maturity, we would now have "duration match" cash flows. However, the convexity attribute would now be much higher for the $9 issue. As you will recall, convexity increases in terms of T^2. Therefore, if two straight issues have the same duration but different maturities, the longer maturity issue will increase in value at a faster rate (higher acceleration) than the shorter maturity issue. The maturity effect was shown in the plot of convexity depicted in Figure 7–2.

Applying the concept from the previous example of two zero-coupon bonds, we can see that if we had two straight bonds with the same maturity, but different coupons, the higher coupon issue would have a relatively lower duration. The high-coupon issue, relative to a low-coupon issue, has a higher proportion of its present value weights in the earlier years. If we wanted to match durations, we would not be able to match maturities. A higher coupon issue would have a longer maturity and, concomitantly, a higher convexity attribute.

Convexity of a Portfolio of Bonds

Convexity can be calculated in a way similar to the calculation of the duration of a portfolio of bonds (see Chapter 6). It is the weighted average of the convexities of all the bonds. We can alter portfolio convexity by changing the portfolio weights in bonds with high or low convexity measures.

Perpetual Bond

Again consider a semiannual coupon-paying bond with infinite maturity. Suppose the annual coupon rate is c. We have shown in the last chapter that the bond price is

$$P = c/r$$

and the duration is

$$D = -1/r$$

We can calculate the convexity by taking the second derivative of the price equation and dividing both sides of the equation by price to get

$$C = 2/r^2$$

Remember that the same factors that affect duration will affect convexity.

Convexity with Credit and Liquidity Spread

The analysis of the impact of the liquidity and credit spread on convexity is similar to that for duration. Once again consider the analysis of the spread on a zero-coupon bond. By the same analysis used to derive Equation 7–1, we can show that the convexity of a zero coupon bond with a spread of sp is given by

$$\frac{T^2 + T}{2(1 + r + sp)^2}$$

As a result, it follows that the convexity decreases with the increase in the spread.

This chapter thus far has provided the mathematical foundation for understanding convexity and its applications. When evaluating more complex instruments, such as bonds with embedded options, the convexity attribute is a significant factor in the bond's return performance.

The following section will highlight some of the dichotomous return patterns.

BOND OPTIONS

Bond options and convexity are closely related. Perhaps one of the most important aspects of holding an option whether a call or put option, is that the downside risk is limited to the invested principal while the upside return can be substantial. As discussed in this chapter's introduction, this aspect is precisely convexity. On the other hand, we have seen that the convexity value is relatively small for a straight bond. That is, for bonds with no embedded options, the performance represented by the convexity measure is relatively negligible when compared with the duration measure. But convexity is particularly useful for discussing bond options (or option-embedded bonds).

In general there is no simple way to compute the convexity measure for bond options. The most common way to simulate the convexity measure is through the use of a bond option model. To avoid some of the complexities of some bond option instruments in our general discussion, we will focus on a Treasury bond option, although the following concepts are applicable to a broad range of options.

Both call and put options, American or European, have high positive convexity. The more an option is out-of-the-money, the higher its leveraged position on the initial investment. It therefore follows that the more an option is out-of-the-money, the more convex is its performance profile.

Option-embedded bonds have different convexity attributes, compared to similar-maturity and similar-coupon straight bonds. The types of convexity deviations are attributable to the types of options that are embedded. Accordingly, the holding period returns one can expect from an option-embedded bond, relative to a straight bond, will also depend on the option's characteristics.

From option pricing theory, we know that the holder of an option (long position) has to pay for the downside protection; the holder pays the premium. By the same token, if a bond has an option such that the option-embedded bond has a high positive convexity (long option position), then the bond price must incorporate the option premium. Conceptually the option price is added to an equivalent straight bond price. This option premium has a relative effect on the option-embedded bond's return. Specifically, assuming no change in other factors affecting option value, the time decay of the option premium causes the holding-period return of the option-embedded bond to be lower than that of a similar straight bond.

Conversely, if a bond has significant negative convexity because of an embedded short option position, then the bond's expected holding-period return is higher in order to compensate for the undesirable performance of negative convexity. A short option position represents the subtraction of the premium from an equivalent straight bond's price. As the option decays over time, the effective holding-period return for the bond would be higher than the straight bond's. The incremental return is attributable to the diminishing premium value. As the option premium approaches zero, the combined postion's fair value rises to approach that of an equivalent straight bond's.

Using option pricing theory, we can extend our discussion of a bond's convexity characteristics to include its relation to market volatility. It is well known that the option value always increases with increases in interest rate volatility. Therefore, if a bond has a high positive convexity because of the embedded option (i.e., long a put option), then the bond value will increase with increasing interest rate volatilty. As long as a bond has high positive or negative convexity, the bond value will be very sensitive to changes in interest rate volatility. If a bond has high positive convexity, the bond value will increase as volatility increases; with high negative convexity, the changes in bond value will be negatively correlated with changes in volatility levels.

FOUR CASES OF A BOND'S ATTRIBUTES

We can think of four cases in describing a bond price in relation to the shift in interest rates. The four cases represent bonds with different types of embedded options. Figure 7–3 illustrates the four cases.

The following is a brief explanation of just two of the four cases.

Case 1: Positive Duration and Negative Convexity (Straight bond short a call option)

In this case, when the interest rate drops, the bond value goes up. But the bond value can go up only to an extent—the value is somewhat

FIGURE 7–3
Performance Profile of Four Basic Option Embedded Bonds

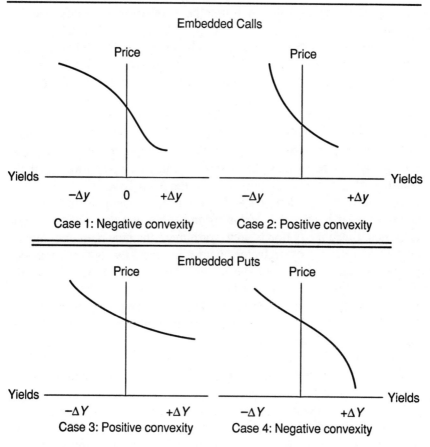

Embedded Calls

Case 1: Negative convexity

Case 2: Positive convexity

Embedded Puts

Case 3: Positive convexity

Case 4: Negative convexity

capped. For example, the bond value of a callable bond is capped at the call price.

Case 3: Positive Duration and Positive Convexity (Straight bond, long a put option)

When the interest rates drop, the bond increases in price. Therefore the bond captures the upside returns. However, if the rates rise, the bond value drops, but only to a certain extent; the downside is protected. For example, for a putable bond the investor has the right to put the bond back to the issuer at a fixed price. Therefore, the investor is protected against large downside returns attributable to an increase in rates.

Since convexity can be beneficial (i.e., when you win, you win more; and when you lose, you lose less), there has to be a cost for it. The cost is the option value built into the prices of bonds with embedded options.

The convexity concept can be applied in any context. For instance, what does it mean to hold a bond in a short position when the bond has positive convexity? It is best to think through an example of a putable bond.

If we have an agreement with someone to *borrow* money at a specific interest rate (i.e., to be a bond issuer), we would be long a liability; this is the same as being short a coupon-paying instrument. Either position gains in value if interest rates go up. However, if the instrument contains a long put—that is, the *bond issuer paid a premium* to be able to put the loan back to the lender at par if interest rates go down—then if interest rate volatility increases, the value of the option increases. Since the option is now worth more than the premium initially paid (assuming all other factors held constant), the option-embedded position increases in value. The increase in value is attributable to the higher probablity of the issuer's being able to call in its debt at par, under declining interest rates, when the market price of the instrument is more than par. Essentially, since the issuer is only required to pay back par, the *issuer* is able to get rid of a high-interest-rate debt and simultaneously exchange it for a low-interest-rate debt. The issuer's position wins both ways; it has unlimited upside gain in an increasing rate environment and limited downside loss in a declining rate environment.

We have completed the theoretical and mathematical discussion of convexity. However, it could be helpful to look at convexity again, this time from the angle of a more technical aspect of its relationship to duration measures. In the next section we explain a second interpretation of convexity and highlight the differences between the interpretations.

DELTA CONVEXITY: CHANGES OF DURATION WITH THE CHANGE IN INTEREST RATES

It is somewhat confusing that convexity is sometimes defined to be the change of duration with the change in interest rates. For clarity, we shall call this performance measure "delta convexity" as distinct from convexity. Now we can draw the subtle difference between them. Recall that duration is defined as the instantaneous return of a bond per unit shift of the yield curve. Therefore, *delta convexity* is the rate of change *of the instantaneous return* per unit shift of the yield curve. In contrast, convexity is concerned with the rate of change *of price* per unit shift of the yield curve per dollar.

In other words, delta convexity, being the change in duration, is a change in the percentage itself. However, convexity is the change of the rate of change in price. We shall illustrate the difference by the following numerical example.

Recall the performance profile example from earlier in the chapter, in which we estimated $\hat{P}_3$ from the initial price of $38.55. The -35 cents represents the change on the inital price using a duration measure. The $+.0017$ is also a change on the intial price, but this is obtained from the convexity measure. Delta convexity, as applied, would be the change in the .35 value if the yield curve shifted. This is not the same as convexity. We are concerned not with the change in duration if the yield curve shifts, but rather with whether the price changes increase or decrease as a proportion of the initial price.

The difference is best demonstrated by a simple example of a zero-coupon bond. We have seen that the duration of the zero-coupon bond is approximately equal to the maturity (T). Therefore, for any small change in interest rates, the change in duration would still be maturity (T) divided by the modifier (see Chapter 6). Hence the delta of duration should be zero. Yet we know that the convexity of a zero-coupon bond is positive, not zero. Upon closer inspection, we can see what causes this discrepency.

Consider what we are really saying when we say convexity is the change in duration:

$$P = \frac{100}{(1 + r)}$$

Duration is

$$D = \frac{\Delta P}{\Delta r / P}$$
$$= \frac{-T}{1 + r}$$

Then the change in duration is

$$\frac{\Delta D}{\Delta r} = \frac{T}{(1 + r)^2}$$

This is not the same as the convexity term, which is

$$\frac{T^2 + T}{2(1 + r)^2}$$

Notice that the change-in-duration term shows the same numerator as duration; hence the acceleration/deceleration in price changes, under delta convexity, is moving at a rate of T. This is distinctly different from convexity, which shows movement occurring at a rate of $T^2 + T$ (with the same modifier).

Consider the case when the rates rise. The bond value drops. Let us say that the bond value drops one point. Now suppose the interest rates rise further. The bond price would drop further but at the same duration. However, the actual price drop is less this time. This is because duration is the *percentage* change in price, and since the price has fallen, the actual price drop should be less. In sum, the positive convexity of a bond may mean increase or decrease of change in duration with the change in interest rates.

Understanding convexity requires understanding effective duration. It is important to remember that effective duration is conceptually different from modified duration. It is not calculated simply as the first-order change at a point, but rather as the *percentage* change between two distinct points on a curve representing computed bond prices at different yield levels. Likewise, convexity is calculated using additional points along the curve and by computing the differences. The Appendix to this chapter provides a numerical example applying the effective duration and convexity concepts.

There is a reason why we do not dwell on delta convexity as a bond performance measure. The reason is that it does not have the two useful properties that the convexity measure has. First, the delta convexity of a portfolio is not simply the weighted sum of the delta convexity of each bond postition. As we have seen, this property is very useful in structuring bond strategies. Second, delta convexity describes the behavior of the bond duration and not the price change. Therefore, unlike convexity, it cannot be directly used for describing a bond's return (the price performance). For these reasons, we focus more on the convexity measure.

Convexity is a summary measure used for calculating a bond's expected price changes. Of course, expected price changes (or price performance) can be converted into projected return measures.

A total return for a security is its percentage change in value from a beginning date to an end date. The initial value is the price plus accrued interest. The ending value includes price appreciation, coupon income, and reinvestment income earned during the holding period. A projected total return for a security can be computed if one knows its initial value and calculates a future value according to a specified future term structure. The following section illustrates how projected return measures can reveal a security's relative convexity characteristics.

CONVEXITY EXHIBITED IN TOTAL RETURNS OF TREASURY ISSUES

Convexity, a characteristic of a bond's expected price performance under changing yield levels, can be intuitively deciphered by comparing a security's expected total return (ETR) against its total return.

Expected Total Return and Total Return

Expected total return (ETR) is a bond's probability-weighted annual return. This measure takes into account coupon income, reinvestment income, and projected principal value under a number of parallel yield curves. The yield curves are established in scenario analysis.

Scenario analysis entails constructing a forecasted yield curve environment expected to materialize by the end of the bond's holding period. In recognition of the difficulty of successfully forecasting an exact yield curve, investors often construct a series of parallel yield curves. These curves represent instantaneous shifts above and below a defined interest rate term structure. A security's total return and probability of occurrence 's computed for each curve. The ETR of a security is the sum of the probability-weighted returns in the forecasted environment.

The convexity attributes of a security will govern its probable range of returns during the unforeseeable future. Reviewing ETRs in conjunction with total returns simplifies the process of identifying the security's price performance characteristics.

A total-return calculation is based on a single forecasted yield curve. ETR, in contrast, is calculated on a series of curves. This methodological difference is the basis of the dual advantage of the ETR measure: that; it is a probability-weighted return that does not require absolute certainty in a forecast, and that it highlights the extent of an issue's convexity. The convexity attribute characterizes the pattern of changes in a security's price associated with each parallel yield-curve structure. A positively convex security has larger differences between the upward scale of projected returns than between the downward scale of returns. This asymmetry causes the ETR to be greater than the total return.

The following section elaborates on the interplay between convexity and return performance for various treasury issues.

Scenario Analysis

Figure 7–4 depicts a forecasted yield-curve environment. The forecasted environment consists of a defined term structure and shifts representing up to three standard deviations above and below the structure. The normal distribution was used for calculating the probability of each shift. The present date is March 29, 1989, and the center curve is the underlying spot curve on that date. The underlying scenario forecast is that the same term structure will exist one year later.

Table 7–1 provides a summary of the calculated returns for a 30-year Treasury issue (9% due 11/18) and a 10-year Treasury issue (9% due 05/98).

The convexity attribute of securities can be readily identified by noting the *percentage differences* between the ETR and the total return associated with the zero-basis-point shift. The preceding table indicates that the difference between ETR and total return increases as the security's convexity increases.

Notice that the long bond's ETR is 0.86 percent higher than its total return. The short bond's ETR is 0.21 percent higher than its total return. Since the long bond's percentage difference is greater than the short bond's, one can deduce that the long bond has a higher convexity. A higher convexity characteristic implies that for the same change in rates, the high convexity issue will accelerate in price change faster, as a proportion of initial price, than a lower convexity issue. The following table displays the duration and convexity computed for both issues.

Description	Duration	Convexity
TN 9.00 5/15/98	5.90	0.5
TB 9.00 11/15/18	10.07	1.8

FIGURE 7–4
Implied Spot Curve

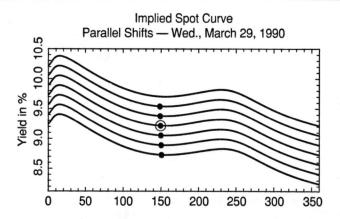

Implied Spot Curve
Parallel Shifts — Wed., March 29, 1990

The center dot, ◉, is the 150-month spot rate on 3/29/90. We will use this rate to highlight the graph's usefulness. The other dots represent where the spot rate would be if the yield curve made instantaneous parallel shifts. The rates can be converted into discount factors or prices, and plotted on another graph. This new graph would be the performance profile for the 150-month issue, depicted as follows:

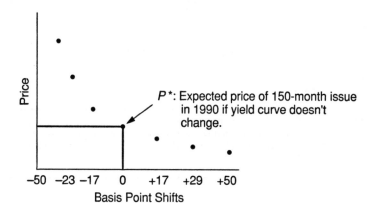

P^*: Expected price of 150-month issue in 1990 if yield curve doesn't change.

TABLE 7–1
Scenario Market Values and Total Returns For Each Shift

Basis Point Shift	Market Value	Return (%)
	9% Treasury Bond Due 11/15/18	
−50	116.57	14.55
−33	114.74	12.76
−17	112.98	11.02
0	111.26	9.33
+17	109.59	7.69
+33	107.97	6.10
+50	106.40	4.55

Summary:

Total Return under Forecasted Yield Curve:	9.33% *	
High Return:	14.55%	
Low Return:	4.55%	
Expected Total Return:	9.41% *	

Basis Point Shift	Market Value	Return (%)
−50	113.43	12.12
−33	112.48	11.18
−17	111.55	10.26
0	110.62	9.34
+17	109.71	8.44
+33	108.80	7.55
+50	107.91	6.66

Summary:

Total Return under Forecasted Yield Curve:	9.34% *	
High Return:	12.12%	
Low Return:	6.66%	
Expected Total Return:	9.36% *	

*The total return displayed for each basis-point shift represents the annualized return attributable solely to the change from today's yield curve to one delineated as the possible future term structure. The expected total return incorporates all the possible yield curves in the forecasted environment.

Generally, positively convex securities have ETRs that are greater than their total returns. Negatively convex securities have inverted performance profiles, and hence their ETRs are less than their total returns.

SUMMARY

This chapter described the conceptual and mathematical elements of convexity as they applies to fixed-income instruments. The last section of the chapter used an example of two Treasury issues to highlight how ETR calculations could be used as a way to readily ascertain the relative magnitude of a security's convexity.

The discussion of convexity has been confined to assuming parallel shift of the yield curve for explanatory purposes. The general principles discussed in this chapter can easily be extended to other types of yield curve movements. These generalizations will be discussed in later chapters.

APPENDIX TO CHAPTER 7: MATHEMATICS OF DURATION AND CONVEXITY

Applying the concepts of the Taylor expansion, we can compute the new price of a bond, given a parallel change in rates, by isolating the components affecting the change in value, duration, and convexity and then summing their effects on the initial price. The application of this concept is provided below. The formulas for duration and convexity are given at the end of this appendix.

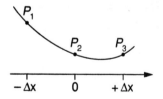

Duration:

$$D = \frac{-\Delta P/\Delta I}{P} = \frac{\frac{-(P_3-P_1)}{\Delta X-(-\Delta X)}}{P_2} = \frac{P_1 - P_3}{2(\Delta X)(P_2)}$$

*Convexity:**

$$C = \frac{\frac{\Delta^2 P}{\Delta I^2}}{100P} = \frac{\frac{\frac{P_3 - P_2}{\Delta X} - \frac{P_2 - P_1}{\Delta X}}{\Delta X}}{P_2} = \frac{P_3 + P_1 - 2P_2}{100(\Delta X)^2 P_2}$$

$$\Delta X = \text{Basis points} \times .0001$$
$$P_i = \text{Price} + \text{Accrued}$$

Example: 10%   12/21/17   Accrued = $4.454

$$D = \frac{P_1 - P_3}{2(\Delta X)(P_2)} = \frac{113.357 - 102.174}{2(.005)(111.971)} = \frac{11.183}{1.1197} = 9.987$$

$$C = \frac{P_3 + P_1 - 2P_2}{100(\Delta X)^2 P_2} = \frac{113.351 - 102.174}{100(.005)^2(111.971)} = \frac{0.497}{0.2799} = 1.775$$

	Basis Points	Price	Duration	Convexity
P_1	−50	113.357		
P_2	0	107.517	9.99	1.775
P_3	+50	102.174		

Duration and convexity are "local" properties. We calculate them as functions of three points. For the above diagram, we can calculate three durations and convexities, which are displayed as follows. On the summary screen that lists all bonds, we would report the numbers for a zero-basis-point shift, P_3, D_3, and C_3, where D_3 and C_3 are functions of P_2, P_3, and P_4 only.

BP	Price	Duration	Convexity
$-2\Delta X$	P_1		
$-1\Delta X$	P_2	D_2	C_2
0	P_3	D_3	C_3
$+\Delta X$	P_4	D_4	C_4
$+2\Delta X$	P_5		

---

*This term represents the change in slope as we move away from point P_2.

MATHEMATICS OF DURATION

Definitions:
P = Price
c = Cash flow (coupon and/or principal)
Y = Yield
N = Number of cash flows
t = Years
    In this chapter we used Δ to represent differences. For purposes of this appendix, ∂ will be used.

$$P = \sum_{t=1}^{N} \frac{C_t}{(1 + Y)^t}$$

Letting $\mu = (1 + Y)$, so that price could be represented as

$$P = \sum_{t=1}^{N} C_t(\mu)^{-t}$$

and then taking the first derivative

$$\frac{\partial P}{\partial Y} = \sum_{t=1}^{N} -t(c_t)(\mu)^{-t-1} \times \frac{\partial(\mu)}{\partial(Y)}$$

we see that

$$\frac{\partial \mu}{\partial Y} = 1$$

and we can now rewrite the equation, multiply by 1 (P/P), and factor out the constant $P/(1 + Y)$ in order to isolate the duration measure as follows:

$$\frac{\partial P}{\partial Y} = \frac{P}{(1 + Y)} \times \frac{\sum_{t=1}^{N} -t(c_t)/(1 + Y)^t}{P}$$

    The second term on the right-hand side of the expression is simply Macaulay duration, D. By dividing both sides by P and multiplying both sides by $\partial(Y)$, we isolate effective duration, the percentage price change measure. Notice that in this specific case, where the yield curve is flat (i.e., y is constant), modified Macaulay duration is exactly equal to effective duration.

We use duration (D) to estimate price change in the following way:

$$\frac{\partial(P)}{P} = \frac{-D}{(1 + Y)} \times \partial(Y)$$

MATHEMATICS OF CONVEXITY

Definitions:
P = Price
c = Cash flow (coupon and/or principal)
Y = Yield
N = Number of cash flows
t = Years (or compounding periods)
In this chapter we used Δ to represent differences. For purposes of this appendix, ∂ will be used.

$$P = \sum_{t=1}^{N} \frac{c_t}{(1 + Y)^t}$$

Letting $\mu = (1 + Y)$, so that price could be represented as

$$P = \sum_{t=1}^{N} c_t(\mu)^{-t}$$

and then taking the first derivative

$$\frac{\partial P}{\partial Y} = \sum_{t=1}^{N} -t(c_t\mu)^{-t-1} \times \frac{\partial \mu}{\partial Y}$$

we see that $\partial(\mu)/\partial(Y) = 1$; and we can now take the second derivative of price as follows

$$\frac{\partial^2 P}{\partial Y^2} = \sum_{t=1}^{N} (-t - 1) - t(c)(\mu)^{-t-2} \times \frac{\partial \mu}{\partial Y}$$

Again, we see that $\frac{\partial \mu}{\partial(Y)} = 1$, or

$$\frac{\partial^2 P}{\partial Y^2} = \sum_{t=1}^{N} (t^2 + t)(c_t)(\mu)^{-t-2}$$

The second-order change in price, or second derivative, can be shown as

$$\frac{\partial^2 P}{\partial Y^2} = \sum_{t=1}^{N} \frac{c_t(t)(t + 1)}{(1 + Y)^t(1 + Y)^2}$$

Rearranging terms, factoring out $1/(1 + Y)^2$, and multiplying by P/P we have

$$\frac{\partial^2 P}{\partial Y^2} = P \times \frac{1}{(1 + Y)^2} \times \frac{\sum_{t=1}^{N} \frac{c_t t(t+1)}{(1+Y)^t}}{P}$$

Isolating the convexity measure, analogous to duration,

$$\frac{\partial^2 P}{\partial Y^2} = P \times C$$

Dividing both sides by P and multiplying both sides by ∂Y^2 give

$$\frac{\partial^2 (P)}{P} = C \partial Y^2$$

If the right-hand side is divided by 2!, it becomes the same as the Taylor expansion term, which then gives us the percentage price change measure:

$$\frac{C}{2} \partial Y^2$$

GRAPHICAL EXPLANATION OF TAYLOR EXPANSION

Recall the equation

$$P_n(x) = f(0) + \frac{f'(0)}{1!}x + \frac{f''(0)}{2!}x^2 + \cdots + \frac{f^n(0)}{n!}x^n$$

This equation can be better understood by comparing Figures 7A–1a and 7A–1b which appear on the following page.

Figure 7A–1
Representation of (a) Change in Interest Rates, (b) Shift in Basis Points

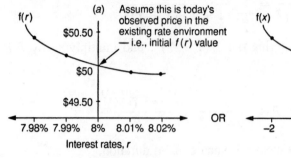
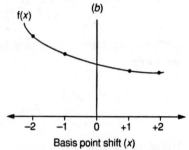

Equation of zero price curve:

$$f(r) = \frac{1}{(1 + r)^n}$$

OR

Equation of zero price curve:

$$f(x) = \frac{1}{(1 + .08 + x)^n}$$

The polynomial $f_n(x) = f(x)$ only when $x = 0$

CHAPTER 8

TREASURY MARKET

An understanding of the treasury market is essential for managing various types of fixed-income securities. The first half of this chapter is a synopsis of not only the types of instruments in this market but also the underlying distribution structure of the market that affects transaction prices. Treasury prices (yields) are used for estimating the nominal yield curve, which is a quasi representation of the time value of money. The second half of this chapter provides a description of the nominal yield curve and the reasons why this curve does not adequately represent the time value of money. This chapter closes with a discussion of a more informative indicator, an implied spot curve.

GOVERNMENT SECURITIES

Description: Bills, Notes, and Bonds

U.S. Treasury securities are issued under the authority of the Second Liberty Bond Act of September 24, 1917, as amended. This act in effect limits the outstanding total face value of U.S. government obligations to a certain level (i.e., $400 billion). However, over the years Congress has exercised its authority under the act to temporarily raise the limit or to provide remedial legislation. Generally, Congress will act when the value of outstanding debt approaches the ceiling and threatens the ability of the government to raise new debt to meet expenses.

The Public Debt Act of 1942 grants the Treasury wide discretion in setting the terms on marketable securities. These securities may be discount or coupon-bearing. They may be sold by auction or by other means. There is no statutory limit on the coupon rate for bills, certificates, or notes. There was, however, a 4.25 percent coupon rate limit on Treasury bonds that Congress had to continually provide exemptions for when the Treasury had a refunding or needed to issue new long-term debt. On November 10, 1988, the statutory limit was finally repealed.

Treasury issues fall into two broad categories: marketable and nonmarketable. Nonmarketable securities do not trade in a secondary market. They must be redeemed by the Treasury department through any Federal Reserve Bank and its branches. The most commonly known nonmarketable securities are the United States Savings Bonds (for example, series EE and HH). Other nonmarketable securities exist for special purposes. For instance, there are securities issued directly to government agencies, trust funds, and accounts as well as to state and local governments. State and local governments use these securities as temporary investments for the proceeds they receive from the advanced refundings of their tax-exempt issues. One other type of nonmarketable security falls under the heading of a Foreign Series; these issues represent debts of foreign governments and monetary authorities.

Almost all other issues of the United States Treasury and Government-Sponsored Organizations are marketable (i.e., they trade in a secondary market). U.S. Treasury-backed sponsorship or guarantees apply to agencies such as the Farm Credit System, World Bank, Federal Home Loan Banks, and many more. The securities may exist in one of three forms: bearer, registered, or book-entry. Bearer securities differ from registered securities in that there is no record of ownership. A "book-entry" issue exists only as a computer entry; there is no physical certificate. In this chapter we are going to focus only on Treasury bills, notes, and bonds. Treasury bonds and notes can exist in any of the three forms, whereas Treasury bills presently are only in book-entry form.

Marketable issues are either discount or coupon-bearing instruments. At the present time, bills are issued at a discount, whereas notes and bonds are issued with semiannual coupons and principal repayment at maturity.

Treasury bills (T bills) are issues that mature in one year or less. These securities do not have periodic interest payments and are in effect pure discount instruments. Because T bills have no intermediate payments, the interest received on them is the difference between the face value and the purchase price. Currently, Treasury bills have a minimum denomination of $10,000 and increase in par value by increments of $5,000.

Coupon-bearing bonds are subdivided into two categories: Treasury notes and Treasury bonds. Treasury notes have maturities ranging from 1 year to 10 years. Treasury bonds have maturities greater than 10 years (currently the longest maturity is 30 years). Coupons on Treasury issues have semiannual payment. Treasury notes with maturities of 3 years or less have denominations ranging from a minimum of $5,000 to a maximum of $500 million. Treasury notes of maturity greater than 3 years, and all Treasury bonds have a minimum denomination of $1,000 and a maximum of $1 million.

The following two sections discuss the two-tiered distribution structure of Treasury securities. The first tier, termed the "primary market," involves the original issuance of securities from the U.S. Treasury. The second tier, termed the "secondary market," handles the broad distribution of post-issue securities.

Primary Market

The U.S. Treasury raises funds for the U.S. government's needs through competitive auctions held by the 12 Federal Reserve banks. New Treasury issues are auctioned off in the primary market, which is composed of U.S. government securities dealers (primary dealers) who are allowed to bid for new issues for their own inventories. This section focuses on the auction process for various types of issues.

In an auction for Treasury bills, bids are quoted on a price basis. The Treasury allocates securities from the highest bid to the lowest bid until it obtains the announced funding needs. Successful bids are ones that obtain Treasury issues at their bid price. Some bids are made on a noncompetitive basis (usually by noninstitutional investors). These bids specify only the quantity wanted and receive an allocation at the end of the auction process. Their price is the average price of the successful bids.

Presently, most coupon issue bids are quoted on the basis of yield. Treasury notes and bonds are allocated according to the ascending schedule of bids (yields) until the announced amount is fully subscribed. At the close of the auction, the Treasury sets the coupon rate slightly below the average yield of the successful bids. The Treasury accepts noncompetitive bids from private or noninstitutional investors. Noncompetitive bids are guaranteed to be filled at the average yield of the open (competitive) bidding process. There are times when an auction for coupon issues is done on a price basis. This usually occurs when the Treasury announces the reissue of an outstanding security. In this case, there is an outstanding bond issue that has a current yield equal to its coupon rate (bond is trading at par), and the outstanding issue has the same maturity as the Treasury's planned new issue.

Procedures for Treasury refunding have become fairly routine in recent years. The following paragraphs highlight a few of the current auction procedures for Treasury issues.

Three- and six-month Treasury bills are normally auctioned weekly on Mondays with payment due the following Thursday. The payment on Thursday coincides with the maturity of "older" three- and six-month issues. The Treasury is not limited to auctioning off a face amount equal to the prior issue.

The 52-week bills are auctioned every four weeks on Thursday. The size of the issue is usually announced in the late afternoon on the Friday preceding the Thursday auction. Once every four weeks, the payment dates for the 52-week, six-month, and three-month bills coincide.

Cash management bills are issued at irregular intervals. Maturities for these bills range from a few days to about six months. Cash management bills are generally issued early in the month, when government spending tends to be heaviest. These bills usually mature after one of the major midmonth tax-receipt dates in March, April, June, September, or December. Maturities of cash management bills are usually set to coincide with the maturities of existing outstanding bill issues. This permits the cash management bill to become interchangeable with existing bills for market trading purposes, thereby improving liquidity. Cash management bills do not refund existing debt; they always raise new cash.

Two-year notes are auctioned in the second-to-last week of every month, generally on a Wednesday. The issue matures at the end of the 24th month from the present issue date. Auction announcements usually occur on the Wednesday preceding the auction.

Three-year to 3.5-year notes are generally included in the Treasury's regular quarterly refundings, which issue intermediate notes and long-term bonds. These refundings occur in February, May, August, and November. Securities sold in these auctions are issued on the 15th of the month and mature on the 15th of the same month at the end of their term.

Before the mid 1980s, Treasury bonds were issued with 20- and 30-year maturities. On April 30, 1986, the Treasury announced the elimination of the regular, quarterly, 20-year bond refunding cycle; only 30-year bonds would continue to be issued.

The 30-year issues that have maturities ranging from 2007 to 2014 have embedded call options. The Treasury has the right to call these bonds at par after their 25-year call protection period expires. Since 1984, callable bonds have not been issued. A major factor for the demise of the callable issues was the explosive growth in coupon stripping activities on Treasury issues that started in 1984. Callable bonds cannot be stripped; hence, they were not as popular as noncallable issues in the primary and secondary markets.

SECONDARY MARKET

After primary dealers know the amount they are allocated from a Treasury auction, they turn around and sell this "post-issue inventory" to their customers. Their customers can range from other registered brokers and dealers or corporations to individuals and foreign governments. The trading of securities obtained from the auctions is termed "secondary market activity." After an auction, there is a brief period (10 days) between a security's auction date and its actual issue date when trades in the security are made on a "when-issued" basis. At all other times, trades are made among existing securities. Post-issue securities are broadly categorized as either on-the-run or off-the-run issues. On-the-run issues are the most recently issued Treasury securities for a given maturity. Off-the-run issues were issued in prior auctions.

Almost all issues have some secondary market activity, but some issues trade more frequently than others. The frequency of a particular instrument's trading activity is a function of various market factors, such as the outstanding size (nominal dollar amount) and whether the instrument is deliverable against future contracts. Future contracts will be covered in Chapter 11.

The secondary Treasury market is very liquid. A liquid market can be measured by the tightness of the spread and the trading size of the quotes. For notes and bonds, the spread of the on-the-run issues is almost nonexistent. Approximately one-third of the issues have a spread of $\frac{1}{32}$. Another third has a spread of $\frac{2}{32}$. The rest are "illiquid" bonds with a spread of 4/32. Considering that the quotes are generally good for a trade of $5 million or more, the market is indeed very active.

Unlike the primary (auction) market, where tenders are delivered to the U.S. Treasury at Federal Reserve banks and branches and at the Bureau of the Public Debt, the trades in the secondary market are over-the-counter (no central geographic location). Buy and sell offers are continually placed by telephone or other electronic devices (e.g., by fax and computer). There are many dealers and brokers in the secondary market. The existence of such a large distribution network is due to the generally high trading volume in treasury securities. Given the large number of participants, quotes are very competitive and bid/ask spreads are generally very tight.

Because of the large volume of activity in the secondary market, the secondary market's trading prices best reflect the consolidated views of the time value of money, which is reflected in the prices (yields) of Treasury securities of different maturities. The monitoring of Treasury prices has led to a process of depicting a nominal yield curve.

THE NOMINAL YIELD CURVE

At the end of every trading day, the closing prices of all *on-the-run* Treasury securities can be obtained and used to calculate equivalent YTMs for each issue. The yield of each issue (*y*-axis) can be plotted against its maturity (*x*-axis). A curve may be fitted using a mathematical method (e.g., least squares) such that the curve approximates the pattern of Treasury yield/maturity relationships at a point in time. This relationship is generally referred to as the "term structure of yields" (nominal yield curve).

It would be helpful if we could use the nominal yield curve to represent a series of one-period spot rates that reflect the time value of money. However, because the nominal yield curve is a blend of many factors, it does not give a clear view of periodic discount rates. A few of the factors that influence the nominal yield curve's structure are coupon effects, tax effects, and embedded call-option effects. The following paragraphs briefly summarize the impact of these effects, which hinder the nominal yield curve's usefulness as a measure of the time value of money.

The problem with using the nominal yield curve as an approximation of the true term structure of interest rates is that the nominal curve does not represent the internal rate of return of $1.00 at different maturities. Instead, the curve represents a series of internal rates of return associated with various flows of funds. A *flow* is a stream of coupon payments and any amortization or accretion of principal for a particular security. A look at the effect of differing coupon rates on bond yield illuminates the differences between the nominal yield curve and the underlying (spot rate) term structure.

Coupon Effects

To illustrate the differences between the nominal yield curve and the spot curve for all bonds (the "term structure"), assume the yield curve is upward sloping. Now compare the YTM of a coupon bond with a zero-coupon bond of the same maturity. Because the yield curve is upward sloping, according to the bond model, the earlier coupon payments should be discounted by a lower rate compared to later payments. The rate for discounting the earlier coupon payments should be lower than the discounting rate used for the zero-coupon bond. However, YTM is the internal rate of return, and it must represent somewhat of an average of underlying spot rates used to determine present values of payments. The coupon bond's yield (YTM) must be lower than the YTM of the zero-coupon bond.

Since the bond yield represents a flow-weighted average of all discount rates, the nominal yield curve, by construction, has a smoothing effect on the underlying spot yield curve. For example, if the underlying spot yield curve has a sharp hump, then the nominal yield curve would have a less acute hump. Conversely, if there is a small hump in the nominal yield curve, the underlying spot yield curve must have a sharper hump.

In a downward-sloping yield-curve environment, the coupon bond yield must be higher than the lowest discount rate applied to a zero-coupon bond with the same maturity; the coupon bond's YTM must be higher than the YTM of a zero-coupon bond.

Tax Effect

Another factor influencing the shape of the nominal yield curve is the status of the federal income tax code. Since income derived from coupon interest and capital gains on U.S. government securities is subject to all federal income taxes but exempt from state and local income taxes, changes in the code will affect the trading volume of different securities. The code contains special provisions that differentiate securities according to whether they were purchased in the secondary market or at an auction. The investor must be aware of the appropriate section governing the calculation of the cost basis and of the taxable income for a particular issue. A change in the tax structure for interest income and capital gains can lead to a change in investor demand between premium and discount issues. Therefore, the shape of the yield curve can be indirectly affected by the volume of trading of certain types of issues. The change in the yield curve attributable to the change in prices/yields of particular coupon issues is not to be construed as representing a change in investors' views of the pure (before-tax) time value of a dollar.

Empirical work to date indicates that the impact of the tax effect is very small relative to the impact of other factors affecting the yield curve. When the tax rates for interest income and capital gains are very similar, an investor deciding between a deep-discount issue and a high-coupon issue is concerned with the present value of the ultimate tax impact. When making comparisons among these issues, investors compare the benefits of deferred taxable income with the benefits of higher, currently taxable income associated with premium securities.

Callability

A call provision on any bond permits the bond issuer to buy back the bond according to a schedule that specifies the dates and prices at which the bond may be called. Notice of such a call must be given four months prior to the call date.

The call provision works to the advantage of the issuer and as such is considered the bond issuer's option. To illustrate the use of a call option, assume a market in which interest rates are falling. The call provision on an outstanding bond permits the borrower to call the bond and issue another at a lower interest rate. In exercising its option, the issuer saves the difference between the present value of future interest payments on the higher-coupon original bond and the present value of interest on the lower coupon bond.

The borrower pays a price for the ability to hold this call option. First, the right to call the bond is not active for a specified period, which may be immediately after issue to five years prior to maturity.

The investor does have certainty with respect to income from the bond's cash flow during this call-protection period. Second, to compensate the lender for the uncertainty of holding a callable bond and the need to reinvest at a lower interest rate, callable bonds always yield more than their noncallable counterparts. As a consequence, the price of a callable bond to the lender is always lower than that of a similar bond. Finally, the bond issuer must pay a call premium to the lender. The call premium, which is always positive, is the difference between the market price of the bond and the call price. (Treasury bonds are always called at par. The call price, then, is par plus the call premium.) Despite this compensation, the purchaser of a callable bond is essentially purchasing a bond whose price will not rise above that specified in the call schedule, no matter how low interest rates drop. In other words, the capital gain on a callable bond under conditions of falling interest rates is capped in two ways:

1. If interest rates drop below a certain point, the bond issuer will call the bond.
2. If the investor sells the bond when the call schedule is effective, he cannot hope to receive a price greater than that specified on the call schedule.

In deciding whether to purchase a callable bond, an investor must weigh the dollar value of the benefits of higher yield for a certain period of time against that of the disadvantages listed above. The issuer must also weigh advantages against disadvantages, not in issuing the callable bond but in determining when to call the bond. The bond issuer has a time-limited option to call the bond. If it waits too long, the value of the option will fall to zero. If the issuer exercises the option while interest rates are falling, but before they have ceased to fall, it will have called the bond prematurely. There is an optimal time at which the issuer will reap the maximum benefit from calling the bond. The method for estimating this optimal time is called the "optimal call strategy," which is fully discussed in Chapter 12.

Callable Treasuries have a major impact on the yield/maturity points for maturities ranging from 10 years to 25 years. Since this represents a large segment of the yield curve, the change in prices/yields, attributable to changes in the call-option component, has a significant impact on the structure of the nominal yield curve. It is difficult to discern the underlying time value of a dollar for this segment of the maturity range.

CONSTRUCTION OF AN APPROPRIATE DISCOUNT FUNCTION

The nominal yield curve is recognized as an inappropriate structure for depicting periodic discount rates, and there is a market view that a more adequate curve can be constructed using Treasury prices.

The Basic Framework

It was shown in Chapter 3 that a bond model can be constructed using the discount function to price any cash flow. In essence, as long as the time value of the money (the discount function) is known, each payment can be discounted by the appropriate discount rate, which is specified by the discount function.

At any time instant, the market determines an implied discount function that represents the market consensus of the time value of money. In an effort to develop a methodology that will reveal the discount function at any point in time, we should try to estimate the discount function from the market prices. The natural choice for these market prices is the range of prices of the Treasury issues.

Briefly, here are a few of the reasons for using Treasuries to estimate the discount function: First, except for a few bonds that have call provisions, most Treasuries are straight issues. Therefore, the expected returns on these bonds do not include any embedded-option returns. The next chapter discusses the discount-estimation process that explicitly models the embedded options in order to obtain an equivalent straight-bond return for the callable instrument. It will be shown that misspecifications in the option values will not lead to gross errors in estimating the discount function.

Second, since Treasury issues are default-free, they do not incorporate a credit premium. Therefore, the yield of a Treasury issue is not confounded with the market price of default risk.

Third, the Treasury market is the most liquid bond market. It provides a foundation of returns that is used for judging returns in other bond markets (e.g., corporate). Most fixed-income professionals use the Treasury issue prices as their benchmark for comparing the relative prices of other issues. They monitor relative prices in order to interpret market movements. For these reasons, it seems natural to use the Treasury market to determine the discount function.

We have discussed the deficiencies of the nominal yield curve attributable to the coupon, tax, and callability effects. How do we construct the spot curve so that it is free of the effects associated with the nominal yield curve?

To answer that question, we have to use a line of logic that runs backward. It goes like this. Suppose we see all the Treasury bond prices, and we are convinced that the market derives these bond prices by using the bond model and that the market has established the underlying spot curve. Unfortunately, we do not know the precise specification of the spot curve. However, we do know that the spot curve manifests itself in the Treasury bond prices. For this reason, we should be able to use the bond prices to infer the underlying spot curve. The procedure goes as follows.

First we assume that we know the spot curve. We assume a curve, say a 10 percent horizontal spot curve.

Now we use this curve to price all the Treasury bonds by applying the bond model. Here, we ignore all the callable Treasury bonds; there are other techniques to deal with these types of bonds, but for simplicity we will ignore them. If we compare the computed theoretical prices against the observed prices, we will notice significant deviations. This result should not be too surprising because we simply guessed the specification of the spot curve. We shall call the difference between the theoretical price and the observed price the "error."

By judging the distribution of errors in the Treasury bond market, we can adjust the shape of the spot curve to reduce the errors. Therefore we have to develop a search procedure to minimize the errors. However, this requires caution. A curve can always be found that almost perfectly fits all the bond prices. But such a curve may be highly discontinuous. Remember, the spot curve should somewhat reflect the time value of money of the market. For this reason, we should expect the curve to be quite smooth.

The search procedure for the spot curve requires a trade-off between the sizes of the errors of the bonds and the meaningful shape of the yield curve. The curve that best satisfies these criteria is called the "implied spot curve." Such a curve is often used in bond pricing models, so we shall call the curve the "spot curve." Since the criteria for picking the spot curve are somewhat subject to individual judgment, there is really no unique spot curve to be determined. However, if the bond model is well-specified and the statistical procedures are properly set

up, spot curves may differ only subject to the different criteria. The
pricing accuracy, however, should not vary greatly.

The next chapter outlines the technical aspects of estimating a
spot curve using all the Treasury issues, including callables, without
incorporating the aforementioned problems of the nominal yield curve.

SUMMARY

After presenting a broad overview of the Treasury market, this chapter
focused on the nominal yield curve, which is constructed from the yields
of issues trading in the secondary market. This topic included a summary
of the factors influencing the shape of the curve and the reasons why
the yield curve does not represent the time value of money. The chapter
closed with a discussion of both the concept of using an implied spot
curve and the relevant factors involved in estimating such a curve. The
next chapter provides a thorough discussion of the estimation process
and the subsequent application of the spot curve.

CHAPTER 9

THE SPOT CURVE

This chapter presents a procedure for estimating the spot curve, or the discount function, using most of the Treasury issues' daily closing prices, then shows some of the empirical results on the behavior of the spot curve, and finally, using these results, proposes how the spot curve can be used for structuring both bond strategies and return attributions.

A SIMPLE DISCOUNT FUNCTION

The price of a T bill for $1 par represents the present value of $1 for the specified maturity. The bill prices plotted against the maturity can represent the time value of money up to a one-year maturity. This simple example of a discount function illustrates some of the complications involved in constructing a discount function for the whole Treasury market and motivates some of the applications of the discount function.

Given the bill prices, we can provide a theoretical price for a cash flow that can be replicated by holding a portfolio of T bills. This portfolio of T bills can be constructed in a straightforward manner. For each payment in the cash flow, we just need a T bill with a maturity matching the payment date and a principal amount equaling the payment amount. A bond that has a cash flow that can be replicated by a portfolio of bills has the same value as the portfolio of bills, by our argument of the law of one price. (This assumes that the bond has no default risk and the marketability level is similar to that of the bills.)

In reality, T bills do not mature each day, and therefore a portfolio of T bills cannot replicate a cash flow with payments on any given day.

For this reason the bill prices must be interpolated so discount factors can be inferred for the days that do not have maturing bills. The underlying assumption here is that the discount function is smooth and the discount factors do not exhibit large changes within any short maturity range.

The observed bill prices may not reflect the market time value of money exactly. For example, there may be different bid/ask spreads or the quotes may not be correctly reported, and the constructed discount function may incorporate these errors (which may be small). A temporal imbalance in supply and demand may also result in the observed price not reflecting the equilibrium time value of money. How should we isolate these deviations from the equilibrium values that we want to estimate? The best approach is to make an even stronger assumption about our bond market and the underlying time value of money: We will assume not only that the points between any two observations can be interpolated, but also that all equilibrium discount factors lie on a smooth curve and that any deviations of the observed bill price from this underlying curve can be treated as observation errors or deviations resulting from temporary supply and demand imbalances. (There may be additional factors that can be explained by the law of one price.) Having made this assumption, we will seek a procedure to construct a smooth curve that best fits the observed bill prices.

BASICS OF THE SPOT CURVE

Now we want to extend the above concept of the discount function for the T bills to the full spectrum of the term structure. The major difference between constructing a spot curve for the bills market and constructing one for the Treasury market is that the bills have no coupons. The T bills without coupons are in fact, as we have argued, discount factors. However, the coupon issues yields are internal rates of return of a cash flow. Therefore the yield to maturity (YTM) of a coupon issue is not the discount rate of any particular principal payment. To handle this problem, we need to think of a coupon bond as a portfolio of zero-coupon bonds. Each zero-coupon bond has its own discount rate. To construct a spot curve is to determine the discount factors that can value this portfolio of zero-coupon bonds to (at least approximately) equal the observed bond price. And this has to hold true for all the other bonds.

There is another difference between the bond market and the bills market. In the bond market, there are callable bonds, which have embedded options and therefore cannot be treated as a portfolio of zero-coupon bonds. Several approaches have been taken to deal with these particular bonds. Some researchers delete these bonds from the estimation procedure. This is somewhat unsatisfactory. If the purpose were to determine the underlying spot curve and not to price the callable Treasuries, then there would be no particular reason to incorporate the callable Treasuries in our estimation sample. However, in this particular estimation problem the callable bond prices are important for the estimation of the discount function.

The callable bonds must be incorporated in the sample because nearly all bonds in the maturity range of 15 to 25 years in the term structure are callable bonds. If all callables in the sample were deleted, we would not have any observations for that maturity range. As a result, interpolating all the observations in such a broad range of years can result in substantial errors.

Another alternative is to use some simple option model to approximate the embedded option value. Since the embedded option is a five-year option that is not going to expire for at least 10 years, one might argue that the present value of the option premium is small enough that some approximation of the option value would suffice for providing a useful estimation procedure of the discount function. Unfortunately, we shall see that these errors in estimating the option value can generate significant errors in estimating the discount function.

To deal with the problem posed by the outstanding callable Treasuries, we need to employ a bond option valuation model. A later chapter provides the details of this model. For the purpose of this chapter, it suffices to state that there are some fairly robust bond option models and these models can relate bond options identical to those embedded in the callable Treasury bonds. These models require information on the specifications of the underlying discount function.

In review, these are the assumptions we have made for this model of the discount function:

Assumptions

1. Any Treasury security (Treasury bills, notes, and bonds), other than the callable Treasuries, can be viewed as a portfolio of zero-coupon bonds, and we can apply the bond model to value each security.

2. A callable Treasury bond can be considered a portfolio composed of a straight Treasury bond (with the same stated maturity and coupon rate) and a short call option on this noncallable bond, with the strike price at par. The call is exercisable anytime after the bond's stipulated call-protection period. For example, 30-year bonds are noncallable for the first 25 years.

3. There is an underlying discount function that determines the bond prices. This discount function is continuous and smooth.

4. The market is sufficiently efficient that the Treasury securities are priced by the underlying discount function.

CALL-ADJUSTED SPOT ESTIMATION PROCEDURE

There are two main features of this four-step procedure. First, the valuation of the call option (embedded in the callable Treasury bonds) depends on the specification of the discount function. Second, the discount function can be estimated only after the call option value is known. This call-adjusted procedure treats the two problems as a simultaneous system.

Step 1. Determining the Initial Discount Function

There are many mathematical formulations for specifying smooth curves. Such curves may be represented by polynomials, but most of the current research uses spline functions. Let us assume some specification of a smooth function to represent the underlying discount function. Also, let us for now assume that the call options all have no value.

We have discussed how we can price any straight bond, in particular the Treasury securities, using the bond-pricing model. We can use a nonlinear estimation technique to determine the discount function that can price all the Treasury securities such that the theoretical prices are closest to the observed prices. Essentially, we seek to minimize the sum of the squared errors in the estimation.

Step 2. Determining the Option Value

Having estimated the discount function, we now apply this discount function to the bond option model to price the call option embedded in each callable Treasury bond. Note that the call-option value is different for each callable bond because these bonds have different maturities and coupon rates. The options have different expiration dates, and they can be in-the-money or out-of-the-money.

Step 3. Readjusting the Callable Treasury Bond Prices

Step 2 provides the first estimate of the call-option value of each callable bond. Adding this option value to the observed callable Treasury price gives an estimate of the equivalent straight Treasury bond. Step 3 is to add the estimated option value to the observed callable Treasury prices and establish a new set of sample bond prices.

Step 4. The Looping Procedure

Now, with the new set of sample prices, we can repeat Step 1 and determine a revised discount function with which to estimate the option prices. After using the revised option prices to adjust the callable Treasury bond prices in Step 3, we are ready to repeat Step 1 again.

   The loop provides convergence to a solution, in the sense that after several iterations the call option values and the discount function do not change in value with further iterations and they satisfy the pricing of both the straight bonds and the callable Treasury bonds simultaneously.

   This procedure is consistent with two aspects of the Treasury market. First, it provides the discount function that best determines the prices of observed Treasury securities, and second, it obtains a discount function that explains callable Treasuries. Earlier we stated that a proper bond-option pricing model is needed. In this iterative procedure, the estimated results are sensitive to any systematic errors in Step 3; the convergence of the iteration can be seriously affected by systematic errors in pricing the call option. Therefore, every effort has to be made to identify the appropriate option value.

ECONOMICS OF THE SPOT CURVE

What can the discount function reveal to us about the Treasury market? Also, how can or should we use the estimated spot curve? The answers to these questions are given below after a brief discussion of the relevant aspects of the spot curve. It is important to note that the spot curve that we have estimated is not constructed to fit the prices that we see. The usefulness of the spot curve consists in the fact that it reveals the underlying economics.

Uniqueness and Existence of the Spot Curve

The constructed spot curve is not unique. It seeks to achieve two objectives: to be smooth and at the same time to best explain the observed Treasuries prices.

These two objectives are somewhat in conflict. First, a curve with many sharp turns that statistically fits and explains the observed bond prices very well will be most unlikely to reveal the underlying time value of money. This is not satisfactory because the purpose is to construct not a curve that fits the bond prices, but one that can reasonably be considered to be the time value of money curve—so that we can interpret the discrepancies between the observed bond price and the theoretical bond price.

Second, the spot curve is not constructed to reflect what we think the spot curve should be, disregarding its ability to explain the observed bond prices. The construction recognizes the importance of the spot curve's ability to explain the observed prices and to behave reasonably well as a spot curve. Decisions about how smooth the curve should be and how well it should explain the observed bond prices are subjective, so the spot curve is not uniquely defined by the observed bond prices.

The issue more important to modeling is not the spot curve's uniqueness but its existence. Of course we can always construct a smooth curve as the "spot curve," but it may be very unsatisfactory in explaining the observed bond prices. In such a case, one could argue that the bond model is not applicable and that the development of an underlying spot curve is suspect.

The existence of a spot curve depends upon identifying a curve that satisfactorily fulfills these two criteria: (1) the curve can be used to interpret the time value of money, and (2) the curve can be used to accurately price the Treasury securities. If such a curve exists, and if we can construct another spot curve that is also a reasonable candidate, then probably the two curves cannot be very different. Therefore, on the practical level it is not important to ensure the uniqueness of a spot curve for the Treasury market.

Perhaps the reason for the prevalent use of the spot curve is that research to date has shown that such a curve does exist, suggesting that the bond model is applicable to the Treasury market. We shall dwell on these empirical results in the following sections. The empirical results use the daily closing prices of all the Treasury securities, which are reported in the *New York Times*. Flower bonds are not applicable to the theory that we have discussed, so they are not included in our analysis, the results of which are reported below.

Robustness of the Model

Figure 9–1 depicts the snapshots of the spot curve for each quarter from March 2, 1987, to June 1, 1989. The long rate of the yield curve rose during this period from the lowest level of 7.5 percent at the beginning of the period to 9 percent at the end of the period. Moreover, the yield curve's configuration also changed rapidly. At the beginning of the period, the curve was sharply upward sloping. Then the short rate gradually moved upward, and by the end of the period the short rate was above the long rate.

FIGURE 9–1
Spot Curves: March 2, 1987 to June 1, 1989

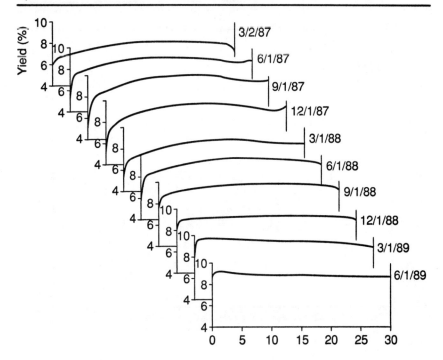

Although the yield curve showed significant movement during this period, its configuration remained somewhat smooth, suggesting that the yield curve can represent the underlying market-perceived yield curve.

After we have estimated the spot yield curve, we can apply the bond model again and determine the theoretical price of each bond. Next, we calculate the difference between the theoretical price and the observed price, with the difference called the "error."

We first investigate the pricing errors of various Treasury securities. Figure 9–2 depicts the distribution of the relative errors for a Treasury note, a Treasury bond, and two callable Treasury bonds. Within the past year, compared to the callable issues, the noncallable issues had much smaller relative pricing errors. This finding is not too surprising, considering that it is more difficult for the market to price these bonds and that these bonds, in general, are not actively traded.

FIGURE 9–2
Pricing Error Trend Analysis: (a) Treasury Note, 8.125, 2/15/1998; (b) Treasury Bond, 7.259, 5/15/2016 (Noncallable); (c) Treasury Call, 13.250, 5/15/2014; (d) Treasury Call, 11.750, 11/15/2014.

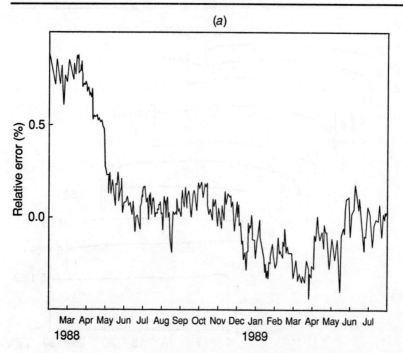

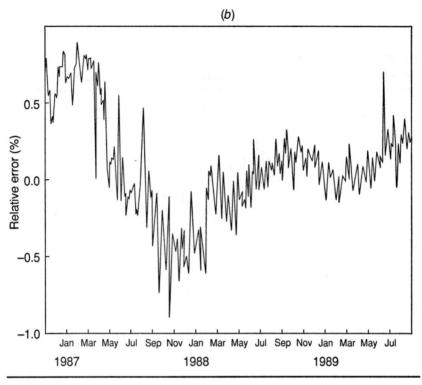

(b)

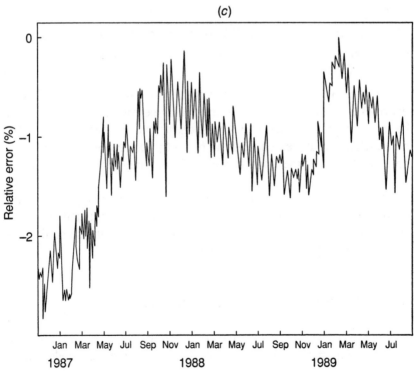

(c)

FIGURE 9–2 (continued)
Pricing Error Trend Analysis: (d) Treasury Call, 11.750, 11/14/2014

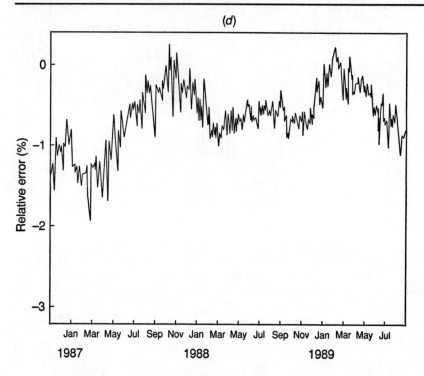

Another interesting result concerns the average error of all Treasury securities over time. We find that the average error has been declining in the last two years, which seems to suggest that the market is becoming more efficient to the extent that the market prices converge over time to those predicted by the bond model. This finding is depicted in Figure 9–3.

We have shown how to use observed Treasury prices to construct a spot curve. Empirically, we have shown that the estimated spot curve can be interpreted as the time value of money and at the same time can price the Treasury securities accurately.

ECONOMICS OF THE PRICING ERRORS

If a bond has a pricing error, we cannot conclude that the bond is mispriced and that the market is inefficient. The bond-pricing model makes

FIGURE 9–3
Average Pricing Error Trend: 1987 to July 1989

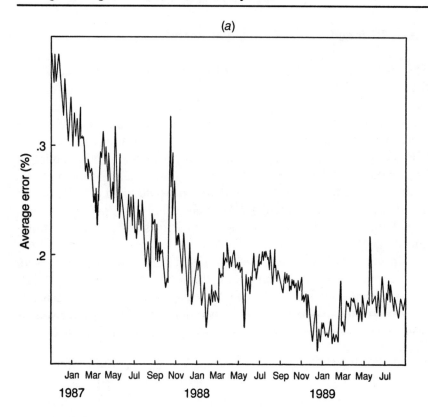

a number of assumptions, all of which must be satisfied before inferring that the pricing error reveals market inefficiencies. However, the above empirical results suggest that by and large the model assumptions are correct.

For simplicity of exposition, let us introduce the following terminology. When the observed bond price is above the theoretical bond price, the bond is *traded rich*. If the observed bond price is below the theoretical price, the bond is *traded cheap*. The differences between the observed and theoretical prices can be simply categorized as follows:

$$\text{Observed} - \text{Theoretical} = +, -, \text{ or } 0 \text{ values}$$

where $(+)$ is rich and $(-)$ is cheap. Later in the chapter we will show that tracking these errors could be quite informative.

Cheap/Rich and Relative Pricing of Bonds

The spot curve can also be viewed as providing useful measures for depicting relative values among bond issues. Its usefulness can be demonstrated by an example. Suppose we have two identical bonds with the same maturities and coupon rates. If one bond is traded above the other, the former is always traded with an error, indicating that it is richer than the other bond. Also, if the cash flow of a bond can be replicated by a portfolio of bonds, and if the bond is traded rich and the portfolio is cheap, then the purchase of the portfolio would yield a higher return than the purchase of the bond. These are simply arbitrage conditions. Therefore, bond errors can provide very useful summary statistics of a traded bond's value.

In the above two cases we considered only cash flows that were perfectly matched. What about cash flows that do not match? Recall that the bond model assumes that the cash flow can be reinvested at the forward rates. When comparing two bonds that do not have similar cash flows, we can always assume that any mismatched cash flow is reinvested at the forward rates.

To illustrate this idea, suppose that the yield curve is flat. Then all the forward rates are the same as the flat rate. When we compare two bonds, we can reinvest the payment at the fixed rate and then line up all the cash flows. Given the same cash flow, the cheaper bond will have a lower observed price. We can extend this argument even further. Let us ignore the callable bonds for the time being and contruct two portfolios of Treasury securities. One is constructed from the cheap bonds and another is constructed from the rich bonds. If we construct the two portfolios in such a way that their cash flows are similar and the portfolios can be made identical by reinvesting their cash flows by the forward rates discussed above, then the portfolio value constructed from the observed prices of cheap bonds will be less costly to buy. Notice how this argument hinges on the forward rates calculated from the spot curve. If the spot curve is erroneously estimated, then the forward rates would have little practical implication and the above arguments would have little economic meaning.

Coupon Effects and the Nominal Yield Curve

In Chapter 8 we discussed the coupon effects that contributed to the differences between the nominal and spot yield curves. As mentioned in that chapter, YTM computations encompass an averaging of spot yields. If there is an upward-sloping yield curve regime, the spot curve rises faster than the nominal curve. The longer the maturity, the more noticeable the difference between the spot rate and the YTM of a coupon bond.

For the purpose of this chapter, we will let the nominal yield curve represent the plot of YTMs of all the Treasury securities—not

FIGURE 9–4
Nominal Yield Curve versus Spot Yield Curve: March 1, 1988

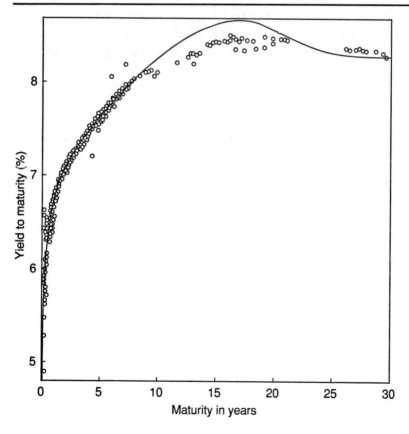

just the on-the-run issues. We can obtain a historical perspective of this relationship by plotting both curves for any given date. Figure 9–4 compares the nominal yield curve and the spot yield curve of March 1, 1988. On that day, the nominal yield has a steep upward slope through the 10-year maturity point. The spot curve is very similar to the nominal curve (YTM curve) for this section of the graph; there are no perceptible differences. In actuality, however, minor differences do exist for securities up to the 10-year maturity range. The differences are increasing gradually and become apparent at approximately the 10-year maturity point. From that point on, we see that the spot curve can differ from the nominal curve by as much as 30 basis points.

On-the-Run Issues

In Chapter 8 we discussed the fact that the on-the-run Treasuries are often traded above similar off-the-run bonds. For this reason we can interpret the bond error of the on-the-run issues to be the premium; we expect the on-the-run bonds to be trading rich.

Indeed, Figure 9–5 shows a typical error of three different long bonds, each over a three-month period. On average the premium for a 30-year Treasury bond is about 0.4 percent, and it declines rapidly as the next on-the-run bond is auctioned. This can be seen by comparing (a) and (b) of Figure 9–5.

Premiums differ for different on-the-run maturities. In general the premium is smaller for the shorter maturities. This result suggests that any investor holding an on-the-run Treasury bond from the auction date to the date on which another new issue is auctioned would lose approximately 0.4 percent of the investment on average.

The estimation of the premium for the on-the-run issue is clearly important for the pricing of the "when issues." If one knows the underlying bond value determined by the spot yield curve and the on-the-run liquidity premium that has been historically embedded in on-the-run securities, then one can use the sum of these elements as the first step toward deriving a fair value and hence the yield or coupon level for securities trading as "when issues." Subsequent steps involve adjusting this yield to reflect other relevant market factors. The following brief overview of "when issue" trading highlights these factors.

Securities begin trading as "when issue" instruments immediately after a public announcement of an issue's auction date and continue

FIGURE 9–5
Pricing Error Trend Analyses for Three Bonds

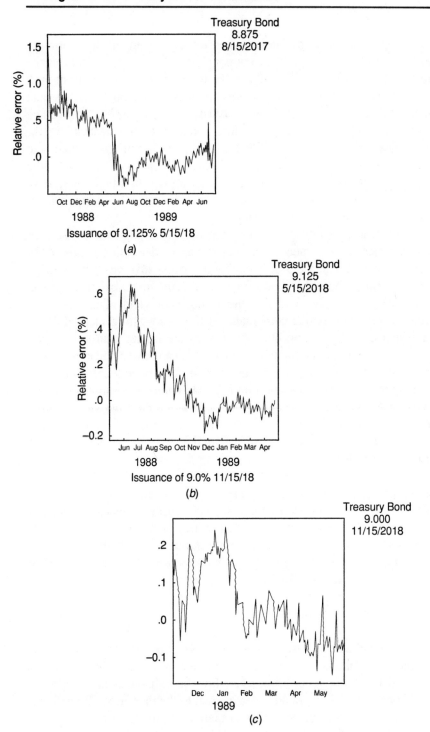

For example, comparing the bond issued in (b) to the bond in (a) — the old on-the-run issue — the bond in (b) trades rich at the same time the bond in (a) becomes more fairly valued.

trading up to the auction. These "when issue" instruments are normally traded on the basis of yield or coupon level. Quotes are based on the subjective views of the fair yield today for a security that will not start accruing interest until a coupon level has been set on its dated date (or auction date). As extensively discussed in Chapter 8, the average of the auction's accepted yield bids, rounded to the nearest eighth, establishes the coupon level. On the new issue's settlement date, the actual price paid by each successful bidder will not necessarily be the same. The differences in the actual price, among the purchasers, arise from a price adjustment for the divergence between the coupon level and the purchaser's accepted yield bid.

"When issue" securities can be viewed as trading in a pre-auction auction process. A "when issue" buyer has to determine a fair YTM or coupon level. The yield determination process involves a knowledge of the overnight borrowing rate for a similar maturity, existing coupon issue trading near par, and the underlying spot yield. This financing spread information is one component of the yield-setting methodology. For instance, if short-term borrowing costs are higher than the coupon level of an existing issue trading near par, this can have a negative impact on market views, and one might therefore make a downward adjustment in the spot plus on-the-run premium yield. Another component of the yield-setting process is the market participant's subjective view of how well the new issue will be accepted in the market or the market's tone. Participants' views of the tone in the market will cause them to either raise or lower the "when issue" yield quote.

The significance of using the spot curve and an estimation of the on-the-run premium arises when one is trying to establish a fair foundation for "when issue" yield levels. First, the spot curve provides a reflection of the time value of money. Second, the historical perspective provides an estimation of the value of liquidity associated with the on-the-run issues. Finally, the existing market environment provides the subjective elements in the yield-determination procedure.

Callable Treasury Bonds

Consider a callable Treasury bond, and compare it with another non-callable bond that has the same coupon rate and maturity. We shall call this bond the "equivalent Treasury." For the callable bond the goverment's option to call the bond is detrimental to the investors. The callable Treasury bond should be priced lower than the equivalent Treasury bond.

On the first call date, if the callable bond trades above the par price, then the goverment should call back the bond at par. However, if the bond is traded below par, the bond would not be called on that first call date. By this argument, it is clear that the callable bond's value on the first call date can at most be par, so the callable Treasury should be priced below an equivalent Treasury bond that has the same coupon rate and a *maturity equal to the first call date.*

The callable Treasury bond therefore should be traded below the minimum of the two equivalent Treasury bonds mentioned above. Using the call-adjusted methodology, we can compare the observed callable Treasury prices against the theoretical prices of the equivalent Treasury bonds.

Each day, we can compare the observed prices or yields of each Treasury issue against its theoretical equivalent. For instance, if a Treasury bond is trading in the market on the basis of its yield to maturity, its price should be compared against the theoretical price of an equivalent maturity issue. Alternatively, if a callable bond is trading based on its yield to call date, the proper equivalent issue to use is one that has a term to maturity equal to the term to the call date. If one does not exist, we can construct one for valuation purposes; we can create an issue that has the same coupon level as the callable Treasury and a maturity date equal to the callable's call date. The spot curve, which has been derived from a call-adjusted estimation procedure, provides the factors for computing all theoretical treasury values. The difference between the observed price and the theoretical price is termed the *cheap/rich* of that bond for that day. For example, say that a bond closed at 100.25 and the theoretical price using the spot function is 100.00. That bond is then said to be 0.25 rich. Alternatively, if the bond had closed at 99.75, it would be said to be 0.25 cheap, and it would be quoted as −0.25.

We can plot the differences for all the Treasury issues in a bellwether portfolio. Figure 9–6 depicts a cheap/rich cluster analysis. It is readily apparent that different maturity regions of the Treasury bellwether have different levels of cheap/rich. Examined over time, it is observed that these clusters may, on average, "move around," but their components remain a distinct cluster. For instance, A, B, C, D, and E are distinct clusters as indicated in Figure 9–6.

By monitoring the daily differences between theoretical and observed prices, we can determine whether the differences fall into a consistent pattern. The implication is clear that the overall cheap/rich for a bond on any given day has two components. The first component

FIGURE 9–6
Treasury Cheap/Rich: March 1, 1989.

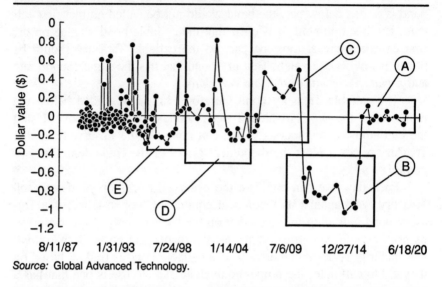

Source: Global Advanced Technology.

is *systematic*, or *persistent*. The commonality of this component is what gives rise to the cluster effect. The second component is *unsystematic*, or *transient*.

This effect shows up as the position of a bond's cheap/rich on a given day, relative to the cluster overall. There are a number of possible causes of persistent cheap/rich behavior. These include

- Mispricing of the call component of callable Treasuries.
- Liquidity discounts and premiums.
- Investor time preferences and market segmentation effects.

Transient cheap/rich should reflect the relative flow of market forces, bid ask spreads, and demand. In addition, around the time of the issuance of a new bond into a cluster, there may be a quasi-transient effect induced as the "old" on-the-run is superseded by the new issue. Transient cheap/rich movements are of direct interest to a trader.

A Cheap/Rich Cluster Analysis (CRCA) may provide insight into any underlying market inefficiencies. Each cluster can be considered a class of bonds. In Figure 9–6, cluster A represents the long-bond class. On a daily basis we can compute a cross-sectional average of the cheap/rich for each class, then directly compare each bond's relative position within its cluster. Each bond's cheap/rich value can be compared to its cluster's average cheap/rich value. The relative positions over time can be analyzed using statistical techniques analogous to the *t*-statistic methodology. Each bond is assigned a divergence factor, which summarizes the relative stability of the bond's cheap/rich position in the cluster. In other words, divergence factors would be the equivalent of *t*-statistics. Large positive numbers indicate that a bond is very rich, relative to the cluster; likewise a large negative number indicates a significantly cheap price. These numbers directly measure transient cheap/rich.

Figures 9–7 through 9–11 depict the persistent attributes of each cluster's cheap/rich analysis. Each graph shows the cluster average as the middle line, and the almost symmetric outer pair of lines represent one standard deviation above and below the mean for each day in the period 12/5/1988 to 4/28/1989. It is apparent that the most dense clusters are the short notes (E-Class) and the long bonds (A-Class), since they have the smallest standard deviation. Also, these two classes have the smallest absolute cheap/rich, which reflects their liquidity and the efficiency of the dealer market. The greatest cheap/rich variability is found in the callable Classes (B and C) and in the illiquid Class D. Note, however, that the averages are all quite stable across the time period. This, then, shows graphically what is meant by the persistent, or systematic, cheap/rich component.

FIGURE 9–7
Average Error of A-Class between 12/5/88 and 4/28/89

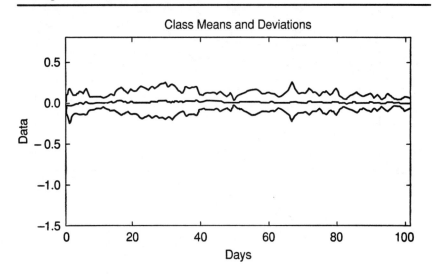

FIGURE 9–8
Average Error of B-Class between 12/5/88 and 4/28/89

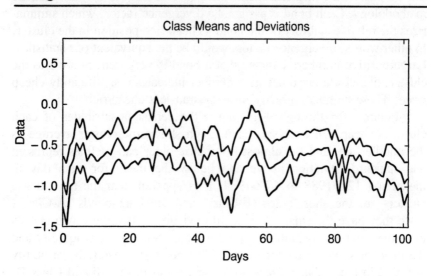

FIGURE 9–9
Average Error of C-Class between 12/5/89 and 4/28/89

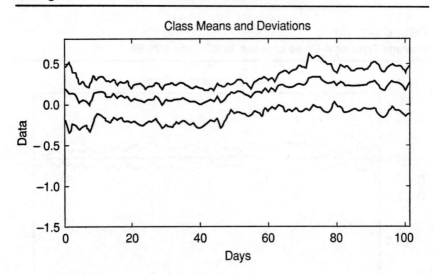

FIGURE 9–10
Average Error of D-Class between 12/5/88 and 4/28/89

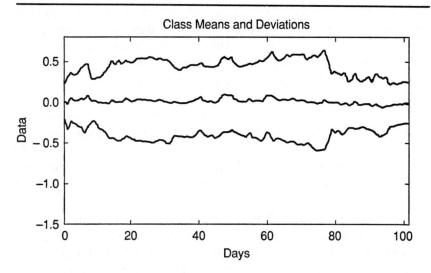

FIGURE 9–11
Average Error of E-Class between 12/5/88 and 4/28/89

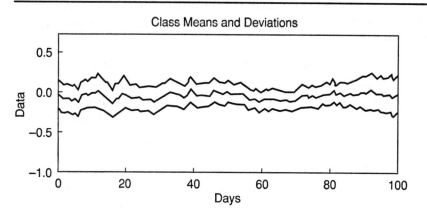

RELATIVE VALUE STRUCTURE

We have been analyzing the cheap/rich characteristics of securities from the perspective of a security's position within a particular maturity group or class. We can also study the errors of a particular bond over time. One way to simultaneously analyze the errors of all the bonds at one time, as well as the errors over time, is through the use of a relative value diagram, depicted in Table 9–1.

In constructing the relative value diagram, we first estimate the errors of all the bonds over a time period. The errors are classified into three types. Errors exceeding 0.25 belong to type 0. Errors below −0.25 belong to type *. Clearly, type 0 represents the rich bonds, type * the cheap bonds. Errors between + .25 and − .25 are depicted by a blank space.

Now we order all the bonds in ascending order of maturities. Table 9–2 is a list of the bonds summarized in the relative value diagram. Columns 90 through 105 of Table 9–1 represent callable bonds, which *have not been included* in this summary format. On the relative value diagram, each column represents the errors of a bond over time; each row in the relative value diagram represents the errors of all the bonds on a particular date. The most recent date is the last row. The patterns of the symbols * and 0 can reveal interesting results of the cheap/rich analysis. Referring to Table 9–1 and Table 9–2, we can observe the following phenomena.

- Bonds can remain rich or cheap over substantially long periods of time. We can clearly reject the hypothesis that these errors are noises in the estimation and are randomly distributed. Of course, it is interesting to investigate the factors determining these errors. Some of these patterns can be explained quite easily.
- The on-the-run issues stand out very clearly in the pattern. As we have discussed before, the on-the-run issues are often traded rich, and these patterns are apparent. We can see that the 0 patterns run downward for about two months before another bond is auctioned and the newly issued bond becomes the on-the-run trading rich. Columns 62 through 66 and columns 111 to 114 depict the appearance of a new issue and its tendency to trade rich for a while and then become more fairly priced.

TABLE 9-1
Relative Value Diagram

Col. #: 1234567890123456789012345678901234567890123456789012345
(10) (20) (30) (40) (50) (60) (70) (80) (90) (100) (110)

11/24/1986
12/ 1/1986
12/15/1986
12/29/1986
1/12/1987
1/26/1987
2/ 9/1987
2/23/1987
3/ 9/1987
3/23/1987
4/ 6/1987
4/20/1987
5/ 4/1987
5/18/1987
6/ 1/1987
6/15/1987
6/29/1987
7/13/1987
7/27/1987
8/10/1987
8/24/1987
9/ 8/1987
9/21/1987
10/ 5/1987
10/19/1987
11/ 2/1987

TABLE 9-1 (continued)
Relative Value Diagram

Col. #: 1234567890123456789012345678901234567890123456789012345678901234567890123456789012345678901234567890123456789012345
       (10)   (20)   (30)   (40)   (50)   (60)   (70)   (80)   (90)   (100)   (110)

11/16/1987
11/30/1987
12/14/1987
12/28/1987
1/11/1988
1/25/1988
2/ 8/1988
2/22/1988
3/ 7/1988
3/21/1988
4/ 4/1988
4/18/1988
5/ 2/1988
5/16/1988
5/31/1988
6/13/1988
6/27/1988
7/11/1988
7/25/1988
8/ 8/1988
8/22/1988
9/ 6/1988
9/19/1988
10/ 3/1988
10/17/1988
10/31/1988
11/14/1988
11/28/1988
12/12/1988

TABLE 9–2
Listing of Bonds in Table 9–1

CUSIP	Coupon	Matures	Seq[a]
912827RT	11.625	1/15/1992	1
912827MW	14.625	2/15/1992	2
912827UH	6.625	2/15/1992	3
912827WA	7.875	3/15/1992	4
912827SB	11.750	4/15/1992	5
912827NE	13.750	5/15/1992	6
912827UQ	6.625	5/15/1992	7
912827WJ	8.250	6/15/1992	8
912827SL	10.375	7/15/1992	9
912810BY	7.250	8/15/1992	10
912827UY	8.250	8/15/1992	11
912827WS	8.750	9/30/1992	12
912827SV	9.750	10/15/1992	13
912827VG	8.375	11/15/1992	14
912827NV	10.500	11/15/1992	15
912827XA	9.125	12/31/1992	16
912827TC	8.750	1/15/1993	17
912827PD	10.875	2/15/1993	18
912827VQ	8.250	2/15/1993	19
912810BN	6.750	2/15/1993	20
912810CA	7.875	2/15/1993	21
912827TM	7,735	4/15/1993	22
912827PM	10.125	5/15/1993	23
912827VY	7.625	5/15/1993	24
912827TV	7.250	7/15/1993	25
912827PV	11.875	8/15/1993	26
912810CB	8.625	8/15/1993	27
912810BQ	7.500	8/15/1993	28
912827WG	8.750	8/15/1993	29
912827UD	7.125	10/15/1993	30
912827QD	11.750	11/15/1993	31
912810CD	8.625	11/15/1993	32
912827WQ	9.000	11/15/1993	33
912827UL	7.000	1/15/1994	34
912827RM	11.625	1/15/1994	35
912810CF	9.000	2/15/1994	36
912827WY	8.875	2/15/1994	37
912827UT	7.000	4/15/1994	38
912827QU	13.125	5/15/1994	39
912827VB	8.000	7/15/1994	40
912827RC	12.625	8/15/1994	41
912810CH	8.750	8/15/1994	42
912827VK	9.500	10/15/1994	43
912810CJ	10.125	11/15/1994	44
912827VT	8.625	1/15/1995	45

TABLE 9–2 *(continued)*
Listing of Bonds in Table 9–1

CUSIP	Coupon	Matures	Seq[a]
912810CL	10.500	2/15/1995	46
912827RW	11.250	2/15/1995	47
912827WB	8.375	4/15/1995	48
912810CN	12.625	5/15/1995	49
912827SE	11.250	5/15/1995	50
912810CQ	10.375	5/15/1995	51
912827WK	8.875	7/15/1995	52
912827SP	10.500	8/15/1995	53
912827WT	8.625	10/15/1995	54
912827SY	9.500	11/15/1995	55
912810CR	11.500	11/15/1995	56
912827XB	8.625	1/15/1996	57
912827TF	8.875	2/15/1996	58
912827TQ	7.375	5/15/1996	59
912827UF	7.250	11/15/1996	60
912827UW	8.500	5/15/1997	61
912827VE	8.625	8/15/1997	62
912827VN	8.875	11/15/1997	63
912827VW	8.125	2/15/1998	64
912810BP	7.000	5/15/1998	65
912827WE	9.000	5/15/1998	66
912827WN	9.250	8/15/1998	67
912827WW	8.875	11/15/1998	68
912810BR	8.500	5/15/1999	69
912810BS	7.875	2/15/2000	70
912810BV	8.375	8/15/2000	71
912810CT	11.750	2/15/2001	72
912810CU	13.125	5/15/2001	73
912810CW	13.375	8/15/2001	74
912810BW	8.000	8/15/2001	75
912810CX	15.750	11/15/2001	76
912810CZ	14.250	2/15/2002	77
912810DA	11.625	11/15/2002	78
912810DC	10.750	2/15/2003	79
912810DD	10.750	5/15/2003	80
912810DE	11.125	8/15/2003	81
912810DG	11.875	11/15/2003	82
912810DH	12.375	5/15/2004	83
912810DK	13.750	8/15/2004	84
912810DM	11.625	11/15/2004	85
912810DQ	12.000	5/15/2005	86
912810BU	8.250	5/15/2005	87
912810DR	10.750	8/15/2005	88
912810DU	9.375	2/15/2006	89

TABLE 9–2 *(continued)*
Listing of Bonds in Table 9–1

CUSIP	Coupon	Matures	Seq[a]
912810BX	7.625	2/15/2007	90
912810BZ	7.875	11/15/2007	91
912810CC	8.375	8/15/2008	92
912810CE	8.750	11/15/2008	93
912810CG	9.125	5/15/2009	94
912810CK	10.375	11/15/2009	95
912810CM	11.750	2/15/2010	96
912810CP	10.000	2/15/2010	97
912810CS	12.750	11/15/2010	98
912810CV	13.875	2/15/2011	99
912810CY	14.000	11/15/2011	100
912810DB	10.375	11/15/2012	101
912810DF	12.000	2/15/2013	102
912810DJ	11.750	2/15/2014	103
912810DL	11.250	2/15/2014	104
912810DN	11.750	11/15/2014	105
912810DP	11.250	2/15/2015	106
912810DS	10.625	2/15/2015	107
912810DT	9.875	11/15/2015	108
912810DV	9.250	2/15/2016	109
912810DW	7.250	2/15/2016	110
912810DX	7.500	11/15/2016	111
912810DY	8.750	2/15/2017	112
912810DZ	8.875	2/15/2017	113
912810EA	9.125	2/15/2018	114
912810EB	9.000	11/15/2018	115

[a] Seq = Col. # in Table 9–1.

- Perhaps the most interesting feature is that the results show how the event of October 19, 1987, has affected the market. Prior to the event, there are relatively few cheap/rich discrepancies; there was a "calm period" for the observable errors. However, after the event there are many significant pricing errors, and, moreover, they last for a substantial period. This shows that cheap/rich is not a riskless arbitrage condition, and the identification of cheap/rich does not imply that there is an immediate arbitrage opportunity available. There is no market mechanism that can eliminate such pricing discrepancies in a riskless fashion. As a result, we see that errors can persist for several months. It is important to note that after three to four months, most pricing discrepancies disappear.

- One may hypothesize that many of the cheap, or type *, bonds are illiquid. Perhaps there is no market for these bonds and for this reason the bond is priced below the fair value. However, current research correlating the cheap/rich level of bonds to liquidity has not revealed any significant relationship. Only the richness of the on-the-run issues have exhibited strong evidence of such a relationship.

RETURN PERFORMANCE

Thus far we have been concerned with the instantaneous total return of a bond or portfolio. It is also useful to analyze the total return of a bond for a specified time horizon. For simplicity we will focus our discussion on a bond, but the theory is equally applicable to the portfolio. We can now use the pricing model developed to specify the total return of a bond. We will let the time interval be Δt.

Suppose the initial bond value is B and the value at the horizon date is B^*. Also assume that the interest (coupons) paid during this period is reinvested at the forward rates to the horizon date. Let the total cash accumulated at the end of the period be I. Then the total return of the bond is

$$\text{Total return} = (B^* - B + I)/B \qquad (9\text{--}1)$$

At the initial date, using the prevailing spot curve, we can calculate the risk-free return over this horizon period (let the rate of return be R). We can also calculate the forward discount function that prevails at the horizon date. Therefore we can calculate the bond value given for the forward curve. The value is denoted by B^{**}. We can also calculate the bond duration at the horizon date, assuming that the forward curve prevails. Let the duration be D_H.

We have shown earlier that all bond returns equal the risk-free rate (R) if the forward curve prevails on the horizon date. For this reason, using Equation (9–1) we see that

$$\text{Total return} = (B^* - B + I)/B = R \text{ only if } B^* = B^{**}$$

But since B^* is rarely equal to B^{**}, total return could be thought of as the expected risk-free rate plus an adjustment for price divergence from the forward price. Equation (9–1) can be rewritten as

$$\text{Total return} = \left[(B^* - B^{**})/B\right] + R \qquad (9\text{–}2)$$

where if $B^* > B^{**}$, total return will be greater than R; and if $B^* < B^{**}$, total return will be less than R.

In Chapter 6 we explained that the effective duration of an issue could be multiplied by the change in yield to determine the issue's percentage change in price. We can calculate a duration measure on the horizon date by implementing instantaneous parallel shifts off the implied forward curve. By the definition of a bond duration, we know that

$$(B^* - B^{**})/B^{**} = -D_H \Delta r \qquad (9\text{–}3)$$

Therefore, we conclude with a very useful bond-return equation:[1]

$$\text{Total return} = T = R - \frac{D_H B^{**}}{B} \Delta r \qquad (9\text{–}4)$$

The usefulness of this total return equation is not limited to a flat yield curve environment or to instantaneous parallel yield shifts. This equation can be easily extended into a return attribution methodology capable of analyzing returns under a myriad of yield curve fluctuations. This application will be discussed in Chapter 15. For now we will focus on the equation's usefulness in the context discussed in the following sections.

We know that the observed return can be very different from the risk-free rate. The difference, called the excess return, can be either a

---

[1]Proof:

$$T = \text{Total return} = \frac{B^* - B^{**}}{B} + R$$

$$= \frac{B^* - B^{**}}{B^{**}} \left(\frac{B^{**}}{B} \right) + R$$

$$= (-D_H \Delta r) \frac{B^{**}}{B} + R$$

negative or positive value. Since identifying the factors that determine the bond's total return would be very helpful, we will focus on a methodology that can be used to dissect the excess return. We will show that the excess return has two components: the interest rate movement and the change in pricing error.

Specifically, we have

$$\text{Excess return } = E = T - R + e = -\frac{D_H B^{**}}{B}\Delta r + e \qquad (9\text{--}5)$$

We can calculate the term $(D_H B^{**}/B)\Delta r$, which represents the interest rate risk component, and we can observe E. Hence we can calculate e, the residual. In this way we can break down the bond return into two parts or attributions.

Another application is to simulate the bond total return for a different shift of the yield curve. That is, for any given value of Δr, we can determine E using the return equation; this allows us to determine or simulate the return of a bond under different yield curve scenarios.

Finally, the return equation gives us another interpretation of convexity. Suppose we are holding a bond with an investment horizon. We are willing to assume that the shift of the yield curve is uncertain and that it distributes normally with mean $M\Delta t$ and variance $V\Delta t$, where the value of M is small (we can ignore any higher-order terms of M).

The bond-return equation can be extended quite simply to

$$T = R - (D_H B^{**}/B)\Delta r + (CB^{**}/B)\Delta r^2 \qquad (9\text{--}6)$$

In this case, we consider Δr to be a random variable. We can represent expectation on both sides of the equation. We get

$$\text{Expected total return } = \text{ Interest return } - \frac{D_H B^{**}}{B}M\Delta t + \frac{CB^{**}}{B}V\Delta t$$

Therefore the equation shows that the expected return is higher for the higher convexity bond. The following example will illustrate the usefulness of the total return equation.

Numerical Example

Consider a two-year zero-coupon bond. Suppose the prevailing spot curve is flat at a rate of 8 percent. Then the implied forward yield curve is also a flat 8 percent. Let the horizon date be one year from now. Then we have

B = the present bond price = $100/(1 + .08)^2$
B^{**} = the forward bond price on the horizon date if the forward curve prevails) = $100/1.08$.
D_H = duration of the bond on the horizon date (if the forward curve prevails), or

$$\frac{\text{maturity}}{(1 + r)} = \frac{1}{1.08}$$

According to the bond total return model (9–4),

$$T = \frac{0.08 - \left(\dfrac{1}{1.08} \times \dfrac{100}{1.08}\right)}{\left[\dfrac{100}{(1.08)^2}\right]\Delta r}$$

$$= 0.08 - \Delta r$$

Now we can cross-check this equation. Suppose that on the horizon date the spot rate prevails at 8.5 percent. The bond price on the horizon date is therefore

$$B^* = \frac{100}{(1.085)}$$

The total return is

$$T = \frac{\dfrac{100}{(1.085)} - \dfrac{100}{(1.08)^2}}{\dfrac{100}{(1.08)^2}}$$

$$= \frac{(1.08)^2}{(1.085)} - 1$$

$$= 0.075023$$

Ignoring the convexity term for the moment, we can use Equation (9–4) to obtain very similar results. With $\Delta r = .005$, we have

$$T = .08 - \Delta r$$
$$= .08 - .005 = .075$$

Although .075 is very close to the actual return of .075023, we can improve our estimation of total return by including the convexity term.

Convexity for a zero-coupon bond is defined as

$$\frac{1}{2}\left(\frac{\text{maturity}(\text{maturity} + 1)}{(1 + \text{spot rate})^2}\right)$$

For the two-year zero bond, on the horizon date, if the forward curve prevails, the bond would have a remaining maturity of one year and its convexity would be

$$C = \frac{1}{2}\left[\frac{2}{(1.08)^2}\right] = \frac{1}{(1.08)^2}$$

Applying Equation (9–6), we solve for total return as follows:

$$T = .08 - \Delta r + \frac{1}{(1.08)^2}\frac{\dfrac{100}{1.08}}{\dfrac{100}{(1.08)^2}}(\Delta r)^2$$

$$= .08 - \Delta r + \frac{(\Delta r)^2}{1.08}$$

For $\Delta r = .005$, we have $T = .075023$.

This shows that after adjusting for the convexity term, the approximation procedure is accurate up to six decimal places. The total return model enables us to represent the bond return very simply.

SUMMARY

This chapter has provided a detailed analysis of the Treasury market. Specifically, the discussions clarified how bond prices are set and discussed the main factors determining the bond prices. Extending the concepts into applicable procedures, we introduced a new methodology for analyzing total return. The advantage of using this format for analyzing returns will become evident when return attribution is discussed in detail in Chapter 15. At this point in the book, we will continue to present information pertaining to the assessment of fair value. The next two chapters will build upon the bond valuation concepts introduced thus far and integrate them with the future contracts and options. By the end of the next two chapters, the reader will be ready for the synoptical presentation of corporate bonds in Chapter 12.

CHAPTER 10

FORWARD AND
FUTURES CONTRACTS

Futures contracts and forward contracts are similar in many ways. For instance, they are both agreements made between two parties on the purchase of an asset on a future date, the "delivery date," and therefore, unlike most other securities, do not require any initial investment. But there are a number of differences in the institutional arrangements between the futures contract and the forward contract. Most fundamentally, the futures market consists of an established intermediary that ensures delivery of positions and enhances liquidity. In this exchange-trading environment, futures are marked to market while forward contracts are not. This difference between the two has an impact on their pricing and their use as hedging instruments. The following sections discuss these issues.

FORWARD CONTRACTS

A *forward contract* is simply an agreement between two individuals. The buyer of the contract (the "long") agrees to buy a specified quantity of an asset (which might be anything from wheat to $100,000 par value 30-year Treasury bonds) at a specified price and future date, the delivery date. The other side of the contract, the seller (or "short") agrees to sell a specified quantity of the asset at a specified price and delivery date. The forward price is therefore the price at which the transaction will take place at the delivery date. Forward contracts, then, permit both the long and the short to "lock in" a price on a set quantity of an asset for delivery at a time acceptable to both buyer and seller.

For example, suppose we enter into an agreement to sell 1 million dollar par value of six-month Treasury bills at 95 to a counter party. The transaction will not take place immediately. It will settle six months from the present date. On the delivery date we will deliver the Treasury bills and receive $950,000 cash. For this forward contract, we will be holding a *short position*. At the time of the initiation of the contract, no money changes hands and there may not be any transaction between the two parties until the delivery date.

Replicating a Forward Contract

To determine the price of a forward contract, we will use an arbitrage argument in which we show that we can replicate the forward contract position using the bonds. Roughly speaking, when one holds a *long position* on a forward contract (i.e., when one is to receive the bond at a future date), it is as if one executed the following simultaneous transactions: (1) borrowing at a fixed interest rate over the term maturing on the delivery date (or short a discount bond with maturity at the delivery date), and (2) using the proceeds from the borrowing or from the shorting of the bond to buy a pure discount bond that matures at some time in the future, that time being the maturity date of the bond specified in the forward contract.

In a perfect capital market where there are no transaction costs, there would be no need for forward contracts because taking a position in a forward contract is no different from taking a long position in one bond and short in another.

We will now show this replication more precisely.

Arbitrage Conditions for a Zero-Coupon Bond Forward Contract

For simplicity, first consider a basic case: a forward contract with a term to delivery represented by t. For instance, for delivery one year later, $t = 1$. Since we will be dealing with forward periods, we will be slightly modifying the notations introduced in the previous chapter. For the purposes of this chapter, the underlying bond to be delivered is the zero-coupon bond with maturity $T-t$, where $T-t$ is the bond's term to maturity on the delivery date. In other words, a bond in the current period with a three-year maturity that will be delivered one year later will be described with $T-t = 2$.

Also, for the purposes of this chapter, let $P(t)$ equal the discount price of the zero-coupon bond with maturity t. [$P(t)$ is the notation in this chapter for discount prices (prices stated as a percentage of par)].

Suppose we sell $P(T)/P(t)$ number of short-term bonds (zero-coupon bonds with maturity t). The proceeds from the sale of the bonds would be

$$[P(T)/P(t)] \times P(t) = P(T)$$

This shows that the proceeds of the sales can purchase exactly one long term bond, a zero-coupon bond with maturity of (T). When we take the position by shorting $P(T)/P(t)$ short-term bonds and buying one long-term bond, the net cash flow at the initial date is zero. But on the delivery date, which is also the maturity date of the short-term bond, the position becomes holding one zero-coupon bond with maturity $T-t$ and shorting cash of $100 \times P(T)/P(t)$. There is no other cash flow between the initial date and the delivery date. But this cash-flow situation is identical to holding a long position in a forward contract where the forward price is $F_t(T-t) = 100 \times P(T)/P(t)$.

In an efficient capital market, the forward contract price has to be $F(T-t)$ to satisfy the arbitrage-free condition; we will show this later. We have shown that a long position in a forward contract can be replicated by the above bond position. By a similar argument, taking a short position in the forward contract is equivalent to shorting one long-term bond and using all the proceeds to buy the short-term bond, the zero-coupon bond maturing at time t.

Pricing of the Forward Contract

Now we proceed to argue that the forward contract should be priced at $F_t(T-t)$. We do so by showing that if the forward contract is priced otherwise, it would provide an arbitrage opportunity.

Suppose the forward contract is priced at F', which is higher than $F_t(T-t)$. Then consider the following position. Sell one forward contract, buy one long-term bond, and short $P(T)/P(t)$ number of short-term bonds. Now there is no net cash flow initially. On the delivery date, we deliver the bond with maturity of $(T-t)$ to satisfy the forward contract obligation. The sale of the bond is guaranteed at the price F'. We can use part of those proceeds to pay off the short position of $F_t(T-t)$ cash. The net cash flow is the arbitrage profit.

Now we can repeat this argument in the alternative scenario. Suppose the forward contract is priced at F' where this time F' is less than the value F_t $(T-t)$. In this case, we hold the forward contract long, short on a long-term bond, and use the proceeds to invest in the zero-coupon bond that matures on the delivery date. Once again, there is no cash flow on the initial date or any other date until the delivery date. On the delivery date, the short-term bond matures, yielding a total cash amount of $F_t(T-t)$. We use a portion to purchase the zero-coupon bond whose original maturity was T when the short position was established one year ago. The price of such a bond was fixed by the forward contract at F' one year ago. This bond can then exactly cover the short position of the long bond. The net result is that we have generated $F_t(T-t)$ − F' arbitrage profit.

The above argument shows that the forward contract price is determined completely by the discount function or the spot curve and that any forward contract position can be replicated by a bond position. Arbitrage conditions also result when the long term bond price F' is less than F. In this case, one wants to be long the forward contract on the long-term bond. To do so, one short-sells a long-term bond while going long on a forward contract for a long-term bond. The proceeds from the sale of the first long-term bond are used to purchase a short-term bond. At the maturity t of the short-term bond, the principal received is used to buy the long-term bond at a price F'. Since the price F of the long-term that has been short-sold is greater than the price F' of the long-term bond of the forward contract, one nets a profit of $F-F'$. The total portfolio renders one short a long-term bond and long a long-term bond, so the long and short positions cancel, and one is left with a profit gained at the maturity of the short-term bond.

Arbitrage Conditions for a Straight-Bond Forward Contract

The pricing for a forward contract on a zero-coupon bond was easily demonstrated in an intuitive manner. The pricing for a contract on a straight bond is also intuitive if the bond is seen as a portfolio of zero-coupon bonds. The forward contract for a straight bond becomes a contract for the purchase of a portfolio of bonds. It follows that this contract may be broken down into a portfolio of several contracts for zero-coupon bonds. The price of one of these individual contracts may be seen as $P(t_i)/P(t)$ as each individual contract matures at t.

The price of the forward contract is the sum of the prices of the individual contracts or

$$F = X_1 P(t_1)/P(t) + X_2 P(t_2)/P(t)$$

Comparing the above result with the definition of the forward discount function defined in Chapter 4, we see that the forward price is the same as the value of the deliverable bond determined by the forward discount function where the forward date is the delivery date.

Forward Price and the Forward Rate

The forward price of a contract for a zero-coupon bond can be used to determine the forward rate of return on a bond specified in the contract. Prices of zero-coupon bonds are often quoted in yield equivalents. Similarly, forward prices are often quoted in terms of discount yield.

$$P(t) = \frac{1}{(1 + r/2)^{2t}}$$

Hence the forward price is determined to be

$$F = \frac{1}{(1 + f/2)^{2t}}$$

where f is the forward rate. When we compare this result with the results in Chapter 4, we see that the forward rate is identical to the forward rate determined by the spot curve.

It is also interesting to note that the forward contract price is not the market expectation of future price of the underlying straight bond; such would be true only if we assumed the expectation hypothesis.

FUTURES VERSUS FORWARDS

Trading Forward Contracts

To understand the fundamental difference between a forward contract and a futures contract, first consider what can happen to a forward contract after the initial agreement and prior to the delivery date. Assume that the forward contract is not negotiable and can be traded in the secondary market.

Suppose that a forward contract has been initiated and that on the following day the price of the underlying asset rises or the short rate changes such that the forward contract has a higher prevailing price. The person who is long the contract should be pleased, as he or she has locked in a future purchase price that is lower than the current market price. The long can sell his or her position and, as the current market price is above the contract price, should be able to do so with a profit.

Assume that the original price of the forward contract is F and the prevailing market price is F'. The long will want to be compensated for the difference between F' and F, wanting to realize a profit on the sale of the contract. Yet it is important to remember that the profit to be realized on the purchase of a contract whose price is less than the value of the underlying asset is a future profit, even though this profit is not subject to any uncertainty. It is realized only on the delivery date. Hence, the profit to be realized in the future must be discounted to its present value. The rate at which the profit is discounted will be the risk-free rate.

In summary, we see that the forward contract can be viewed as a security. Although there is no initial investment required, the forward contract yields profits and losses with the change in the interest rates. The profits and losses are determined by the present value of the change in the forward price.

Futures Contracts

A *futures contract* is in principle similar to a forward contract: the holder of a futures contract (the long) is to pay a specified price for a given amount of the underlying asset at a specified delivery date. The primary difference between a forward contract and a futures contract is that the latter is designed to be traded. Forward contracts, which are highly diverse in nature (i.e., not standardized) and are not "collateralized," are negotiable only between two (or a slightly greater number when traded) people who can accept the following two conditions: (1) the clearly specified (often immutable) terms of the contract, and (2) the possibility that the other side of the contract will renege. Futures contracts, whose terms and underlying assets are highly standardized, are meant to be actively traded in markets. The standardization of underlying assets, such as in futures contracts, assures the availability of the assets on the delivery date.

Futures are traded on exchanges such as the Chicago Board of Trade and the New York Futures Exchange, whose members (whether affiliated with financial institutions or independent) pay to belong to a clearinghouse. The clearinghouse acts as the counter party to both sides of a trade, ensuring that neither side of the trade will default on or be unable to fulfill the specifications of the trade. The clearinghouse acts as a seller to the buyer and a buyer to the seller. It does so by requiring a margin (down payment) from each side of the trade. In other words, when one strikes a trade, one is obligated not to the other party but to the clearinghouse of the exchange on which the trade is made. The clearinghouses are financially supported by their members and require margins on trades; the probability for clearinghouse default is negligible.

Margin Requirements

As mentioned above, futures traders must secure their positions through the clearinghouse with a margin, which is a percentage of the value of the futures contract. If the total dollar value of the position has increased (i.e., more contracts have been purchased), the margin must be increased immediately to remain a set percentage of the total position. If the total value of the position has decreased (i.e., contracts have been sold), the holder of the position is notified as well, as he or she may withdraw funds tied up by the margin. This notification of change in the required margin is a *margin call*.

The initial margin, then, is seen to fluctuate based on the value of the futures contract (or rather, on the total value of the underlying assets). The initial margin is supplemented by the *variation margin*, which is a separate margin that also represents a percentage of the value of the underlying asset, and that changes as a result of matching the value of the contract with the underlying asset. This matching is called "marking-to-market." Marking-to-market is used by clearinghouses as a means or assuring the continuing solvency of the holder of an open position.

As indicated previously, the required margin will fluctuate to reflect the changes in price of the underlying asset. These price changes are posted daily, and both sides of the trade must alter their margins accordingly. Suppose that $F(t)$ is the price of a futures contract at time t. If the price on the following day becomes $F(t+1)$, the holder of the long position receives $[(F(t+1) - F(t))]$ in cash while the short pays $F(t+1) - F(t)$ If a futures contract has risen in price more than it has decreased in price (i.e., if the net value has increased), the price of the contract at the expiration date will reflect the payments made to increase the margin in the time between the initiation of the contract and the delivery date. In this case, the price paid for the contract will be the original settlement price minus the payments to increase the margin over time. On the other hand, if the net value of the futures contract has decreased in the time between the initiation of the contract and the delivery date, the settlement price at delivery will be more than the original settlement price to reflect payments to the holder of the long position. Marking-to-market does not change the ultimate value of the contract. However, it does provide immediately available funds for the holder of the long position, should his or her expectations of price increases for the underlying asset be realized.

Impact of Marking-to-Market on the Traded Price

Futures contracts are fundamentally distinguished from forward contracts by marking-to-market. The price of a futures contract as a result of marking-to-market differs from that of a forward contract. Marking-to-market creates a reinvestment risk for futures contracts that is not implicit in forward contracts. Suppose the dollar values of marking-to-market were stated as the present values of future price changes (i.e., if they were discounted). This would mean that marking-to-market price changes would be treated as though they occurred on the settlement date. In other words, the settlement price would not be altered by marking-to-market, and the futures contract would be priced the same as the forward contract.

However, marking-to-market occurs at *current prices*. The profit and loss from marking-to-market would be reinvested at the prevailing market rate. For this reason, a position in a futures contract has a cash flow different from that of a forward contract. Furthermore, futures positions can no longer be replicated by a simple strategy of buying one bond, shorting another, and holding the position until the delivery date. However, if we assume that the daily rate is known (nonstochastic) from the present date until the delivery date, we can replicate the futures position using dynamic hedging strategies, assuming the underlying bond price follows a binomial process. The dynamic hedging strategy is the standard approach taken in the stock return models. In replicating the futures position, we find that the futures price is the same as the forward price.

In summary, if we assume, as an approximation, that the daily interest rate is nonstochastic, then the futures contract will be valued at the same price as the forward contract. This is perhaps one of the most interesting results in recent research on futures and forwards. In the pricing of bond futures, we are concerned with interest rate risks, and therefore it would be consistent to assume that the daily interest rate risk is minimal, at least until the delivery date. The daily interest rate risk affects the futures price to the extent that the reinvestment of the profit and loss of the marking-to-market is uncertain. When the delivery date is not too distant, the effect is generally rather small.

Aside from the aspect of marking-to-market, a feature that causes the futures price to differ from the forward is the right of the holder of a short contract to choose which specific instrument to deliver against the contract. Usually a number of issues qualify as a deliverable security for each futures contract. This feature is also known as the "cheapest to deliver" option.

Cheapest to Deliver

On the delivery date, when the person in the short position has to deliver the underlying bonds, he or she can deliver any bond that qualifies for delivery. Clearly, the cheapest bond that can be purchased would be delivered. To determine the cheapest-to-deliver bond, we have to take the bond's market price and conversion factor (CF) into account. More precisely, we can divide the market price of each bond in the deliverable basket by its conversion factor to determine the number of bonds to deliver against the contract. The issue with the lowest ratio (lowest number of bonds) for delivery is the cheapest to deliver. By definition, as people expect the cheapest bond to be delivered, the futures price converges to the price of the cheapest bond in the basket. Before expiration of the futures contract, the futures price will follow the price of the expected cheapest-to-deliver instrument. The relationship between the underlying's price and future contract's price is represented by the cost-to-carry model described below.

COST-TO-CARRY MODEL

Any time the futures price is relatively high, one can buy a deliverable bond and short a futures in order to lock in the future "sale" price. For obtaining the deliverable bond, the *objective* is to minimize the invoice price less forthcoming coupons until the delivery date.

Minimize: Invoice price (1/CF) − PV(coupon/CF)

With respect to the total cost to short at delivery, the present value of the futures price cannot exceed the cost of holding inventory, or inventory will be shorted. The cost-of-carry model says nothing about how the futures price is traded relative to the bond price. The cost-of-carry model depends on the coupon level, the time value of money, and the bond's conversion factor. At any time, the difference between the futures price and the cheapest-to-deliver's price is called the "basis." The variation of the basis over time is called the "basis risk."

The basis risk characterizes the sensitivity of the futures price relative to the underlying market basket's interest rate sensitivities. The basis changes are attributable to changes in market interest rates that affect the determination of a cheapest-to-deliver instrument. One may question whether the futures price must be exactly specified by the cost-to-carry model. The answer to this query is: not necessarily. At the time of delivery there can be another bond that would be cheaper than the one used in the computations prior to the delivery date. Since only the short position holds the option (the option to deliver the cheapest bond at delivery date), this option has value; therefore one expects futures to trade at a price lower than the one specified by a model that does not account for the option component. In other words, one can consider the true future price as representing a cost-of-carry theoretical price with an embedded short option.

PERFORMANCE PROFILE FOR FUTURES CONTRACTS

The performance of a futures contract is particularly useful when we use futures positions to hedge the bond positions. Futures are different from other securities in that they do not require an initial investment and they are marked to market daily, so they have a value not in a monetary context but rather as an index. The performance profile (PP) of a futures position is defined to be the instantaneous profit and loss associated with the parallel shift of the yield curve.

To determine the PP of a futures contract, it is helpful to equate a futures contract with a forward contract. For a forward contract, the long position is seen as borrowing short term and holding long term. The short position is seen as lending short term (lending until the delivery date). Thus, the PP of the long position is downward sloping: if interest rates rise, the price of the bond decreases. In contrast, the PP for the short is upward sloping: if interest rates rise, the value owed is less. The PP of a forward contract, then, is a combination of both positions.

Figure 10–1 depicts the PP of a long position in a forward contract. Recall that holding a long position in a forward contract is equivalent to selling a short-term bond (or short-term borrowing) and using the proceeds to buy a long-term bond. The sale of the short-term bond represents a liability, and the short-term bond is represented by curve EF. Since the full proceeds of the sale of the short-term bond are used to purchase the long-term bond (the long-term bond has the same dollar value as the short-term), point G is constructed such that GO and OH are equidistant. The curve CD represents the PP of the long-term bond. Note that CD has a greater slope than EF because the long-term bond has higher duration. The net position (i.e., the net distance of XZ and

FIGURE 10–1
Performance Profile of a Forward Contract

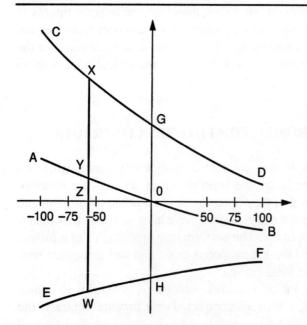

ZW for any point Z along the abscisin is YZ. The PP of the forward contract is represented by line AB.

The PP of a forward contract should be interpreted differently than that of a straight bond. The PP of a forward contract does not depict the future price of a bond given different interest rate levels. Rather, the curve represents the the mark-to-market profit and loss when an instantaneous shift of the yield curve occurs. For example, if the interest rate drops to point Z, the mark-to-market account would increase to the dollar value represented by YZ. The PP of a forward contract is not useful for analysis of price or yield changes because investors do not "pay" to hold a forward contract, as they would to hold a bond. Therefore, the PP of a forward or futures contract cannot be depicted as a net sum of long and short positions, as is the case with a straight bond.

By the same token, the PP of a forward contract in a short position can be constructed. Assume a long-term bond is sold to buy a short-term instrument (e.g., a CD). Figure 10–2 shows that curve EF now has a greater slope, as it represents the liability of the long-term bond that has been sold. The net position of curves EF and CD is AB, which is the short position of the forward curve. In comparing Figure 10–2 to Figure 10–1, it is clear that the position yields a profit when the interest rate increases.

Following this argument, it becomes evident that with an increasingly greater number of forward contracts, the PP curve will always go through the origin. The PPs of the additional forward contracts will be increasingly steep. That is, with an increasing number of contracts, the PP, negative in slope, will rotate clockwise. In contrast, the short position is always represented by a positively sloped curve. In shorting more contracts, the PP curve will rotate counterclockwise.

Note that the PP for futures on bonds with short delivery dates (under one year) will nearly replicate the PP of the underlying asset, which has a significantly longer maturity (e.g., 10 years).

The short position is equivalent to shorting the long term and buying the short term. With additional contracts, the curves simply rotate around the origin and become steeper.

Duration for Futures Contracts

Duration is defined as the percentage change in the futures price when a parallel shift in the yield curve occurs. Since futures contract prices differ

FIGURE 10-2
Performance Profile of a Forward Contract in a Short Position

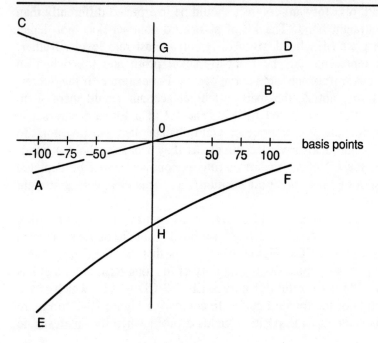

from the spot (cash) price of the underlying asset in that the futures price is not the cost of an investment, the futures price should not be reflected in the value of the portfolio. Only the change in the futures price, based on marking-to-market changes, is relevant. Hence, futures duration is defined as follows (its use will be given in Hedge Ratio section).

$$D = \frac{-\Delta F / \Delta r}{F}$$

with

$$F = P(T)/P(t)$$

Here, for simplicity, one assumes the futures price is approximated by the forward price.

Convexity

By the same line of argument, we can define the convexity of futures as follows.

Consider a zero-coupon-bond forward contract with the deliverable bond's term to maturity represented as T_t and with term to delivery t. T_t is the bond's term to maturity in the forward period (e.g., one year from now), not the zero bond's current period term to maturity. For instance, a zero bond with an existing maturity term of three-years (T) is also represented on a one-year forward basis as having a maturity term of two years for $t=1$, which would be shown as $(T_t) = (2_1)$. The yield curve is represented by r.

In Chapter 9 we used F to represent discount factors or prices as a percent of par. In this chapter F symbolizes forward price, distinctly different from current price P. The price of a forward is

$$F = \frac{100}{(1 + r)^{T_t}}$$

The convexity of a forward contract is just the convexity of the underlying deliverable bond.

CANONICAL EXAMPLE

Hedge Ratios

Now we can show how the duration measure can be used for hedging purposes. Suppose that we have a portfolio with value V. The portfolio duration is D. Suppose we want to determine the number of contracts that we should long (short) such that the portfolio, together with the futures position, would not be subject to any interest rate risk instantaneously. Note that the concept of matching duration does not apply, since the futures position has no *dollar* value. The concept we use is *dollar duration*; that is, we need to determine the futures position such that the total portfolio value in dollars is insensitive to the parallel shift of the yield curve.

By the definition of portfolio duration, we know that

$$\Delta P = -D \times P\Delta r \qquad (10\text{--}1)$$

By the definition of futures duration, we have

$$\Delta F = -d \times F \Delta r \qquad (10\text{--}2)$$

where d is the futures duration.

Suppose the number of futures contracts is N. Then the requirement of the futures position to be able to hedge the interest rate risk exposure of the portfolio is given by

$$\Delta P + [N \times \Delta F] = 0 \qquad (10\text{--}3)$$

Substituting Equations 10–1 and 10–2 into Equation 10–3, we can solve for the appropriate number of futures contracts.

The following is an example of how the spot discount factors can be used to determine the forward factor for the construction of a PP of a forward contract. The spot factors for the one-year and three-year zero were introduced in the canonical section of Chapter 3. Chapter 4's canonical section presented the computation of forward factors (or prices stated as a percentage of par). The following example shows these same factors (or prices) for the initial position or 0-basis-point shifts (BPShifts).

Example

Performance Profile of forward contract: Delivery of a two-year zero-coupon bond in one year (using the current period's three-year zero as the deliverable instrument).

BP Shifts	-100	-50	0	50	100
1-year	.901866	.897818	.8938	.8898	.88588
3-year	.821227	.809790	.79858	.787570	.776760
Forward					
Price	.9106	.9020	.89347	.8859	.8768
PP	.0171	.0085	0	.0076	.0167

The change in forward prices (or theoretical futures prices), ΔF, for given parallel shifts in the yield curve, was obtained by using spot prices. Notice in the above example that the last row is just the price changes from the initial forward price. This row represents the profit/loss profile of the forward position, otherwise known as the "variation margin" of a futures contract. It is the values in this row that lead to the determination of how many contracts (N) must be used in a hedge to offset the determined ΔP.

SUMMARY

This chapter presented a complete discussion of the forward market activities, including arbitrage positions, emphasizing the establishment of forward contract prices through the integration of short and long Treasury positions. The arbitrage relationships were similar for futures contracts. The variation margin and cheapest-to-deliver discussions provided added insight into the cash-flow risks of futures contracts over forward contracts. The performance profiles of different positions highlighted the sensitivity to interest rates. The following chapter draws upon the arbitrage relationships and interest rate sensitivities for a coherent progression into fixed-income options.

CHAPTER 11

BOND OPTIONS

There are many actively traded options in the market, as well as many option-embedded bonds. This chapter extends our earlier discussions on the spot curve and instruments whose prices are closely related to the spot curve. Options cannot be priced and analyzed by the spot curve alone; their study requires the use of option-pricing models. This chapter shows stock option models are not adequate for evaluating bond options.

BASICS OF OPTIONS

A fixed-income option is a contract for a future transaction with initially specified terms, at the election of one of the parties (referred to as the "buyer," "holder," or "long side" of the option). If the buyer can exercise the option at any time up to the expiration date, the option is said to be "American"; if exercise is permitted only on the expiration date, the option is said to be "European."

Different contracts exist for the purchase ("calls") or sale ("puts") of a fixed-income security. Unlike equity options, however, an option may actually be embedded in the terms of the security. Options that stand alone and those that are embedded in fixed-income securities are analyzed similarly.

There are three broad categories of fixed-income options:

- Exchange-traded options
- Over-the-counter options
- Embedded options

For *exchange-traded options*, organized exchanges, notably the Chicago Board of Trade and the Chicago Mercantile Exchange, offer trading of standardized put and call options on interest-rate-sensitive instruments. Standardization allows these options to be traded in a central location. Trade data, transaction prices, and volume information are readily available for the public market. Exchange-traded options, noted for their liquidity and conceptual simplicity, are used in many hedging and speculative strategies. Options on the futures contracts for 20-year Treasury bonds and 10-year Treasury notes, and on short-term Eurodollar futures, are *among the most actively traded instruments in our fixed-income securities market.* All active exchange-traded fixed-income options are for *futures contracts* rather than for underlying cash instruments. This serves to enhance liquidity and promote standardization.

Over-the-counter (OTC) options are special, or "custom," options on fixed-income securities, portfolios, or loans; their market is created by various brokerage firms and commercial banks. In principle, these options can be designed in any way that serves the requirements of the market's participants.

The interest rate "caps-and-floors" market is an important OTC market. Many commercial loans are now written with interest rates that float in parity with some key rate such as the LIBOR rate, T-bill rate, or prime rate. Cap-and-floor agreements attached to such a loan specify that the rate charged will not exceed, or fall below, the cap and floor levels, respectively. The market for these agreements is large and growing. Many banks and other primary lenders look first to major brokers, dealers, or larger institutions to underwrite the option component, and then the primary lenders "resell" the combined option/loan commitment to their commercial clients.

The third category, *embedded options*, is comprised of options embedded in bonds and other interest-rate-sensitive instruments. In many ways, these options are the most complex, least understood, and most interesting of the three categories. "Embedded" means that the options cannot be traded in isolation but must be bought and sold along with the underlying security. Embedded-option valuation is thus an integral part of analysis of such securities. The oldest and most familiar type of embedded option is the *call* feature of a bond. A call feature typically gives the *issuer* of a bond the right to buy the bond back from the holders at a specified price, regardless of the market price of the bond at the time of call. This means that the holder of a callable bond is effectively "long" the bond and "short" the call option.

Even a simple European-type bond call feature is inherently complex. Table 11–1 illustrates relative valuation of a 15-year bond with a par call in 10 years. The value of the (embedded) European call is related to the value of an equivalent payoff position comprised of a noncallable bond and a European option on an extension of the maturity.

Clearly, in this case what sometimes is termed an "interest rate" option is actually an option on future cash flows. As indicated in Table 11-1, exercise affects the series of cash flows from the 11th to the 15th year of the bond's life. Since the receipt of the cash flows is conditional on the option's exercise, both put and call values must be related to the present values of those contingent cash flows. The exact nature of the relationship between option values and the cash flows is not easy to characterize. Methods suitable for the analysis of simple options on interest rates or simple bonds are generally not valid for embedded options. A discussion of these limited methods and of the evolution of a viable solution will be presented shortly.

Our discussion of bond options extends from the basic stock option framework, so we will first cover briefly some of the basics in stock options.

TABLE 11–1
Relative Valuation

	Cash Flows If Rates Are . . .	
Position	High	Low
15-year Callable	Years 1–15	Years 1–10 (bond called)
15-year noncallable —and— Write call option for a 5-year bond exercisable in 10 years	Years 1–15 (Call expires)	Years 1–10 (Call excercised)
10-year noncallable —and— Write put option for a 5-year bond exercisable in 10 years	Years 1–15 (Put exercised)	Years 1–10 (Put expires)

Concepts Underlying Stock Call Options

Definitions and Notations:

1. The *premium* is the price of the option. We denote the call option and put option by C and P respectively.
2. The *strike* (exercise) *price*, the fixed price at which the option holder can buy or sell the underlying asset, is denoted by X.
3. *Intrinsic* value for call options is the amount by which the asset value exceeds the strike price; for put options, it is the amount by which the strike price exceeds the asset value.
4. *Time premium* is the difference between the option price and the intrinsic value.
5. The period from settlement date to expiration is denoted by τ, the time to expiration.
6. The expected rate of return of the asset is μ, and the standard deviation of return is σ, which is also called the "volatility."

Given the above description of an option and the following assumptions, we can derive the Black-Scholes model. The model assumptions are

- The financial capital market is frictionless.
- The risk-free rate is constant over the life of the option. The continuously compounding rate is denoted by r.
- The underlying security pays no dividend.
- The underlying security has a lognormal return pattern with mean $\mu\tau$ and standard deviation $\sigma\sqrt{\tau}$.
- The option value depends only on two state parameters: asset value S and the time to expiration τ. We denote the put price and the call price as follows:

$$P = P(S, \tau) \text{ for put option}$$

and

$$C = C(S, \tau) \text{ for call option}$$

We say the option is "out-of-the-money" when the intrinsic value is zero and that it is "in-the-money" when the intrinsic value is positive. The option is traded at parity, or "at-the-money," if the security is traded at the strike price.

Given these assumptions, we can derive the Black-Scholes model:

$$C = SN(d_1) - Xe^{-r\tau}N(d_1 - \sigma\sqrt{\tau})$$

$$d_1 = \frac{\ln(S/Xe^{-r\tau}) + \frac{1}{2}\sigma^2\tau}{\sigma\sqrt{\tau}}$$

N = normal distribution function

and

$N(d_1)$ = the probability that a deviation less than d_1 will occur in a normal distribution (mean = 0, σ = 1)

The reader interested in a more thorough discussion of the Black-Scholes model should consult a book on options.

It is very useful to depict the option value in terms of the underlying security price. After all, the stochastic variations of the option price depend on the underlying security price. Figure 11–1 shows the call option price variations with the stock price on the x-axis. The call option price is given by the Black-Scholes equation. Notice that as the option becomes significantly in-the-money, the option value approaches the present security price net of the present value of the strike price. The value does not approach the intrinsic value but exceeds it.

Also note that the time premium is always positive and that it is highest when the option is about at-the-money. When the holder of the option exercises the option, he or she will receive the intrinsic value.

FIGURE 11–1
Call Option Price Variations

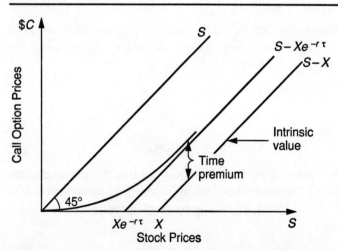

It follows that the holder is always better off selling the option in the secondary market than exercising the option. From this argument, we conclude that there is no early exercise of an American call option, and a call option should be priced as if it were European.

Comparative Statistics

Using the Black-Scholes model, we can show how a small change in a parameter affects the price change, holding all other parameters constant.

1. Hedge Ratio.

$$\delta = \frac{\partial C}{\partial S} = N(d_1) > 0$$

The hedge ratio, or δ (delta), is positive. The δ gives the number of unit changes in option value for a unit change in stock value. For instance, if $\delta = .5$, then a \$1 increase (decrease) in stock value leads to a \$0.50 increase (decrease) in option value for calls. Therefore, for each call option, if one shorts δ shares of stock, the position would be hedged (instantaneously). Conversely, to hedge a position of stock, one can write $\frac{1}{\delta}$ call option contracts for each share.

2. Gamma (Γ).

$$\Gamma = \frac{\partial^2 C}{\partial S^2} = \frac{1}{S\sigma\sqrt{\tau}} N'(d_1) > 0$$

Γ is positive, showing that the call option value in relation to the stock value is concave. The hedge position described above is an approximation, appropriate only for a short interval. The approximation error grows with time. If $\Gamma \approx 0$, the error would be small; otherwise the error is large.

3. Elasticity.
Elasticity, denoted by η, is defined as follows:

$$\eta = \frac{\partial C}{\partial S} \frac{S}{C} = \frac{SN(d_1)}{C} > 0$$

Another term for elasticity is *leverage*. The η gives the percentage increase in call option price for each unit of percentage increase in stock price. η has other economic meanings. For instance, it relates the stock volatility to the option volatility. Specifically,

Volatility of option $= \eta$ (Volatility of stock)

It also relates the return premium of the option to the stock by

Expected return of option $-$ Risk-free rate $=$
η^* (Expected return of stock $-$ Risk-free rate)

4. The Time-Value Premium Decay. Time value, denoted by θ, is

$$\theta = \frac{\partial C}{\partial \tau} = \frac{S\sigma}{2\sqrt{\tau}}N'(d_1) + Xe^{-r\tau}rN(d_1 - \sigma\sqrt{\tau}) > 0$$

The option price decreases over time, holding all other parameters constant. The time-value premium decays much more rapidly in the last few weeks of the option's life compared to the first few weeks in the option's life.

5. Relationship to Exercise Price.

$$\frac{\partial C}{\partial X} < 0$$

In differentiating the call option price with respect to exercise price, we can show that it is negative. That is, for calls, the increase in the exercise price leads to a drop in the premium.

6. Relationship to Volatility.

$$\frac{\partial C}{\partial \sigma} = S\sqrt{\tau}N'(d_1) > 0$$

Increase in stock volatility results in higher call premium.

7. Relationship to Risk-Free Rate.

$$\frac{\partial C}{\partial r} = \tau Xe^{-r\tau}N(d_1 - \sigma\sqrt{\tau}) > 0$$

When the risk-free rate falls, the call premium would also fall.

Extension to Other Options

This basic model can be extended quite simply to European put options and options on dividend-paying stocks. Likewise, we can also use it to value European options (put and call) on futures.

European Put Option

The European put option premium is completely determined by the asset price and call option value. Specifically we have

$$P = C - S + de^{-r\tau} - Xe^{-r\tau}$$

where d is the dividend paid between the settlement date and the expiration date.

Option on Futures

Let F be the futures price. Let

$$C = C(F, \tau)$$

be the premium of the options on futures. Then the pricing model is simply the option model substituting S in terms of F given by

$$S = Fe^{-r\tau}$$

The argument follows directly from the risk-neutral arguments.

Early Exercise of an Option

We have shown that there should be no optimal early exercise of a call option, and therefore that the American call option value should be the same as the European call option. Such is not the case for European put options and options on futures. In these cases, the early exercise decision is more complex (see Appendix A for further discussion).

PRICING INTEREST RATE OPTIONS

A common base of all modern option models is that each employs a model of the value of the underlying asset in the future. A statement of mathematical rules that define the probabilistic nature of uncertain future value and rates of return is termed a "stochastic process." Stochastic processes define ways in which value or return changes over time. A particular stochastic process implies a corresponding probability distribution of the value of the underlying asset. Option models throughout this book depend upon stochastic models of future underlying prices.

Option-pricing methodology follows a simple and logical sequence of analysis. Using the stochastic specification, the evolution of the price of the underlying asset through time can be identified, and subsequently the probability of every feasible price at all points in time can be inferred. For a European call option, the analysis next makes use of the "boundary conditions" of the call option at expiration. If the price of the underlying asset is P, a call option's value at expiration is Max$[(P - X),0]$, where X is the strike or exercise price. If the probability distribution of P at maturity can be identified, the expected value of the boundary value follows directly. Discounting this expected value to the present provides the value of the option.

The Black-Scholes model [3] is developed under the assumption that returns obey the most simple and natural of all stochastic processes, Brownian motion, or Wiener diffusion. The Wiener process can be defined by a differential equation describing the dynamics of the way returns on stock change over time. This differential equation and the boundary conditions give the well-known closed-form solution, which was presented earlier.

Equivalently, the process can be described by the probability distribution of security value at expiration. The Wiener process implies that the continuously compounded rate of return obtained by holding an asset for a given interval of time is normally distributed with a variance that is proportional to the holding period. This basic assumption can be expressed as follows:

$$P(T + t) = P(T)\exp(Rt)$$

or

$$\ln[P(T + t)/P(t)] = Rt$$

Since R has a normal distribution with variance proportional to t, the price is said to have a "lognormal" distribution.

The Black-Scholes solution could be obtained by taking the expected value of the boundary conditions over the appropriate lognormal distribution of value of the underlying stock at expiration.

As long as there is correspondence between a stochastic process and an implied probability distribution, there are two equivalent approaches for option evaluation. The choice of methodology is generally motivated by consideration of the simplicity and relative lucidity of the alternatives. Some alternatives use methods based on the differential expression of stochastic processes; we will concentrate on the binomial approximations of probability distributions. In either case, once some fundamental principles of construction are accepted and verified, it is possible to price options on assets with very complex assumed distributions of returns. It is critically important to recognize that an option model will be appropriate for valuation only if the assumed stochastic process is an adequate description of the returns generated from holding the underlying instrument.

In modeling stock returns, one stock is conceptually very much like another. The returns process of IBM can be viewed as the same as that of, say, General Motors, up to differences only in the values of such parameters as volatility and dividend rate. There is nothing, other than nonnegative prices, that constrains the domain of possible future prices. In other words, the nature of equity returns does not require volatility to be different at different points in time.

In contrast to the simple dynamics of equity prices, a stochastic description of fixed-income prices is complicated by several factors. The domain of reasonable bond prices is constrained on both the upside and the downside. Like stocks, bond prices cannot fall below zero. But on the upside a bond has a defined, time-dependent maximum price. If interest rates cannot be negative, the upper bound for the price of a series of cash flows is the sum of the cash flows: the present value at a discount rate of zero. Further, the price of a bond will converge to its face value at maturity, regardless of discount rates.

An important concept for formalizing the concept of yield is that of holding-period return, (HPR). The holding-period return of an asset is the measure of the value of all cash flows received over a period of time plus the market value of the asset at the end of the period, relative to the beginning market value.

Bond-return modeling is complicated by an institutional peculiarity in the way a bond's coupon payments are reflected in quoted prices. In general, market value and quoted price are not the same.

Bonds operate under a pricing convention different from that of stocks. Stocks pay dividends to the holder of record on a particular day, regardless of how long the holder has owned the stock. On the ex-dividend date, the stock price is marked down by the amount of the dividend payment. In contrast, the transaction or *invoice* price of a bond incorporates proportional coupon payments. In effect, the seller of a bond receives all coupon interest that has accrued from the date of the last payment to the transaction date.

TIME-DEPENDENT NATURE OF FIXED-INCOME ASSET VOLATILITY

The principal complication in modeling fixed-income returns is that bond returns cannot have a constant variance over the life of the bond.

Figure 11–2 shows two possible paths a coupon-bond price could take until maturity. For a certain period after issuance, the value of the bond can substantially rise or fall, due to the fact that the price will reflect the present value of the remaining coupons. From issue date, T_0, to a time point T^*, the distribution of bond prices is increasingly dispersed, reflecting more opportunities for large changes to occur in yield. After T^* until maturity, T_M, the effect of the diffusion of possible yield states is increasingly offset by the effect of the "pull to par" of the bond. In other words, T^* represents the crossover point in time where the pull-to-par effect starts to offset the diffusion effect. The specific value of T^* is unique for each bond and is determined by such factors as coupon rate and remaining term to maturity.

As bond life shortens, these two effects work to restrict price movement. With fewer discounting periods until maturity and fewer remaining payments for coupon issues, the upper bound on possible price is relatively lower. Therefore, as the bond is approaching maturity, the maximum attainable price is decreasing, and the probable minimum price is increasing. At maturity, of course, both of these effects converge to the face value of the bond.

The change in variance of bond returns over time has been investigated by a number of researchers. Three alternative specifications are discussed below.

The Merton Model

Merton's model of the risk structure of interest rates [12] was the first to describe use of time-dependent variance to price bond options. Merton showed that it is theoretically possible to value a debt option, assuming the underlying bond returns follow a Wiener process, by generalizing the solution obtained by Black and Scholes to the case where variance is a function of time. He applied continuous arbitrage arguments to derive an expression for the value of a debt option.

Essentially, the solution of option value requires two components: (1) the specification of the bond-return variance, and (2) an expression

FIGURE 11–2
Two Price Paths over a Bond's Life, Showing "Pull to Par"

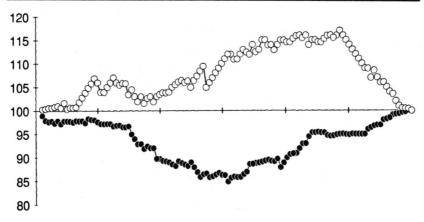

that contains not only an integral of return variance but also a bond's return covariance with a short-term rate, over the time interval until expiration. It is difficult to estimate the values for the parameters of this integral, and thus the model has limited appeal.

Merton's model was an immediate extension of his often-cited compendium of work on generalized option pricing [13]. Together with the Black-Scholes model, which appeared at the same time, Merton's analysis forms the cornerstone of modern option theory.

The Brownian Bridge Model

This model specifies bond returns as a stochastic process with variance that first increases and then decreases over time. Ball and Torous [1] suggested that bond returns can be modeled by a "Brownian Bridge" process. This process, sometimes termed "tied-down Brownian motion," defines random motion when both the beginning and ending points are determined *ex ante*. This circumstance describes well the certainty of the current and maturity values for a bond.

This ingenious idea models the price of a discount bond as it converges to its face value at maturity in such a way that the variance of the rate of return is constant over time. Ball and Torous then make use of Merton's specification of stochastic interest rate options to determine a form for the value of a European option on a discount bond.

The instantaneous variance and expected-return parameters of the Bridge process cannot describe all of the characteristics of bond return. Further, a significant weakness of the approach is that the constant variance of return implies that the variablility of yield to maturity increases without bound as the bond approaches maturity. However, the Brownian Bridge is still an important normative characterization of bond-return behavior under the constraint of bond-price behavior, and in part it suggested the following development.

The Schaefer and Schwartz Duration Model

This third approach models bond returns by a Wiener process augmented by an explicit model of the instantaneous variance of bond return.

Schaefer and Schwartz [14] developed a model that relates the instantaneous return variance to bond duration. Specifically, they assume that the standard deviation of return on bonds is proportional to the bond's duration. This explanation of bond price-changes over time is both simple and realistic.

As will be discussed below, there is a well-defined link between bond return and duration. For simple, riskless bonds, an explicit formulation of duration is possible, and the instantaneous variance of the bond-return process can be identified. However, implementation of the model, especially for general-purpose use, is again quite involved.

Each of these three models was motivated by the goal of pricing options on bonds. A taxonomy would place all three in the family defined by the solution methods of Black-Scholes and Merton. Their common root is the recognition of changing bond-return variance. The primary difference between them is the specification of the nature of change.

An alternative line of development has given rise to fixed-income option models that have begun to dominate securities applications. These techniques relate values of the debt option to movements in the term structure of interest rates.

EQUILIBRIUM TERM-STRUCTURE MODELS AND OPTION VALUATION

Figure 11–1 illustrated that the value of a debt option should depend on the present value of the cash flows being optioned. It logically follows that option value must be a function of the term structure of rates corresponding to the present value factors used to value those cash flows.

The aforementioned models of bond-price behavior all specified the HPR of a specific bond or type of bond. Modeling of the term structure of interest rates avoids the need for explicit explanations of the complex structure of holding-period returns. Once a term-structure model is specified, any bond price, the bond's HPR behavior over time, and option values on that bond can all be examined as consequences of that common underlying structure.

A term-structure model must perform two tasks for option valuation purposes. First, the model must involve a stochastic process or probability distribution that identifies the possible future term structures. The evolution of the term structure into the future implied by the stochastic process must be economically rational and consistent with observed behavior. Second, the model should be consistent with the term structure observed at any point in time.

A number of different theories of equilibrium term structure have been proposed in finance and economics. Interested readers are encouraged to study the papers by Cox, Ingersoll, and Ross [6], Vasicek [15], Brennan and Schwartz [4], and Courtadon [5], and their references, to gain insight into this important arena of theory.

An important virtue of equilibrium term-structure models is that they provide *arbitrage-free rate movements*. An easy and valid "reality check" on a model is whether it can be used to answer the question: "If the market actually functions according to the model, can trading strategies be developed that yield superior returns?" If no such strategies can be found, then the model is arbitrage-free. Formally, an arbitrage-free term structure implies that no security or combination of securities can provide consistently higher expected holding-period returns than any other. The arbitrage-free condition is a necessary condition for maximum validity and practical acceptance of an option model. Correct relative pricing of options on different cash flows relies on the condition. Accordingly, arbitrage-free rate movements play an important role in the model development below.

All equilibrium term-structure models are derived by assigning stochastic processes to one or more term interest rates. The models of Vasicek and Courtadon are single-factor models, where the state variable is the "short rate" of interest. Equilibrium levels of all other rates are derived therefrom. Brennan and Schwartz present a two-factor model in which the dynamics of the term structure are related to the rate on a perpetuity, or "consol rate," in addition to the short rate. Cox, Ingersoll, and Ross provide a general equilibrium structure. Although they explicitly study a one-factor model, the basis can be generalized to higher-factor dimensions as well.

Practical difficulties restrict the use of equilibrium term-structure models for pricing debt options. First, the models require estimation of, or belief in the assumption of, the stochastic process of one- or two-term interest rates. Second, they require the estimation of a parameter determined by investor utility. This parameter relates to risk aversion and is termed the "market price of risk." The final practical barrier to implementation is that generally the methodology for option valuation involves the numerical solution of differential equations. This barrier is not insurmountable for those who have access to powerful computers and have advanced mathematical skills. However, if a procedure is to be widely accepted and implemented, it should be as easy to comprehend and apply as the Black-Scholes model or as solutions based on the direct modeling of the probability distribution of future term rates.

As previously mentioned, equilibrium models of term structure, which possess the necessary property of arbitrage-free rate movements, should be consistent with an observed term structure. It is possible, within the context of option pricing, that an exogenous specification of the conditions of equilibrium could imply that an observed term structure is not in equilibrium. To avoid this, an alternative specification procedure has been developed.

The alternative to specification of equilibrium parameters is to implicitly accept the current observed term structure as consistent with an unobserved and unspecified equilibrium. From this platform, feasible subsequent movements of term rates can be modeled so that they are arbitrage-free. The first such approach was that of Ho and Lee [9], the *arbitrage-free rate movements* (*AR*) model. This approach has immediate advantages for option pricing while it avoids some of the problems that attend *a priori* equilibrium specifications.

The main advantage of the AR model is that it utilizes the full information about the term structure to price options. By tautology, the market's price of risk and general time preferences must be reflected in the the array of current term rates. Moreover, the shape of the yield curve directly determines the present values of cash flows and thereby affects prices of options on those flows.

Most importantly, the use of term-structure information automatically determines option prices that are consistent with underlying asset values, and all other fixed-income security prices as well. The arbitrage-free property of feasible rate movements ensures that "straight" bond prices derived from the model are identical to the market prices determined by the current term structure. This has practical importance for the valuation of embedded options. By construction, the value of an embedded option feature is the price difference between the bond with the option feature and the same bond without the option. This allows the direct attribution, or separation, of value and return to the option features and straight cash-flow features of any bond.

The AR model possesses a relatively simple and straightforward binomial representation. Evaluation of option prices, using a binomial model, provides ready insight into the properties and behavior of debt options.

DEVELOPING AN OPTION-PRICING FRAMEWORK FROM THE AR MODEL

Essentially, an AR model derives a structure that governs possible interest rate movements through time by using an observed term structure to define periodic spot rates while maintaining an arbitrage-free condition.

Because the structure governing rate movement was an outcome, not an input, in the construction of the AR model, the lattice of zero bond prices, also generated by the AR model, is inherently arbitrage-free. In other words, *prices* of bonds in future states preclude arbitrage.

For conceptual clarity, assume that the bonds and embedded options are riskless in the sense that all cash flows will be paid when promised. Of course, this basic assumption can be modified to handle bonds with credit risk. The concepts underlying "riskless" securities can also be extended to account for credit risk. We will discuss these aspects later.

In binomial modeling, possible prices for a discount bond at the end of a period are represented by two values—the "upstate" and the "downstate." Figure 11–3 shows a four-period binomial lattice. At $t = 0$, the prices of the four discount bonds are determined by the spot term structure, which is a "flat" yield curve of 8 percent in the example.

From these initial conditions, prices at the subsequent nodes of the lattice are constructed so that the prices are arbitrage-free. In the binomial model of Figure 11–3, it is assumed that the probability of an upmove is the same as that of a downmove:

$$\pi = (1 - \pi) = .5$$

For an initial term structure, a set of *forward prices* (and forward rates) can be derived. Forward prices can be explained by reference to Figure 11–3. We will let *P(T)* be the existing discount prices (percent of par), depicted in Figure 11–3, and *F(T)* the forward discount prices.

With an investment horizon of two years, an investor could buy a two-year zero-coupon bond for 85.734 [$P(2) \times 100$] and be assured of 100 at maturity. Alternatively, a one-period bond could be purchased at time 0 for 92.593 [$P(1) \times 100$]. After one year, the 100 could be reinvested for the next year, buying 1.08 units face value of (then) one-year bonds at the market price. If the market price of one-year bonds in one year were 92.593, the return from the "rollover" would be exactly that of the two-year investment.

The discount price of a one-year zero bond in one year that would equate the returns of the two strategies is termed the *forward discount function*, *F(1)*. In this example, *F(1)* has the same value as *P(1)*. In general this is not true; here, it reflects the flat yield curve. In every case, however, the forward discount function is completely specified by the initial discount function. The forward discount of a *T*-period bond, determined for time *n*, is given by

$$F_i^n(T) = \frac{P_i^n(T + 1)}{P_i^n(1)} \tag{11-1}$$

At any node (n,i) on a lattice, the upstate price beyond that node, for a bond with maturity *T*: is expressed in terms of the forward prices

$$P_{i+1}^{n+1}(T) = F_i^n(T)h(T) \tag{11-2}$$

In the downstate, the definition is

$$P_{i+1}^{n+1}(T) = F_i^n(T)h^*(T) \tag{11-3}$$

Arbitrage-free bond price equilibrium requires the expected HPR to be equal for all bonds. Equivalently, the AR condition can be expressed in terms of the ratio of prices. At any node, the ratio of the *expected* price at the end of the period divided by the price at that node must be the same for all maturities. This is true everywhere in Figure 11–3, as can be easily verified.

FIGURE 11–3
An Arbitrage-Free Binomial Term Structure

Spot Discount Factors

t = 0	t = 1	t = 2	t = 3	t = 4
				0 1.00000
			0 1.00000	
			1 0.93988	
		0 1.00000		0 1.00000
		1 0.93523		0 1.00000
		2 0.87461		
	0 1.00000		0 1.00000	
	1 0.93058		1 0.93048	
0 1.00000	2 0.86596			
1 0.92593	3 0.80580	0 1.00000		
2 0.85734		1 0.92588		
3 0.79383		2 0.85721		
4 0.73503	0 1.00000		0 1.00000	
	1 0.92127		1 0.92118	
	2 0.84872			0 1.00000
	3 0.78187	0 1.00000		
		1 0.91662		
		2 0.84015	0 1.00000	
			0 0.91197	
				0 1.00000

Spot Discount Rates

t = 0	t = 1	t = 2	t = 3	t = 4
			node 3,3	
			1 6.40	
		node 2,2		
		1 6.93		
	node 1,1	2 6.93		
	1 7.46		node 3,2	
node 0,0	2 7.46		1 7.47	
1 8.00	3 7.46	node 2,1		
2 8.00		1 8.01		
3 8.00	node 1,0	2 8.01	node 3,1	
4 8.00	1 8.55		1 8.56	
	2 8.55			
	3 8.55	node 2,0		
		1 9.10		
		2 9.10	node 3,0	
			1 9.65	

Because the AR condition must hold for the one-period bond, then

$$\frac{[\pi P_i^n(T+1)h(T)]/P_i^n(1) + [(1-\pi)P_i^n(T+1)h^*(T)]/P_i^n(1)}{P_i^n(T+1)}$$

$$= \frac{1}{P_i^n(1)} \tag{11--4}$$

Clearing terms common to both side gives this result:

$$\pi h(T) + (1-\pi)h^*(T) = 1 \text{ for all } T$$

One additional constraint on the binomial lattice allows specification of the AR prices at every node of the lattice. This constraint is the *path independence condition*. Path independence means that the discount function at node (2,1), for example, should be the same whether that node is reached with a downmove to (1,0) followed by an upmove, or by an upmove first to (1,1) followed by a downmove.

The AR condition and the path independence condition combine to express $h(T)$ uniquely in terms of π, $h(1)$, and $h^*(1)$. If δ is defined as $h(1)/h^*(1)$, it can be shown (refer to Ho and Lee [9] for details) that

$$h(T) = \frac{1}{\pi + (1-\pi)\delta} \tag{11--5a}$$

and

$$h^*(T) = \delta^T h(T) \tag{11--5b}$$

This result can be applied recursively to specify the AR term structure at each node. That is, at time n and state i,

$$P_i^n(T) = \frac{P(T+n)h(T+n-1)h(T+n-2)\ldots h(T)}{P(n)h(n-1)h(n-2)\ldots h(0)} \delta^{T(n-i)} \tag{11--6}$$

With this AR specification, all discount bonds and portfolios of discount bonds are priced correctly, relative to the spot curve and to each other. Any bond's cash-flow stream can be considered to be sums of discount bonds. Any two bonds' prices will likewise be consistent and arbitrage-free. By extension, options on the cash-flow stream of any bond can then be valued in the same relative pricing framework.

The AR model is a statement of subsequent equilibrium, given the spot discount function prevailing at a point in time. It does not insist that subsequent movements of the spot curve must be arbitrage-free, nor does the model really forecast the shape or level of subsequent spot curves.

The important point is that the price of an arbitrary fixed-income asset or option obtained by the AR model will be in arbitrage-free equilibrium with all other assets at the time of pricing.

APPLICATION OF THE SPOT FUNCTION

In Chapter 3 we have discussed various procedures for estimating the spot curve. Once a spot curve has been derived, a binomial lattice of future interest rate paths can be generated using the AR model. The following sections will elaborate on this methodology.

ESTIMATION OF AR BINOMIAL PARAMETERS USING BELLWETHERS

The lattice in Figure 11–3 was constructed with assumed values for pi (π), $h(T)$, and $h^*(T)$. In practice, these parameters may be estimated in order to implement the AR model for option valuation. Because the AR approach is built upon a foundation of current market information, these parameters are estimated from the current bond price environment. This process is termed "fitting" or "tuning up" the model.

The AR model will provide consistent relative prices for any non-callable security, irrespective of the values of the three parameters. To provide relative prices for observable callable securities in the market, the next step in implementation of the AR model is estimation of parameter values that are most consistent with a population of observed prices of callable bonds.

The population of callable bonds used to estimate pi and delta is a *bellwether portfolio*. The estimation procedure is conceptually very simple. Essentially, the estimation searches for the values that minimize the difference between the prices of the bellwether bonds and the AR model prices. In practice, this requires a criterion of "goodness of fit" and a systematic and robust procedure to search among the pairs of possible values for the best fit. Current practice employs nonlinear estimation algorithms to find the values of pi and delta that best explain the prices of the bellwether bonds.

The bellwether portfolio employed to estimate the AR model's parameters is usually a population of callable bonds. In principle, the bellwether should be chosen to most closely replicate the type of security on which options are to be evaluated. For example, for custom options to be written on bonds, observed prices of similar options would comprise the most useful bellwether to ensure that values would be relative to similiar other offerings in the market.

Best-fit estimates of pi and delta, relative to the bellwether portfolio, combine with the estimated spot curve to fully identify the AR model. When this is accomplished, the model can be used to value any security, option, or embedded option.

A simplified procedure can be used if exogenous estimates of volatility are available and equal probabilities of up and down moves on the lattice are accepted. The delta parameter is functionally related to the variance of the short rate. Specifically, if σ is given exogenously (in basis points per year) and S is the number of lattice nodes per year, then for $\pi = .5$, delta (δ) is given by

$$\delta = \exp(-2\sigma/S^{3/2}) \tag{11-8}$$

VALUATION OF CALLABLE BONDS USING THE AR MODEL

Pricing a fixed-income security with the AR model is accomplished by "backwardation," or rolling back, of the successive cash flows of the bond, beginning at maturity and discounting back to the present.

Figure 11–4 illustrates the valuation procedure applied to an 8 percent annual-coupon bond of four-year maturity. At every node (n,i), the value is the sum of two terms. The first term is the expectation, or weighted average, of the bond values at nodes $(n + 1,i)$ and $(n + 1, i + 1)$, discounted at the one-period rate at that node, $P(1)$. This is then added to the cash flow at node (n,i). Each node in Figure 11–4 also shows the one-period discount factor that would prevail under the AR specification. For reference, at node $(1,1)$, Figure 11–3 shows that the spot rate would be 7.46 percent; the spot one-period discount factor would be .93058. In Figure 11–4, the price of the bond, then, with three years to maturity, would be 101.40. Since the value at that node includes the coupon payment of 8.00, the total value is 109.40. As required, the price of the bond at time 0 is par.

Backward substitution uses only the one-period rates at each node. The complete term structure, shown in the upper panel of Figure 11–3,

FIGURE 11–4
Valuation of a Noncallable 4-year Note (Discount Factors in Parentheses)

t = 0	t = 1	t = 2	t = 3	t = 4
				108.00
			109.51 (0.93988)	
		109.94 (0.93523)		108.00
			108.49 (0.93048)	
	109.40 (0.93058)			
		107.99 (0.92588)		108.00
100.00 (0.92593)			107.49 (0.92118)	
	106.60 (0.92127)			
		106.07 (0.91662)		108.00
			106.49 (0.91197)	
				108.00

is not required. The price at each node can alternatively be obtained by discounting the bond's remaining cash flows using the complete discount function. Because of the AR construction, there is no need to take on this additional work. The price thus obtained will always be equal to the answers given by backward substitution. It is precisely this fact that facilitates use of the binomial lattice to price callable securities.

Figure 11–5 values a four-year note callable at 101 on or after the first year. In time 3, the values at node (3,3) is replaced with the call price plus the coupon payment, 109.00. This value is employed in the subsequent rollback to node (2,2). It was found that node (2,2) also has a value greater than 109.00, and therefore its value, too, is replaced by the call price plus the interest payment. After the rollback is completed, the price of the callable note is shown to be 99.80. It is important to note that in Figure 11–4, the noncallable bond's value at node (1,1) is 101.40 (109.40 with coupon). Yet Figure 11–5 indicates the callable bond would not be called at that node. In other words, compared to the

FIGURE 11–5
Valuation of a 4-Year Note Callable at 101 Plus Interest (Discount Factors in Parentheses)

t = 0	t = 1	t = 2	t = 3	t = 4
				108.00
			109.00 (0.93988)	
		109.00 (0.93523)		
	108.96 (0.93058)		108.49 (0.93048)	
99.80 (0.92593)		107.99 (0.92588)		108.00
	106.60 (0.92127)		107.49 (0.92118)	
		106.07 (0.91662)		108.00
			106.49 (0.91197)	
				108.00

straight bond depcited in Figure 11–4, the cap of 101 on future price levels diminished the upside range of potential values. Therefore, this bond's value evaluated for node (1,1), 108.96,* is lower than the non-callable security and also turns out to be less than the mininum call price of 101 ($109.1 with coupon).

In general, the price that would prevail at a particular node for a noncallable bond with the same maturity and coupon does not provide an inference about the optimal time to call. The "called" states for a bond are given only by the lattice of that bond. The time of call is also the earliest node of substitution along an up diagonal of the lattice. In the case of Figure 11–5, the bond would be called at state (2,2).

---

*Price + Coupon = Total; $100.96 + $8 = $108.96.

The AR model could be used to verify the following general principles regarding pricing callable bonds relative to similar bonds without call features:

- For premium high-coupon bonds with deferred calls, the price of the callable bond will be less than the price of a similar straight bond that matures on the first call date.
- For discount low-coupon bonds with deferred calls, the price of the callable bond will be less than the price of a similar bond that matures at the same time as the callable issue.
- The above two statements will certainly hold if yields over the call period are generally flat. However, it will always be true that the price of a callable bond will be less than the minimum of the prices of the two straight bonds with maturities equal to the callable's maturity and the date of first call, respectively.

Other Binomial Models

The AR model is not the only possible binomial representation of rate movements. Dyer and Jacob [7] provide an interesting informal discussion of some alternatives. In every case, the condition of arbitrage freedom constrains the way the models can be developed and solved. One of the advantages of the AR model is that it incorporates a systematic and insightful method for making arbitrage freedom endogenous to the construction.

Comparative Results of Alternative Models

The models that have been presented can be compared in terms of ease of application. The Black-Scholes model can be implemented on a hand-held calculator. Binomial models require a modest amount of computer programming, and simplified versions can be written for Lotus 1-2-3. Equilibrium specifications require sophisticated econometric estimation and software for solution of differential equations.

However, it is not possible to make direct comparisons of the alternatives. No set of inputs can simultaneously satisfy all of the assumptions because they are conjointly incompatible. Any test against actual data is subject to a type of selection bias. All of the models require parameter estimation or "tuning up" to actual data via different parameters This itself would destroy comparability.

For a practitioner, the most important comparison would probably be between the Black-Scholes model and the results obtained from binomial lattice pricing implementations. Accordingly, Black-Scholes call option results for both zero-coupon bonds and a par-coupon bond will be compared to those obtained with a commercially available implementation of the AR model [8].

Table 11–2 shows the results of the two models, for the parameters shown. The initial spot curve is flat at 10 percent. For the zero bond, exercise prices of the calls are the compound values of the initial price, so the present value of the exercise price is in every case equal to the

TABLE 11–2

Comparative Pricing of Interest Rate Options (Black-Scholes Model and AR Model)

| | 10-Year Zero-Coupon Bond: | Current price | = 37.69 |
| | | Volatility | = 9.58 % p. a. |

Expiration (Years)	Strike Price	AR Model Price	Black Scholes Price
3 mo	38.63	0.64	0.73
6 mo	39.59	0.85	1.00
9 mo	40.54	1.04	1.26
1 yr	41.55	1.17	1.48
2 yr	45.80	1.36	2.09
5 yr	61.40	1.40	3.29
9 yr	90.71	0.36	4.41

	10-Year 10% Coupon Bond:	Current price	= 100.00
		Volatility	= 9.58 % p. a.
			= (102 bp)

Expiration (Years)	Strike Price	AR Model Price	Black Scholes Price
3 mo	100.00	1.10	1.88
6 mo	100.00	1.47	2.58
9 mo	100.00	1.72	3.09
1 yr	100.00	1.94	3.48
2 yr	100.00	2.19	N/A
5 yr	100.00	1.83	N/A
9 yr	100.00	0.35	N/A

current price. These calls are the term structure equivalent of at-the-money options. For the calls on the par bond, the strike price is always 100.

The Black-Scholes prices increase monotonically with time to expiration for both bonds because the model assumes that the bond prices can drift without bound and with constant variance. Alternatively, the AR prices are not monotonic. This is a direct reflection of the pull-to-par effect on both bonds, as evidenced by the significant reduction in value of the options with nine-year term.

The two models produce significantly different results even for very short-term options. This can be partially attributed to different amounts of "drift" in the two stochastic processes, even though the two possess the same variance. In the Black-Scholes model, the prices drift but the rates do not. In the AR model that was used in the comparison, expected price does not drift significantly; moreover, price changes of the bonds are automatically associated with changes in the discount rates of the cash flows and the present value of the boundary conditions.

The clear implication is that the Black-Scholes model is not appropriate for use with debt options. However, this is not true for analysis of traded options on Treasury bond and Treasury note futures contracts.

Black [2] gives a model for use with futures options that is very close to his original option model. The futures option model, referred to informally as "Black '76" in reference to the year of publication, is identical to the original, except for one substitution. For every occurrence of the current price, S^* (in this case, the trading price of the futures contract) in the original formulation, the future option model replaces the current price with the future price, F, discounted continuously at the riskless rate from the expiration of the option. The model can then be given as

$$w(F,t) = e^{-r\tau}[FN(d_1) - XN(d_1 - \sigma\sqrt{\tau})]$$

$$d_1 = \left[\ln\left(\frac{F}{X}\right) + \frac{\sigma^2\tau}{2}\right] \Big/ \sigma\sqrt{\tau}$$

Table 11–3 compares the results of AR pricing with prices calculated from the Black '76 model. June 1989 Treasury bond futures

---

*S replaced with $Fe^{-r\tau}$; see page 177.

TABLE 11–3

Comparative Pricing of Interest Rate Options (Black-Scholes Model and AR Model, on 11/15/88)

	June 1989 futures price	= 88.13
	Standard Deviation	= 11.85% p. a.
	Riskless Rate	= 8.35% continuous

Option	Observed	AR Model	Black '76
88 put	2.81	2.82	2.82
88 call	2.97	2.93	2.99
90 put	3.91	3.92	3.90
90 call	2.06	2.09	2.10
92 put	5.19	5.21	5.16
92 call	1.41	1.44	1.46

contracts prices are shown for November 15, 1988. Both models provide results that are quite close to the closing prices. This happens because the constant variance assumption is quite accurate when the underlying asset is a futures contract. Here, the underlying security is a price for a standardized, hypothetical bond of 20-year maturity (10-year in the case of notes) with an 8 percent coupon rate. The futures price could be considered to be an index on the 20-year bond yield. Therefore, changes in the underlying price do not imply changes in the riskless rate, nor do changes imply any particular movement of the term structure.

Effective Duration of Debt Options

Valuation of debt options is a vital input into portfolio analysis and management. Thus far, this chapter has dealt with the construction and use of debt option models. This section relates debt options to the tasks of fixed-income portfolio management.

Effective duration can be determined for debt options as well as bonds. Table 11–5 illustrates effective duration and option elasticity for some options on the 10-year security in Table 11–4, obtained with an AR model.

Before discussing the concept of the *duration* of an option, we will briefly discuss elasticity, a measure closely related to the effective duration of an option. The *elasticity* of an option characterizes relative

TABLE 11–4
Effective Duration for Zero-Coupon Bonds

		Priced for Basis Point Shifts				
Maturity	Effective Duration	−50	−17	0	+17	+50
1 year	0.953	92.74	92.47	92.32	92.18	91.89
5 years	4.789	67.67	66.60	66.07	65.54	64.51
10 years	9.574	44.38	42.99	42.31	41.64	40.33
20 years	19.142	18.15	17.58	17.03	16.50	14.99
30 years	28.876	9.60	8.72	8.31	7.92	7.20

TABLE 11–5
Duration and Elasticity for Interest Rate Options

10-year zero bond, 9% yield, with price of 42.31 (see Table 11–4)

	Strike = 40		Strike = 42		Strike = 44	
	Put	Call	Put	Call	Put	Call
Price	0.32	4.08	0.88	2.59	1.97	1.45
Duration	−205.86	82.43	−169.46	107.42	−138.98	139.06
Elasticity	−21.50	8.61	−17.70	11.22	−4.52	14.52

price movement with the underlying price in terms of a ratio of percentage movements, not a ratio of absolute value movements. Price elasticity is the expected percentage change in the option premium given a small percentage change (e.g., 1 percent) in the underlying security's price.

With c and P denoting option price and underlying security price, respectively, and Δ denoting small changes,

$$\text{Elasticity} = \frac{\Delta c/c}{\Delta P/P} \qquad (11\text{--}9)$$

and by transformation,

$$\frac{\Delta c}{c} = \text{Elasticity} \times \frac{\Delta P}{P} \qquad (11\text{--}10a)$$

Dividing both sides of this expression by Δr, it follows immediately that effective duration, D, for the option is equal to the duration of the underlying security times the elasticity of the option.

$$D(\text{option}) = \text{elasticity} \times D(\text{underlying}) \qquad (11\text{--}10b)$$

Elasticity is increasingly large for an out-of-the-money option; therefore, so is the duration. For options in-the-money, the elasticity approaches unity, and the duration of the option approaches the duration of the underlying bond. These relationships can be seen in Table 11–5.

Effective duration has the same interpretation for any interest-rate-sensitive security, so the duration measures in Table 11–5 directly assess the interest rate exposure of options. For example, Tables 11–4 and 11–5 together show that an at-the-money call option on a 10-year zero bond has a duration of 107.42, compared with the underlying's duration of 9.574. This means that the call price is (107.42/ 9.574) = 11.25 times more sensitive to interest rate changes than the underlying asset.

These observations are equally applicable to put options, except movements are of opposite direction. A put option price rises along with rising interest rates. Therefore, the put option has negative elasticity, and, as noted above, duration is also negative.

Effective duration plays a central role in hedging applications, somewhat similar to the hedge ratio in equity options analysis. However, duration is not as straightforward as the hedge ratio. The latter statistic defines a *dollar* change in option price with respect to stock price change. Duration of a bond and an option provide *proportional* changes with respect to interest rate changes. Simple ratios of duration, then, will not provide hedge amounts directly.

PERFORMANCE PROFILES

The additional complexities of using debt options to hedge bonds is simplified by development of performance profiles. A performance profile is a graphic representation of the risk exposure showing how asset value changes with respect to instantaneous parallel shifts of the yield curve.

Table 11–6 shows prices for zero-coupon bonds with maturities of 10 years and 2 years. These prices are the most simple performance profiles, being the the present values of the $100 face value, discounted

TABLE 11–6
Prices of 2-Year and 10-Year Zero-Coupons under Various Yields

Yield	2-Year	10-Year
7.0%	87.50	49.31
8.0%	85.83	44.79
9.0%	84.20	40.69
9.5%	82.61	36.99
10.0%	81.06	33.65
Duration	1.91	9.56

at 9 percent. Throughout this section, a flat yield curve of 9 percent will be assumed.

ANALYZING INTEREST RATE OPTIONS USING PERFORMANCE PROFILES

Since there is little that is subtle or complex about zero-coupon bond prices, performance profiles of straight bonds do not provide much insight. For debt options, however, performance profiles are much more valuable.

The price of a debt option incorporates a trade-off between two fundamental sources of price risk. First, the option price incorporates the price risk of the underlying asset by fairly reflecting the relative chances of favorable and unfavorable price change due to shifts in market yields. Second, option value reflects the loss of value that the option itself faces until its expiration. Because options generally have a shorter life than their underlying assets, an option will decline in value even when the value of the underlying asset is constant. This phenonomon is termed "time decay" of the option. As time to expiration increases, however, performance profiles show that debt options lose more and more of the character of equity options.

Figure 11–6 shows performance profiles for simple call options on a 10-year zero-coupon bond with a present yield of 9 percent. The strike price for each option is the price of the bond to yield 9 percent at expiration. The performance profile for the one-year call is quite

FIGURE 11–6
Performance Profiles for Simple Call Options

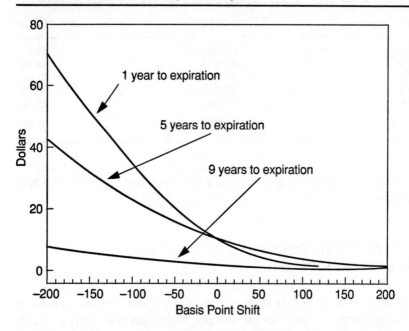

like the profiles for equity options. It falls to zero asymptotically as the underlying asset price moves out-of-the-money and rises rapidly for underlying prices in-the-money. On the other hand, the performance profile for the longest term option, with nine years of time to expiration, is quite flat and almost linear, similar in shape to the performance profile of the underlying asset. The intermediate option, with five years to expiration, is less convex than the one-year but decidedly more "option-like" in appearance than the nine-year. Interestingly, the value of the five-year and one-year calls are almost the same at-the-money. This could never be true of two different term equity calls, and it illustrates that the intuition, like the models, of pricing equity options is often out of place in debt option analysis.

Figure 11–7 shows the performance profiles of puts corresponding to the calls above. As is the case in equity options, put prices are not precise mirror images of corresponding calls. In the case of debt options, a simple explanation of this is that the convexity of an underlying bond is not symmetric around the strike price, so the profiles of the put and call cannot be symmetric either.

FIGURE 11–7
Performance Profiles of Put Options

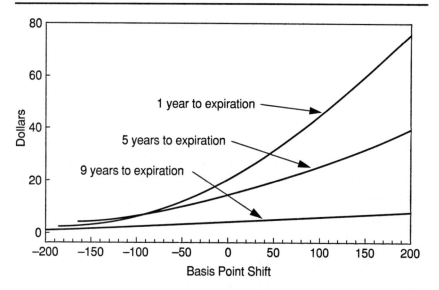

For European equity options, the passage of time reduces the value of a call option for a fixed stock price, whether the stock price is in-, out-of-, or at-the-money. Debt options do not have an unambiguous time-decay effect. This effect is shown in Figure 11–6.

To understand this effect, consider an extreme case when a call is so much in-the-money that the possiblity of the option expiring with no value is negligibly low. This would be represented by options toward the left of Figure 11–6. With the passage of time, the price of a zero-coupon bond will almost certainly appreciate. This effect dominates the time-decay effect. On the other hand, if the option is deeply out-of-the-money, any final value depends on the chance of a favorable bond price change. Then, as in the equity case, the less time for favorable outcome remaining, the lower the option price will be. Time decay can then dominate the price appreciation effect of the bond.

Time decay is even more complicated in the case of coupon bonds. With the passage of time, constant yield results in either an increase or a decrease in price, depending on low or high coupon rates. The behavior of options on coupon-bearing bonds can only be established by the application of a pricing model and consideration of the option's performance profile.

COMPLETE SPECIFICATION OF BOND PRICE CHANGE

Effective duration was defined earlier as the link between relative bond price change and yield change:

$$\frac{\Delta P}{P} = -D\Delta r$$

But duration alone is not sufficient for characterizing debt option price changes. As previously mentioned, there are other influences that combine with duration to provide a more comprehensive representation of an option's price change. These factors can be included as explicit factors in the pricing of underlying bonds as well. These additional factors are

- Convexity (C)
- Time effect (θ)
- Volatility effect (vega)

The extended specification of relative price is then

$$\Delta P/P = -D\Delta r + C(\Delta r^2) + \theta\Delta t + \text{vega}\Delta\delta \qquad (11\text{--}11)$$

Fixed-income portfolio immunization is a strategy designed to eliminate the interest rate sensitivity of a portfolio.

If, for a portfolio, the following values and option descriptions are known,

Duration
Convexity
Option type (put or call)
Theta
Vega
Option strike price and expiration date

then options can be directly applied in immunization. Elementary immunization typically concentrates only on duration, by forming a hedge that makes the first term equal to zero. However, the portfolio will still face price risks associated with the effects of convexity, time to option's expiration, and changing volatility. Among these factors, with respect to options, the convexity effect will generally have the greatest impact. Accordingly, hedges involving options perform much better when both convexity and duration are included in the hedge ratio's computations.

Table 11–7 illustrates the magnitude of the four factors described in Equation 11–11. The data are generated by a straightforward application of that equation. Closed forms are not available for these factors, as they are in the case of equity options using the Black-Scholes model. Therefore, all elements must be approximated by differences.

To estimate the duration, first each Treasury bond future's option price c_0 is calculated. Then the yield curve is shifted a small amount, such as 5 basis points, both up and down. These new yields give two new T-bond futures prices, which in turn provide two more observations on the call price, $c(up)$ and $c(dn)$. Considering only the duration term of Equation 11–11, ceteris paribus, duration is approximated by:

$$D(\text{up}) = -\{c(\text{up}) - c_0\}/(c_0 \times .0005) \qquad (11\text{–}12a)$$
$$D(\text{dn}) = -\{c_0 - c(\text{dn})\}/(c_0 \times .0005) \qquad (11\text{–}12b)$$

A good estimate of duration is obtained by the average of these two numbers.

Two duration approximations are used because convexity is the rate of change of duration. Therefore, the estimate of convexity follows immediately:

$$C = \{D(\text{up}) - D(\text{dn})\}/(c_0 \times .0005) \qquad (11\text{–}13a)$$
$$= \{c(\text{up}) + c(\text{dn}) - 2c_0\}/(c_0 \times .0005 \times .0005) \quad (11\text{–}13b)$$

Because of the large magnitude of the convexity number, "street" practice is to report the convexity figure divided by 100. This is done in Table 11–7.

The other two factors are provided by a similar perturbation of time to expiration and then of sigma.

A number of general characteristics can be observed in the data of Table 11–7.

- Price behavior is similar to the character of equity options. Call prices increase as the options are more in-the-money, and the time decay is evident between the prices of the March and December expirations.
- The duration of the calls increases for out-of-the-money calls. This effect is the same in puts, where out-of-the-money means lower strike prices. The durations of puts are negative numbers. As time to expiration increases, the duration of both puts and calls falls in absolute value. Convexity also increases for out-of-the-money options. Unlike duration, convexity of both calls and

TABLE 11–7
Price Risk Components for T-Bond Futures Put and Call

Price data for October 11, 1988.
Futures prices : Dec = 89.97
Mar = 89.38

Strike		December		March	
		Call	*Put*	*Call*	*Put*
	Price	2.55	0.58	3.19	1.83
	D	271.13	−403.98	181.45	−178.97
88	C	357.50	2155.34	183.08	74.63
	\<theta\>	2.02	8.82	1.09	1.96
	\<vega\>	3.93	16.68	6.65	11.56
	Price	1.25	1.30	2.14	2.75
	D	378.93	−358.08	209.58	−167.76
90	C	1590.90	1587.15	256.04	282.37
	\<theta\>	4.60	4.49	1.64	1.26
	\<vega\>	9.69	9.45	10.24	7.97
	Price	0.55	2.56	1.38	3.91
	D	475.24	−261.52	240.70	−146.73
92	C	1657.84	338.75	400.70	152.75
	\<theta\>	9.02	1.88	2.35	0.78
	\<vega\>	18.44	3.96	14.74	5.17

puts is positive. This reflects the fact that both options provide their holders with unlimited upside return and protection from downside risk.

- Because convexity is positive for a holder of a call option, it can be inferred that the presence of an embedded call will diminish the convexity of a bond, since a bondholder is short an embedded call. As bond prices increase from falling yields, callable bonds will not increase in price above their call prices. This situation must be taken into account in the hedging of callable bonds with noncallable issues. On the other hand, a putable bond increases convexity, since a holder is then long a put with positive convexity.

- The time effect, theta (θ), shows that near-term options tend to lose value the fastest, particularly the out-of-the-money options.

- The volatility effect, vega, increases for puts and calls out-of-the-money. In-the-money, the effect of volatility on short-term contracts is smaller because the price behavior of the underlying bond is more homogenous in the smaller time interval. At-the-money, vega tends to be quite similar for puts and calls. It was demonstrated earlier that futures options can be priced by the constant-variance Black '76 model. This implies that the vega of the underlying futures contract must be quite close to zero, so there is little "directional" difference reflected between puts and calls. While not necessarily an optimal strategy, it is clear that buying a put and selling a call will tend to hedge away volatility risk.

EXAMPLES OF OPTIONS STRATEGIES

As a practical matter, hedging and immunization can be concentrated on duration and convexity if options are used as the hedge vehicles. Option positions used in hedges always need periodic monitoring and possibly must be adjusted. Therefore, any improvement in hedge effectiveness that would accrue to immunization in all four factors would be largely theoretical.

Table 11–8 shows the results of immunization by matching both duration and convexity. This is accomplished by solving a system of equations with two unknowns. One equation equates duration, the other convexity. These equations match the product of the duration and price of the bond portfolio prior to being hedged with weighted products for a put and call:

$$-P_b \times D_b = n_c \times P_c \times D_c + n_p \times P_p \times D_p \qquad (11\text{--}14a)$$

$$-P_b \times C_b = n_c \times P_c \times C_c + n_p \times P_p \times C_p \qquad (11\text{--}14b)$$

A hedge of 10,000,000 face-value 30-year Treasury bonds on October 31, 1988, is illustrated. Duration/convexity immunization, through solution of Equations 11–14a and 11–14b, requires (rounded) transactions of 118 put contracts long against 114 call contracts short.

The initial option transaction had a net inflow of $101,531, and the margin on the short transaction would be covered by the long bond position. When the hedge was sold out on November 30, the transaction

TABLE 11–8

Duration and Convexity Hedge Using Treasury Bond Futures Put and Call

Securities

	T-Bond 9 1/8s 5/18	TB Futures 90 Call	TB Futures 90 Put
Price 10/31/88:	104.09375	2.671875	1.875000
Duration :	10.14	203.32	−210.49
Convexity :		213.15	231.13
Price 11/30/88:	100.25000	1.046875	2.859375

Transactions/Values

T-bond 9 1/8s, May, 2018	(10,409,375)	10,025,000
accrued interest	(419,056)	37,811
Short 114 March 90 Call	315,281	(123,531)
Long 118 March 90 Put	(213,750)	325,969
Portfolio value with hedge	(10,726,900)	10,265,249
Coupon paid 11/15/88 :		456,250
7% interest on coupon :		1,314
		10,722,813

Portfolio Value Under Parallel Yield Shifts

	Basis Point Change				
	−200	−100	0	100	200
Bond alone:	168.44	116.39	104.44	94.45	86.05
With hedge:	107.92	107.20	107.17	107.24	107.26

inflow was $202,438. Also, a coupon payment of $456,250 was received on November 15. The sum of these three cash flows offsets the decline experienced in bond value due to changing interest rates. Including the reinvestment income on the coupon payment, using a 7 percent per annum rate, the net result of the hedge was a cost of about $4,000.

Considering the magnitude of the transactions and the fact that the bond changed about 4 percent (almost $400,000) in value, this "zero duration/convexity" hedge shows practice almost perfectly converging to theory.

Next, we can illustrate the use of options to alter the performance profiles of a bond. The same bond is combined with a short call and then a long put in two different cases.

Case 1: Hold $10 million position in the long bond.

Case 2: Hold the same bond as in Case 1, and write 100 contracts of the 88 strike price March futures calls shown in Table 11–7.

Case 3: Hold the same positions as in Case 2, and additionally buy 100 put contracts with 92 strike March futures puts shown in the Table 11–7.

Table 11–9 shows the ex ante holding period returns (not annualized) for the term October 31, 1988, to January 31, 1989, for five different rate scenarios.

In Case 1, one can observe the convexity of the long bond; for the lower rate scenarios, the magnitude of the return is greater than the loss in the higher rate scenarios.

In Case 2, the addition of the option premiums captured from the writing of the calls increases the return in the "no change" scenario, but at the expense of lower returns when the bond increases in value. Note further that the writing of the calls provides almost no downside protection for the bond position.

In Case 3, the addition of the put options to the position provides substantial downside protection. Also, the range of results over the five scenarios is less than in either of the other cases. The net effect of this position is to significantly lower the effective duration. Note, however, that the convexity of the position remains positive.

TABLE 11–9
Holding Period Returns for Different Rate Scenarios

	Basis Point Change				
	−200	−100	0	100	200
Case 1	25.91	12.99	2.22	−6.82	−14.46
Case 2	9.10	6.83	3.16	−5.79	−13.52
Case 3	7.35	5.11	1.88	−0.66	−1.41

One may be tempted to draw a conclusion that one of these positions is superior to the other two. In fact, no such "global" assertion can be made: as a consequence of the options model, the expected value of each position, analyzed over all possible scenarios, will be equivalent. However, in terms of individual risk preferences, one position will be superior to another. Of the cases above, Case 3 is clearly the best choice for an investor who wishes to face as little interest rate risk as possible, even at the expense of foregoing the chance of large gains. Similarly, Case 2 would be the best choice for one who envisions little change in interest rates in the near future.

SUMMARY

This chapter described the attributes of options on interest-rate-sensitive securities. Options on, or embedded in, fixed-income securities have proliferated in recent years. The material in this chapter discussed why equity options models are generally not appropriate for the pricing of debt options and proceeded to describe an AR model, a model more suitable for pricing interest rate options. This discussion was supported with examples of trading strategies utilizing the AR model's computations of option values.

REFERENCES

1. Ball, C. A., and W. Torous, 1983. Bond price dynamics and options. *Journal of Finance and Quantitative Analysis*, 18, 517–530.
2. Black, F., 1976. The pricing of commodity contracts. *Journal of Financial Economics*, 3, 167–179.
3. Black, F., and M. Scholes, 1973. The pricing of options and corporate liabilities. *Journal of Political Economy*, 81 (May/June), 637–654.
4. Brennan, M. J., and E. S. Schwartz, 1982. An equilibrium model of bond pricing and a test of market efficiency. *Journal of Finance and Quantitative Analysis*, 17 (September), 303–329.
5. Courtadon, G., 1982. The pricing of options on default free bonds. *Journal of Finance and Quantitative Analysis*, 17 (September), 75–100.
6. Cox, J. C., J. E. Ingersoll, and S. A. Ross, 1985. A theory of the term structure of interest rates. *Econometrica*, 53 (March), 385–407

7. Dyer, L. T., and D. P. Jacob, 1988. *A practioner's guide to fixed income option models.* New York: Morgan Stanley Research.
8. Global Advanced Technology Corporation, 1988. *Integrative bond system.* New York: Author.
9. Ho, T. S. Y., and S. B. Lee, 1986. Term structure movements and pricing interest rate contingent claims. *Journal of Finance.* 41 (December), 1011–1029.
10. Litzenberger, R. H., and J. Rolfo, 1984. An international study of tax effects on government bonds. *Journal of Finance*, 38 (March), 1–22.
1. McCulloch, J. H., 1975. On the pricing of corporate debt: The risk structure of interest rates. *Journal of Finance*, 30 (June), 811–830.
12. Merton, R. C., 1975. On the pricing of corporate debt: The risk structure of interest rates. *Journal of Finance*, 29 (March), 449–470.
13. Merton, R. C., 1973. Rational theory of option pricing. *Bell Journal of Economics and Management Science*, 4, 141–183.
14. Schaefer, S. M., and E. S. Schwartz, 1987. Time dependent variance and the pricing of bond options. *Journal of Finance*, 42, 1113–1128.
15. Vasicek, O. A., 1977. An equilibrium characterization of the term structure. *Journal of Financial Economics*, 5 (November), 177–188.

CHAPTER 12

CORPORATE BONDS (INVESTMENT GRADE)

Corporate bonds are an amalgamation of the concerns of both the issuers and the investors. Issuers seek to minimize the costs of debt issues, and investors seek to maximize the safety and yield of the loaned funds. These parties, with their respective interests, forge complex agreements before a bond is issued. Unfortunately, there is no such thing as industry standard agreements, so each bond is unique. An issue's contractual terms reflect the market concerns at the time of issuance; these concerns range from existing interest rate levels and the probability of the company's default on the bond to the supply and demand for a particular type of bond. After issuance, the market will change (for example, the yield curve will change its shape), but the agreements will not. In secondary market trading, market participants need to evaluate the risks and potential rewards embedded in each corporate issue.

This chapter will draw upon the concepts of the previous chapters in its discussion of a framework for assessing fair value. This framework, otherwise known as the bond model, will be useful for synthesizing the diverse attributes of a single bond or a portfolio of fixed-income instruments. The determination of fair value rests upon the investor's ability to correctly identify all the distinct elements of the bond and then to properly consolidate each element's fair value.

We will illustrate that any corporate bond can be subdivided into elements that fall into one of two groups. The first group represents the bond's broad characteristics that are similar to other fixed-income instruments. This group may include such things as the present value of the bond's cash flows or the average incremental yield that serves as compensation for default risk. The second group can be described as containing the characteristics that are company or industry specific. These can be such things as the fair value of the options associated with the embedded call and sinking fund schedules.

This chapter will first provide a broad overview of the corporate bond industry and then delve into the specific attributes common to all corporate bonds. We will then present a corporate bond pricing model. The model's usefulness is not limited to valuing fixed-income securities; it can be used in a portfolio management context for constructing bond strategies. The applicability of the model in this circumstance is fully discussed in Chapter 14.

DESCRIPTIONS

Corporate bonds are issued by corporations for the purpose of raising funds. The bonds are issued to the public through a trustee, generally an investment or commercial bank, which receives a fee for its services. The trustee represents the interests of the bondholders and oversees interest payments.

Although similar to U.S. Treasury bonds in that they have coupons and maturities, corporate bonds are much less homogeneous than Treasuries. Corporate issues have a broad range of maturities, from short-term, 1-year bonds to long-term, 50-year issues. In addition, the coupon rate of each issue varies. Unlike Treasury bonds, not all corporates are issued near par value (the coupon rate does not represent the YTM at issuance). Some bonds may be issued as discount securities with zero or very low coupon rates. Another distinction is that corporate bonds have two features that are nonexistent among Treasury bonds. They are (1) the covenant, and (2) provisions on the bond. A fair value assessment for a corporate issue must properly capture these two features.

The Instruments: Covenants and Provisions

The covenant states the obligations of the corporation to the investors. Among these obligations is the responsibility of the corporation to pay interest in a timely fashion and keep its corporate status. The corporation also indicates under what conditions it would declare bankruptcy. There may be a number of conditions that can trigger a bond default. For example, the cross default clause stipulates that the bond is in default if any other bond of the firm is in default. Some clauses specify courses of action that are contingent on the values of standardized financial ratios. For instance, a clause may provide investors with the right to the prepayment of principal if the debt ratio exceeds a stated limit. If the firm cannot raise the funds to pay the principal, then the bond is in default.

When a bond is in default, the firm is rarely liquidated to use the proceeds to pay its creditors. More often, the firm files for protection from creditors while undergoing reorganization under chapter 11 of the bankruptcy laws. While in this stage, the firm's management negotiates a debt restructuring plan with all outstanding creditors. If the negotiations fail (that is, an agreement is not reached to the satisfaction of either party), the final option is to convert from a chapter 11 filing into a chapter 13, liquidation of the company.

When a firm is in chapter 11, there is speculative value in its bonds since investors recognize the possibility of a negotiated agreement and the continued payment of some interest and principal or the exchange into another security. If a firm is in chapter 13, there may still be some value associated with the bonds. This value, if any, would be the present value of an expected nominal payment arising from the liquidating distribution of the firm's assets.

Bond provisions stipulate ways the issuer may pay back the investors other than the scheduled payments: the coupons on the coupon-paying date and the principal on maturity. The two most important and prevalent bond provisions are the call provision and the sinking fund provision. The call provision is similar to the call provision on U.S. Treasury bonds in that both are callable at a specified price on or after a certain date. When the bond is called, the firm has to pay the bondholder the call price plus the accrued interest. Except for this similarity, there are many differences between corporate and Treasury call provisions. With corporate bonds (unlike Treasury bonds), the call price is not always at par and the first call date need not be five years from maturity. Corporate bonds have precise call schedules stating the call price at corresponding dates. Call schedules vary greatly among bonds. Typically, there is a first call date that stipulates the first date that the bond is callable. A bond may be immediately callable (that is, starting on the issuance date), or the first call date may be deferred for 10 or more years after issuance. Call prices linearly decline to par some time before maturity and remain at par until maturity.

Sinking fund provisions are almost as common as, and usually accompany, call provisions. The sinking fund provision requires the firm to retire portions of the bond over a period of time. Typically, there is no sinking fund requirement at the beginning of the life of the bond. After a deferment period, which is usually five years or more, a fixed amount of the par value of the outstanding bond must be retired to the trustee of the bond. There are two ways to retire the bond in this manner. First, the firm that has issued the bond can buy portions of it back in the open market and then surrender required periodic payments to the trustee. Second, the firm can make payments to the trustee, which will then call a set number of bonds chosen by lottery. If the firm fails to satisfy the sinking fund obligation (i.e., cannot get the required number of bonds to surrender to the trustee), the firm is considered in default of its debt.

On the one hand, the sinking fund provision is an onerous obligation of the firm, which must produce funds to pay back its investors via the trustee. On the other hand, it can be a valuable strategy in anticipating changes in market rates. The benefit for the firm is that it can exercise its option in the implementation of its procedures: The firm may retire the bond at market price by buying back the bond in the secondary market, or it may retire the bond at par by permitting the trustee to call bonds by lottery.

Sometimes, all of a public issue's outstanding balance is held by a single investor or a small group of investors. This is known as an accumulated position. In this case the company cannot buy the bonds back at competitive market prices, so it must execute its sinking fund obligations through the lottery process. It is possible that if the bond had traded in the market, its price would have been lower than its call price.

Private placements are bonds arranged between two parties. Very often, a private placement is a bond issued by a corporation to an insurance company. The sinking fund provision for a private placement will be very specific in that the firm must retire each portion of the bond holding at the prespecified "sink" call price(s).

Economics of the Call and Sinking Fund Provisions

The call provision is clearly valuable to the issuer because it gives the issuer the right to call the bond when it chooses, or not to call it at all. If interest rates drop, the firm will find it advantageous to retire outstanding debt by calling the bond and replacing the called bond with a lower-coupon issue. This calling and replacing of bonds is termed *refinancing*. Refinancing is done to the detriment of investors, who will receive only the call price and the accrued interest when the bond is called, despite the fact that interest rates have dropped and the present value of the bond's cash flows should exceed the call price.

In essence, a callable corporate bond is an option-embedded bond. Holding a callable bond can be viewed as a combined holding: a long position in a straight bond with the coupon rate and maturity the same as the callable bond and a written (short) call option to the issuer. Of course, the call option is not a simple European option that can be described simply by one strike price and an expiration date. The call option is exercisable at different strike prices prescribed by the call schedule. Since the option always has positive value, the price of the callable bond is always lower than the market price of a similar noncallable bond (the yield is higher) as a form of compensation for the call provision.

The call option offers the issuer a higher return on invested capital by providing an avenue for lowering the cost of funds (borrowing costs). Under a declining interest rate environment, the cost of the option will increase in an efficient market. This increase in option costs should offset the higher expected return attributable to lowering interest costs (refinancing in lower interest rate environment). For this reason the firm should be indifferent between issuing bonds with or without call provisions. Thus far our discussion has focused only on the changes in interest rate levels as affecting option value. Of course, as discussed in Chapter 11, there are other factors (e.g., volatility) that affect option values. We have held these other factors constant in an attempt to highlight that the option's fair value should result in no riskless profit opportunities through issuance of a straight bond instead of a callable bond. The present value of the issuer's expected returns should equal the cost of the option the issuer is purchasing to call back the bonds.

Another important point is that a call provision offers the issuer an option to retire debt from the capital market for managerial reasons, independent of the market value of the bond issue. This nonquantitative aspect may explain the prevalent use of call provisions among corporate bonds.

In a perfect capital market, where the bond price reflects the economic value of the bond, the option value embedded in the sinking fund provision is correctly reflected in the bond price. The price is *correct* in the sense that the issuer should be indifferent between issuing a sinking fund bond or a straight bond. The value advantage for the issuer of a bond with sinking fund options should be offset by the higher issuing costs; the bonds are issued with a higher YTM relative to an equivalent straight bond. By the same token, an investor should be indifferent between investing in a sinking fund bond or a straight bond because the issuer's option is already incorporated in the higher bond yield.

Of course, a perfect market does not often exist, and hence, given reality, there are at least two reasons for the prevalence of sinking fund provisions.

1. An active secondary market is maintained by the firm's buying back the bonds on the open market.
2. From a managerial perspective sinking fund options provide a way to shorten the effective maturity of the bond since the issuer is able to buy back or call the bond.

RATING AND SECTORS

There are two main credit rating agencies: Standard & Poor's and Moody's. Bond ratings reflect the ability of a firm to pay the principal and interest on its outstanding bonds in a timely manner, as judged by the rating firms. Bonds can have ratings ranging from AAA (indicating no or negligible probability of default) to D (indicating bond default). Bonds with ratings of BBB and above are considered to be investment grade. Many managed funds are required to invest only in investment grade bonds. For this reason, investment grade bonds enjoy a broader spectrum of investors and are generally more liquid. Bonds with ratings lower than BBB are called high-yield, or junk, bonds. Investors are compensated for this higher default risk by relatively higher interest payments.

Corporate bonds can be classified under one of the following four major sectors: utilities, transportation, financial, and industrial. Each sector's bonds possess different characteristics because each sector has different motives for issuing debt. Utility companies, for example, issue bonds to support power plants. Since the plants represent long-term assets, bonds of utility companies tend to have very long maturities.

There are different types of credit risks among the sectors. For instance, at the same point in time, an AAA rated bond in one sector may provide a higher yield than another sector's AAA bond, given the same coupon, maturity, and bond provisions. This difference is attributable to unique, nonfinancial risk factors such as political or environmental issues. For example, utility companies are regulated by state or federal agencies that have control over many aspects of the company's rate-setting practices. Utility bonds may have higher yields than industrial bonds as compensation to investors for waiting through lengthy regulatory procedures if major company problems arise in the future.

Thus far we have provided a summary of some relevant aspects of the corporate bond market in general. The following sections will focus on the valuation of corporate bonds and what the market prices can reveal about an issue's relative attributes.

YIELD SPREAD PRICING AND YIELD DIAGRAMS

Given a corporate bond, we can calculate its yield to maturity (the internal rate of return of the bond if held to maturity) from the stated maturity, coupon rate, and quoted price. Investors in corporate bonds will demand a higher rate of return than investors in Treasury bonds because of the credit risks, decreased marketability, and call provisions common among corporate bonds. Investors frequently refer to the incremental yield over Treasuries as the corporate bond's *spread*. Technically, there are many ways to compute a spread; for instance, here are three possible ways.

1. The *pure yield spread* is the YTW (yield to worst: represents the lower of yield to call or YTM) of the corporate bond net of the YTM of a same maturity Treasury bond. If a similar Treasury issue does not exist, one can use the time value of money concepts discussed in Chapter 9 for valuing a constructed similar maturity, similar coupon, riskless security. We can then compute a price and a YTM measure for comparison with a corporate issue.

2. The *spot yield spread* is the difference between a corporate bond's yield and an equivalent-duration, zero-coupon bond's yield. The zero's yield is obtained from the spot rate curve. Since a zero bond's maturity is essentially equal to its duration, we select the zero bond with a maturity equal to the corporate bond's duration. This type of spread is the most accurate representation of the risk/return trade-off between a corporate issue and a riskless issue. Duration is essentially the interest rate risk

measure of an issue; hence, by matching these measures, one can observe the incremental yield available for taking on non–interest-rate risks, such as default risk or liquidity risk.

3. The *nominal spread* is the yield difference between the corporate issue's YTW and the nearest on-the-run Treasury issue's YTM. In other words, it is a comparison against the most recently issued Treasury security that has a similar maturity. The nominal spread is the most commonly used measure in the investment community because Treasury yields and prices are readily observable in the market.

Regardless of the type of spread one is dealing with, the size of the spread should be somewhat dictated by the corporate bond's attributes, such as credit risk and others highlighted above. As will be discussed below, the spread is an important component in valuing corporate bonds.

One approach in valuing corporate bonds is to determine the price. Suppose we specify the yield spread of a corporate bond. Then by observing the corresponding Treasury's yield to maturity, we can calculate the yield to maturity of the corporate bond by adding this spread to the Treasury's YTM. We can then derive the price through the price-yield relationship. Suppose the yield curve shifts and, as a result, the Treasury's YTM changes. If we are willing to assume that the yield spread remains constant because the credit risk is not affected by the changing market environment, we can use the same spread to determine the revised yield to maturity of the corporate bond, and hence the bond price.

The Matrix Pricing Model

We shall now describe a methodology for determining the yield spread of a bond. It uses a mathematical formulation that seeks to explain the yield spread by using empirical data. A thorough analysis of the data reveals how the yield spread can be explained by possible relevant factors such as corporate debt/equity ratios, earnings, and bond marketability. This model of the yield spread is often called a *matrix pricing model*. Since the yield spread is equal to the difference between yields on corporate and Treasury bonds, the equation can be written as

$$\text{Corporate yield} - \text{Treasury yield} = (\text{leverage})^{\alpha} \times (\text{working capital})^{\beta}$$
$$\times (\text{amount outstanding})^{\gamma}$$

Since Treasury bond yields are readily observable, the corporate bond yield becomes apparent by manipulating the equation. The coefficients of data on corporate leverage, working capital, and amount outstanding—α, β, and γ respectively—are estimated by multiple regression analysis of statistics on groups of bond-issuing corporations. Once the corporate yield is known, and assuming maturity and coupon payments are known, the bond price can be determined through the yield to maturity formula.

The matrix pricing model is a relative pricing model. A bond is priced relative to other corporate bonds in the same category from which α, β, and γ were estimated. For example, long-term debentures might form one category. All long-term bank bonds, then, are priced relative to one another because the statistics that calculate their yields are in part based on group statistics. For any given bond whose characteristics are known (for any bond that can be classified), we can calculate a price.

Defects of the Model

Matrix pricing is limited in its applications for a variety of reasons.

1. The right-hand side parameters cannot encompass all the economic variables. For example, the schedule of a callable bond, clearly important for price determination, is not included in the scheme. The relationship of the schedule to the yield spread is highly complicated. Hence, the simple determination of the spread through the formula does not suffice.

2. The formula assumes that the spread relationship remains consistent even when yield levels change, yet this is not true. Recall that if the market interest rates fall, the bond price will rise and the call value (which is based on the interest rates at the time the bond is issued) will also increase. The price of a callable bond is prevented from rising above the call price despite declining interest rates. Hence, the yield on the callable bond will stabilize to correspond to its call price and will remain above an equivalent straight Treasury bond yield. The yield spread is altered by the characteristics of the embedded call option. These changes in the yield spread as a function of changing interest rate levels cannot be captured by the equation.

3. The model lacks predictive value. Often, models are used to predict a bond value in simulating possible changes in the yield

curve. The model assumes a constant yield spread in different interest rate scenarios. Therefore, changes in the yield spread, which affect the price of the bond, cannot be evaluated by the model. For example, when the yield curve changes (i.e., the market interest rates fall), the call option value will be affected and the yield spread will change. Therefore, it is inappropriate to assume that the yield spread remains constant in simulations.

4. The first three points show that the model is ad hoc: It does not account for changes resulting from investment strategy or human behavior. It is not an economic model showing exactly why the spread exists. The model hypothesizes a relationship and estimates parameters. At best, the model approximates a relationship between a bond's yield and estimated parameters. The model does not relate observed bond prices, a major determinant of the yield spread, with the economic parameters (such as those imposed by a call provision). Much of financial research, then, is conducted to develop models that incorporate economic parameters.

Yield Diagrams

In Chapter 1 we discussed the construction of a yield diagram. Yield diagrams can be used to relate the yield to maturity of the corporate bond with the yield to maturity of the Treasury bond. As the market interest rates change, the YTM of a corporate bond with a call provision should change less than the YTM of the Treasury bond. Figure 12–1 shows the yield diagram of the Michigan Bell 9.125 percent due February 1, 2018 and the nearest on-the-run Treasury issue, 9 percent due November 15, 2018. It also displays a portion of the corporate bond's call schedule.

Figure 12–1a shows that the slope of the line of best fit is less than 1. That is, for each basis point shift in the Treasury yield, the corporate bond's YTM would change by less than 1. If both bond yields had changed in lockstep fashion, the yields would have been distributed along the 45 degree line.

In Chapter 6, we explained the differences between modified duration and effective duration. Recall that modified duration is the proportional change in the bond price with a unit shift in the yield to maturity. Effective duration, on the other hand, is the proportional change in the bond price with a unit shift in the market yields (parallel shift in the

FIGURE 12–1
Michigan Bell 9.125 Percent Bond Due February 1, 2018: (a) Yield Diagram; (b) Bond Information and Call Schedule

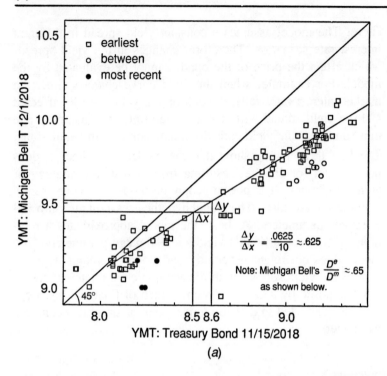

(a)

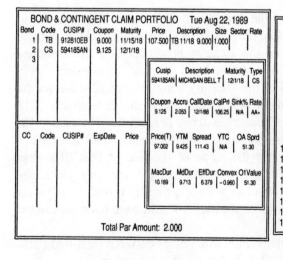

Total Par Amount: 2.000

CALL SCHEDULE			
Date	Price	Date	Price
1 12/1/83	107.500	18 12/1/00	103.250
2 12/1/84	107.250	19 12/1/01	103.000
3 12/1/85	107.000	20 12/1/02	102.750
4 12/1/86	106.750	21 12/1/03	102.500
5 12/1/87	106.500	22 12/1/04	102.250
6 12/1/88	106.250	23 12/1/05	102.000
7 12/1/89	106.000	24 12/1/06	101.750
8 12/1/90	105.750	25 12/1/07	101.500
9 12/1/91	105.500	26 12/1/08	101.250
10 12/1/92	105.250	27 12/1/09	101.000
11 12/1/93	105.000	28 12/1/10	100.750
12 12/1/94	104.750	29 12/1/11	100.500
13 12/1/95	104.500	30 12/1/12	100.250
14 12/1/96	104.250	31 12/1/13	100.000
15 12/1/97	104.000	32 12/1/14	100.000
16 12/1/98	103.750	33 12/1/15	100.000
17 12/1/99	103.500	34 12/1/16	100.000

spot yield curve). We will now show how one can estimate an issue's effective duration from its modified duration by using a yield diagram.

As an approximation, we will assume that the yield curve is flat. As a result, the change in a straight Treasury bond's YTM is approximately the same as a parallel shift in the yield curve. In this particular case, when the yield curve (spot curve) is flat, the modified duration is computationally the same as the effective duration for the Treasury issue. That is, for a Treasury issue at par, a change in market yield (r) is the same as the change in YTM, and both durations are the same.

This result is not surprising because Treasuries reflect the risk-free time value of money, as explained in Chapter 9. Therefore, any change in the spot curve is reflected in Treasury yields and vice versa. For corporates, however, the relation between spots yields or market yield changes and YTM changes is not as coherent. We know that ΔYTM is rarely equal to Δr. Therefore, the effective duration for a corporate issue will be different from its modified duration.

We can quickly estimate a corporate issue's effective duration by reviewing the relationship of its YTM to an on-the-run Treasury's YTM. Since we know the Δr is the same as the ΔYTM for the Treasury, we can substitute the Treasury's ΔYTM for computing the corporate's effective duration. We can compute the corporate's modified duration because we have its observed ΔYTM. Better yet, we do not need to make the computations. We can just use the slope of the line of best fit in the yield diagram as the ratio of the corporate's effective duration to its modified duration. Notice that for a callable bond the slope will always be less than unity.

This relationship can be mathematically depicted as follows.

D^m is the modified duration,
D^e is the effective duration.
P_c and YTM$_c$ are the price and YTM of the corporate bond.
r is the market rate (or YTM$_T$) for the Treasury issue.

If $\Delta r = \Delta\text{YTM}_T$, then

$$D^e = \frac{-\Delta P_c / \Delta r}{P_c}$$

$$D^m = \frac{-\Delta P_c / \Delta\text{YTM}_c}{P_c}$$

Therefore,

$$D^e/D^m = \frac{\Delta YTM_c}{\Delta r}$$

This result is the same as the slope of best fit.

The estimated slope of scattered plots in Figure 12–1a is 0.625. Using a corporate bond model results in a D^e/D^m ratio of 0.65. The two estimates are therefore quite close. Note that D^e is determined by a bond pricing model, but the yield diagram shows that we can estimate D^e from the observed bond prices.

This concludes our overview of yield pricing and yield diagrams. The points made provide one aspect of corporate bond characteristics and considerations. Another important, but subtle, concern is whether option values provide indications of whether the options will be exercised. The following section will be elaborate on this particular point.

OPTIMAL CALL STRATEGY

As mentioned in the discussion of the matrix pricing model, the call provision greatly affects bond value. The value of the call option is determined by first understanding the optimal call strategy of the firm. In other words, we must consider the time at which the firm will want to refinance.

Assume a firm has a bond with a remaining life of five years. The bond has reached its first call date and is priced at par. If market interest rates drop, the bond can be refunded at a coupon rate lower than the outstanding coupon rate, and the firm is able to save money by refinancing. Yet if the bond is refinanced now, the firm loses the option to call the bond in the future.

Using Net Present Value (NPV)

If the bond must be refinanced now (meaning the call option will be lost if not exercised), the decision to refinance is simplified. The net present value (NPV) method permits a comparison of the financial benefits of calling a bond with those of not calling a bond. Should the firm call a bond with the intention of refinancing at lower interest rates, the benefit to the firm of calling the bond is the present value of the net interest costs; that is, the present value of the savings in interest expenses net of the refinancing costs. The costs of refinancing include the value of the call premium (the difference between the call and par price) and transaction costs. For proper comparison, we assume that the firm will issue a new bond (in refinancing) that has the same maturity as the outstanding bond and no call provision (for ease of comparison, we will not have to consider option values). Moreover, the coupon rate of the new bond is set such that the bond can be issued at par (its coupon rate will be lower than the outstanding bond's coupon). The net present value of a refinancing project is

NPV = PV(original interest payments − new interest payments)

−Call premium − Transaction costs

The firm should refinance if the NPV is greater than 0. For example, consider a callable bond with five years remaining to maturity. The bond is now at its first call date at par value, and the issuer has no option afterwards. The issuer, in deciding whether or not to call the bond, acts in the optimal interests of its shareholders and thus applies the NPV rule. In this case the call's strike price premium is nil (as the bond is callable at par) and transaction costs are negligible. The NPV rule says that the issuer should refinance as soon as the market rate on a five-year bond is lower than the coupon rate on the callable bond.

It must be pointed out that the rule is correct only if the issuer has the option on one date. In general, such is not the case. A call schedule of bond allows the issuer to exercise the options any time up to maturity. In this case, if the issuer waits, the rates may drop further. In this sense, the NPV method recommends premature refinancing.

Timing Issues

Once the bond is refinanced, the value of the call option is zero. When there is a call schedule for a bond, the problem of determining the optimal time to call the bond remains. The firm must weigh the value of retaining the option against the value of the interest payments saved by refinancing the bond at a lower rate. We first construct a corresponding noncallable straight bond (same maturity and coupon rate) as the standard for value-added comparison. This corresponding straight bond is identical to the firm's bond except that it is noncallable.

If the call provision only allows the issuer to refinance now, then as long as the corresponding bond is traded at a premium, it is profitable for the firm to refinance (assuming the call price is at par). Note that the bond to be refinanced (callable) is traded at a higher yield (lower price) than the corresponding bond's yield because of its call provision. The more likely the bond is to be refinanced, the greater the divergence from the corresponding bond's yield (price) will be.

To illustrate how to use the optimizing rule, we should compare a corresponding straight bond value against the schedule of possible strike prices established in a call schedule. Consider the scenario of a world of certainty: no interest rate risk and a horizontal yield curve. The forward yield curve will be the same as the spot yield curve. Once the forward yield curve is known, the future price of the bond can be calculated. And, based on the future bond price, the present value of interest rate savings can be calculated. To maximize the value of the option, the firm will choose to sell the bond on the date that will provide the greatest interest rate savings. This date may not be the first call date.

This example illustrates the need to look into the future to determine the optimal time to refinance the bond. Simply because it is profitable to refund the bond at the present time does not mean that the present time is the optimal time for refunding. The market price of the callable bond will take optimal refinancing into account by assuming that the bond issuer will optimally refinance the bond. The investor will conclude that the bond will have an actual maturity of time T, before which the market does not anticipate refinancing of the bond. The bond will be priced accordingly at P_m.

$$P - P_m = \text{the call value of the option}$$

where P_m is the market price of issue and P is the price of the underlying straight bond.

Is it possible for the market price to be above the call price? If the market is efficient, the answer is no. If a bond is traded above its call price, that means some investor is willing to pay at this price. Then the investor runs the risk of getting the bond called at the lower price (the call price)immediately. If a bond is traded above the call price, it means the bond, as evaluated by the market, is worth more than the call price. In effect, it is as if the market was stating that it would be willing to lend more than the call value of the bonds or that the market would be willing to exchange the existing bonds for a greater face value of lower coupon bonds. This would be an immediate signal to the firm to execute its right to buy back the bond at a lower price and maximize firm value (i.e., maximize its invested capital returns by lowering the cost of funds) In anticipating these events, the market should not price a bond above the call price. Further the market will trade at the call price only when it anticipates that the bond will be called.

Other Issues

In this discussion, we have ignored other considerations that have to be incorporated into the refinancing decision. They are rate uncertainties, call schedules, and tax and transactions costs.

1. Rate uncertainties. An interest rate increase may increase the option value because the issuer will be more likely to wait to call the bond. The issuer's downside risk is limited. In other words, if interest rates rise after the bond has been called, the issuer will at worst miss the opportunity to refinance. As the rate on the bond is fixed, any rise in the interest rate does not affect the issuer. If the interest rate drops, the issuer will profit with each point decrease in rates. The upside potential is not unlimited (interest rates won't drop below zero), but it is substantial.

2. Call schedule. We assume the call price to be par, yet the illustration of optimal call timing indicates that it includes a premium.

3. Tax and transactions costs. The interest rate savings should be considered net of taxes. The call premium is tax deductible; hence, the deduction on the premium could motivate earlier refinancing. The transactions costs will delay refinancing so that the price at which the bond is traded will be above the call price.

In light of our discussion, the optimal decision in refinancing a bond is the same optimal decision in early exercise of an American option. The bond issuer has to weigh the costs and benefits of waiting. If the firm waits, then the firm has to pay the high interest costs. But the benefit is that the interest rates may drop further. Moreover, the more the interest rates drop, the more interest costs the firm can save. Meanwhile, if the interest rates rise, at worst the firm loses the profitable opportunity of refinancing for the time being. As we have seen, there is no simple rule for such a decision. The only way is to apply the pricing model that can predict the optimal timing in early exercise of the option. We will discuss this pricing model later.

As we've discussed, if the issuer believes in an efficient capital market that accurately evaluates bonds, then the issuer will use the market as an indicator of when it should exercise its call options. If the bond is trading at the call price, then the market is anticipating that the firm is going to act rationally and call the bond.

PRICING OF CORPORATE BONDS

In this section, we will discuss the methodology for pricing corporate bonds. We will show how any corporate bond value can be broken down into three components: the cash flow value, the credit/liquidity premium, and the embedded option value. Each will be valued by a systematic procedure we call "value attribution."

Value attribution not only enables us to identify the sources of bond value but also to structure comparisons among bonds. The process entails using a pricing methodology that stems from the information depicted in performance profiles. Specificially, we first develop the performance profiles of different types of bonds, and then we analyze the parameters that determine the bond's performance. These parameters include duration, convexity, time decay, and vega risk. It is the assessment of these parameters that will enable us to specify the return attribution of a corporate bond.

Finally, we will use our analysis to discuss a broad range of bond strategies. These strategies are applicable for dealing with an individual bond as well as with a portfolio. These bond strategies are primarily concerned with controlling the holding period risks of a bond or a portfolio while increasing the return.

The Basics

Pricing investment-grade corporate bonds is more involved than pricing Treasury bonds or traded options on bonds. Embedded options in most corporate bonds are often very complex, so we will focus just on the embedded options associated with a scheduled call provision. Since the bond can be called at the call price, when interest rates are sufficiently low, the bond issuers would call the bond. As a result, investors would not receive the balance of the scheduled coupon payments, and the principal would be prepaid. Therefore, a callable bond provides a probable cash flow and not a certain cash flow. These embedded options should affect the bond price. The uncertainty of the cash flow because of the call provision is called the *call risk*.

Furthermore, corporate bonds are subject to default risk. In the event of default, the investors would not receive the full promised amount of coupons and principal. Therefore, we can no longer price a corporate bond based upon the assumption of known cash flows. The pricing of a corporate bond must take the probability of default into consideration.

Since the call risk and the default risk have different characteristics, they both affect a bond's price. The call risk effect is more easily assessed than the default risk. The value of a call provision crucially depends on investors' receiving a significant amount of cash flow when interest rates are low. The investor has to forfeit a higher-yielding instrument for cash that will be reinvested at a lower market rate. For this reason, the call provision lowers the bond price. In contrast, default risk is not concerned with the reinvestment of cash flows. Default risk simply reduces the promised payments to the bondholders. In other words, the embedded options are interest-rate-contingent claims, whereas the default risk has a negligible relationship with the variations in the interest rate levels. The pricing methodology must take these factors into account.

We shall discuss the modeling of the default risk and the call risk separately. First it is useful to describe a particular corporate bond, which will be used as an example throughout the rest of this chapter.

Bond Description: American Standard; 9.25% coupon rate; maturity 12/1/16
Sector: Industrial
Rating: AAA
Call Schedule: First call on 12/01/88 at 108.325, and then call prices decline linearly to par on 12/01/06.

This section will describe a methodology for pricing this particular bond. On 6/30/89 the bond is priced at 100.50, and at this price the yield to maturity of the bond is 9.194 percent.

Treasury Equivalent Value

The most fundamental part of a corporate bond is the cash flow of the coupons and principal. Suppose that this cash flow is not subject to call risk or default risk. Then the cash flow can be discounted by the spot yield curve as if the bond were a straight Treasury bond. Such a bond value is called the *Treasury equivalent*.

Since both the call risk and the default risk are detrimental to the investor, the Treasury equivalent value always exceeds the fair value of the bond. If a portfolio of Treasury securities can be constructed such that the cash flow of the portfolio is identical to the promised payments of the bond, then the value of the portfolio is the Treasury equivalent value of the corporate bond.

Determination of the Treasury equivalent value of a corporate bond is rather straight forward by now. In Chapter 10, we discussed at length the estimation of the spot curve from the Treasury securities prices on a particular day. If we use the spot curve to discount the promised payment of the corporate bond, we can obtain the Treasury equivalent value of the bond.

We will now refer to the numerical example. The Treasury equivalent bond for American Standard is a 9.25 percent coupon bond with a maturity of 12/1/16. On 6/30/89, when we discount this cash flow by the prevailing spot yield curve, the Treasury equivalent bond value can be calculated as $111.835. The yield to maturity of the Treasury equivalent bond at this price is 8.162 percent. We see that the Treasury equivalent bond value exceeds the underlying bond by $11.335. This difference has to be accounted for by the call risk and the default risk. We will first analyze the default risk.

Default Risk

Corporate bonds face the possibility of default by the firm. As a result, there will be a loss of coupons or principals to the investor. To compensate for the loss of the promised income, a bond with default risk would have a lower price or higher yield relative to a default-free bond with the same coupon rate, maturity, and other attributes. This difference in price is called the *credit premium*. The difference in yield (in terms of yield to maturity) is called the *credit spread*.

The likelihood of default for a particular bond depends on the perceived viability of the issuing firm and the protective provisions underlying that particular bond. Therefore, the price or yield adjustment to account for this default risk is not the same for all bonds. We need to first determine the default probability of a bond and then show how the bond has to be priced taking the assessed probability of default into account.

It is beyond the scope of this chapter to describe how to assess the default risk of a bond. This chapter is primarily concerned with investment grade bonds; therefore an elaborate procedure for evaluating the default risk of a bond is not necessary. Instead, we will assume that the bonds with the same bond rating have the same default risk and hence the same credit premium. So far we have not really defined default risk. We have kept the discussion somewhat intuitive.

A bond rating characterizes the default risk of a firm by indicating the likelihood of default of the firm; the rating does not necessarily indicate the likelihood of default of each individual bond. Therefore, it is not clear how one can consider all the bonds with the same rating to have the same default risk. For example, a long-term bond and a short-term bond may both have the same rating, but one tends to think that the long-term bond should be ascribed a higher default risk. Therefore, how should one decide on the credit premium of the two bonds relative to each other? To deal with these questions, we have to establish a framework for analyzing default risk.

Term Structure of Credit Spread

One way to determine the credit premium of a bond is to determine the prevailing value of credit premium for a sample of bonds that have a similar default risk. A direct approach to this problem is to determine the term structure of credit spread.

The term structure of credit spread is similiar to the term structure of interest rates. In dealing with the credit spread, we first group all the bonds with the same rating. For example, we will consider a sample of AAA industrial bonds. Assume that we have many bonds in each sector and rating category, and assume that these bonds have no embedded options.

Now we analyze this sample of corporate bonds in a sector of a particular rating group. Recall how we use the sample of Treasury bond prices to estimate the underlying spot curve. Here we will follow the same procedure. Again, we consider each bond as a portfolio of zero-coupon corporate bonds in the same rating and sector group. Using the bonds, we can always estimate the underlying yield curve so that the corporate bond prices can best be explained by discounting the cash flows of each bond by this yield curve. At any maturity, the yield of this curve must be higher than the spot curve yield because of the default risk. The difference is the term structure of credit spread.

A zero-coupon bond with default risk should have a higher yield to maturity than the same maturity zero-coupon bond without default risk. The difference in yield is precisely given by the term structure of credit spread for the bond maturity. It has also been argued that the bond with longer maturity should have a higher default risk. Therefore, a bond with longer maturity should have a higher yield to maturity than a bond in the same rating group and sector with a shorter maturity. Hence, the term structure of credit spread should be an upward-sloping curve with the credit spread increasing with the maturity.

This approach is very appealing for pricing corporate bonds since it is very straightforward. In essence, it is a direct extension of the spot-curve-estimation procedure, and it can provide a systematic procedure for pricing corporate bonds with default risk.

Unfortunately, there are a number of problems with this methodology. First, there are very few actively traded corporate bonds in a particular sector and rating group with no embedded options. As we've discussed, most bonds have call provisions. Lacking a sufficient sample of these straight bonds, it is quite problematic to estimate the term structure of credit premiums. Therefore, it is somewhat difficult to construct this term structure of credit spread with few practical examples.

Second, even if we can construct such a yield curve we cannot be sure what the yield curve represents. The construction of the credit spread assumes that the methodology for estimating the spot curve can also apply to the bond subject to default risk. Unfortunately, such is not the case. Although we have shown that a default-free coupon bond can be viewed as a portfolio of default-free zero-coupon bonds, we should note that a bond that has default risk cannot be identified as a portfolio of zero-coupon bonds with default risk; when a firm defaults on one payment, the firm defaults on all the payments. Therefore, the default risk of a payment of a bond is not independent of the default risk of another payment of the bond. To demonstrate, let us use a simple, numerical example.

Consider firms A, B, and C. These firms are identical except for their debt structure. Firm A has one bond with two payments X and Y (with the Y payment due later). Firm B has one bond, which is identical to X, and firm C has one bond, which is identical to payment Y. From the investor's point of view, holding the portfolio of bonds of firm B and C is not the same as holding firm A's bond. For example, when firm A defaults on payment X, payment Y is also in default. However, when firm B defaults, firm C does not automatically go into default. Hence, we cannot replicate cash flows of the corporate bond in the same way as the Treasury bonds. So it is not clear what it means to use the term structure of credit premium to price a cash flow of a corporate bond.

Thirdly, the estimation procedure of the term structure of the credit premium is not based in any analytical framework. Therefore, it is not possible to interpret the estimated result to decide whether the results are meaningful or not. For this reason, it is not clear why the term structure of credit premium should be an upward-sloping curve. Further, when we compare the term structure of credit spread for different bond ratings, it is hard to interpret whether or not the spread justifies the difference in default risks.

Recognizing some of the restrictions in the term structure of credit spread theory for building a coherent analytical model of credit spreads, we will use a framework that provides more flexibility. First, we will explain a component of this framework, the *mortality table*.

The Survival Rate of a Bond

Let us establish a simple bond model with default risk. Altman has proposed a way to think about the default risk of a bond. In essence, we can think of a bond as analogous to an individual. A bond in default (as defined by filing for bankruptcy protection) is an event analogous to an individual's death. And so we can compute the mortality table of a bond that is issued at a particular rating.

In calculating the mortality rate of a bond, we consider a sample of bonds belonging to a sample group such as an AA bond. Then we can follow the "lives" of these bonds and determine the portion that survive the first year, the second year, and so on. The proportion of bonds that survive a certain age is called the *survival rate*. So we can estimate the survival rate of the first year, second year, and so on up to the maturity date of the bonds.

It is clear that bonds with a high rating should have a higher survival rate; the low rating bonds should have a low survival rate. After constructing the survival rate for a rating group, we can then calculate the mortality of a bond, the default probability of a bond at a certain age.

A mortality table of bonds with default risk refers to the mortality rate we can calculate for each rating group over the ages of the bonds. There are, however, some differences between the mortality table of a bond compared with that of an individual. A bond must "die" on the maturity date. But that does not mean that the bond's "health" has to deteriorate in the final years of the bond. In fact, the mortality rate can remain very low just before maturity. Of course, such is not the case for people. Although there is no definite life span for an individual, the mortality rate of the "aged" group must necessarily be high.

The importance of a mortality table for bonds is that the table enables us to make some judgments about the default risk of a bond and, hence, the return of a bond with default risk. Altman's studies seek to develop the mortality tables empirically. Considering that the growth of bonds with default risk is a rather recent phenomenon and is closely paralleled by the growth in leveraged buy-out activities, current empirical studies should lead to additional insights and extensions of current theories. The pricing model is constructed in such a way that any developments that further elucidate the credit spread assignment to a bond can be easily incorporated into the framework.

The mortality table framework is a theoretically relevant approximation of credit spread structure; hence we will use some of its aspects to model default risk. To start this model, we use a simple example to demonstrate the idea. We will begin with some simple assumptions before we relax some of these assumptions later to make the model more realistic.

- First, let us assume that there are many corporate bonds outstanding. The defaults of the firms are uncorrelated, so the default risk of the bonds can be diversified away. Thus in the portfolio context, we do not need to incorporate the risk premium for default arising from the risk aversion of the investors. However, we need to calculate the expected return of a bond.

- Second, let us assume that the spot curve is horizontal and that there is no interest rate risk. This way, we can concentrate on the default risk without confounding the interest rate risk.

- Third, when a bond is in default, the bondholder does not receive any payment. This assumption simply makes our arguments clearer. Clearly, the bondholders often receive a portion of their investment in the event of a default or reorganization. We will relax this assumption later.

- Fourth, let us consider only a zero-coupon bond. For now the bond can default only on the maturity date. The probability of default is pi (π).

Although these assumptions seem very restrictive, they do allow us to set up a useful framework for analyzing the default risk of a bond for now.

Our assumptions help us determine the credit spread required to price the bond. Suppose the spread is delta (Δ). In this approach, we first calculate the bond's expected value on the maturity date. Then we consider the alternative investment. Instead of purchasing the corporate bond, we can always invest in the risk-free rate. Since the default risk is diversifiable, the expected value of the corporate bond at maturity must be the same as the value of the alternative investment on the horizon date.

Since the credit spread is delta, the bond price is by definition

$$P = \frac{100}{(1 + r + \Delta)^T} \qquad (12\text{--}1)$$

If we leave the investment in risk-free rate instead of purchasing the corporate bond, the value of this investment on the maturity date must be 100. Since the bond will pay the principal on maturity conditional upon the firm's not defaulting on the bond, the expected value of the bond at mutrity is $\pi \times 100$. In equating the expected values in both cases, we show that

$$\frac{100(1 + r)^T}{(1 + r + \Delta)^T} = 100(1 - \pi) \qquad (12\text{--}2)$$

This result provides the useful relationship between the credit spread and the probability of default. Although the result is simple, it gives us some useful insights. Let lambda (λ) be a constant for the survival rate of the bond. That is, lambda represents the probability of the bond's not defaulting over one period, and that probability remains constant over the life of the bond. There are T periods for this bond; therefore the probability for the bond to survive through T periods is

$$\pi = 1 - \lambda^T \qquad (12\text{--}3)$$

Substituting for π in Equation 12–2 and simplifying, we obtain a very simple relationship:

$$\frac{1 + r}{1 + r + \Delta} = \lambda \qquad (12\text{--}4)$$

The survival rate of a bond is a useful concept. It is not necessary that a zero-coupon bond default only on the maturity date. After all, when the firm has other bonds in its debt structure and if the firm defaults on other bonds because of the cross default clause, the zero-coupon bond can be in default also. Therefore, it is more useful to think of the survival rate of a bond.

Thus far, we have assumed a constant survival rate of a bond for the life of the bond. This assumption is used for simplicity of exposition. More generally, the survival rate need not be constant and can vary with maturity.

Our discussion suggests that for any bond, the default risk should be quantified by the survival rate, lambda. Here we shall use a simple model for the default risk of a bond: the survival rate is constant over the life of the bond. For a constant survival rate, the default risk is not constant over the life of the bond but in fact the default probability (i.e., $1 - \lambda^T$) increases over time. Under this assumption, we obtain a very simple expression relating the survival rate to the credit spread of the bond, as stated in Equation (12–2).

At this point we should point out that a rating itself does not define the default risk of a bond. A rating is simply a way to describe the credit-worthiness of the bonds or the firm. To be precise about the default risk and hence the pricing of the bond, one can assign a survival rate of a bond either explicitly or implicitly.

A General Constant-Survival-Rate Model

In this section, we will relax the previous assumptions. First, we can relax the assumption about a zero-coupon bond. We will show that the argument applies to any bond with different payments. Also we do not need to assume that the bond does not make any payment to the bond-holders in default. Indeed, Altman's studies have shown that the bond in default can actually pay the bondholders a significant amount, generally 41 percent of par. This amount is called the recovery percentage.

Here are the assumptions that we will make for a general constant-survival-rate model. Let us assume that the bond is a zero-coupon bond and that it is priced with a constant credit spread delta. Further, the constant survival rate of the bond is lambda. Knowing the spread, we can calculate the imputed bond value at any time of the bond life. It is the present value of all the future cash flows discounted by the market rate with the spread. Now let us assume that the bond will pay alpha (α) portion of the imputed bond value at the time of default, alpha being the recovery percentage.

Given these assumptions, we can show that the survival rate, the spread, and alpha are related by the following simple equation (the deriviation is given later).

$$\alpha(1 - \lambda) = \mu - \lambda \qquad (12\text{--}5)$$

where

$$\mu = \frac{1 + r + \Delta}{1 + r}$$

If we can estimate the credit spread of a corporate bond and if we are willing to make some assumptions about alpha (the remaining value of a bond at default), we can estimate the survival rate of the bonds, using historical experience. We will later use this methodology to report the survival rate of the bonds implied by estimating the spread delta.

Now we can illustrate this calculation by using our American Standard example (we will later describe the procedure for estimating the spread delta). Suppose that the spread for the AAA industrial sector on 6/30/89 is 33 basis points. Then we can add this spread to the spot curve and then discount the promised payments of American Standard by this yield curve. The value we obtain is $108.18. At this price, the yield to maturity is 8.476 percent. Therefore the credit premium is $3.655 ($111.835 − $108.180) and the credit spread is 31.4 basis points (8.476 percent − 8.162 percent). Note that the credit spread is not necessarily the delta value. The reason is that the prevailing spot curve estimated from the market bond prices need not be flat curve, so the difference between the yield to maturity of the bond and the default-free bond is not the same as the value of delta.

As a result of this analysis, the constant-survival-rate model implies that the spread for the credit risk is constant. Since it seems reasonable to assume that the survival rate of a bond is constant, we can infer that a constant delta for the life of the bond also seems reasonable.

COMPARATIVE METHODS USING CONSTANT SURVIVAL RATES

There are three ways to think about how a bond with a constant survival rate should be priced. First, we will consider the expected value of a bond on the maturity date. Second, we will consider the present value of the expected cash flow. Finally, assuming the investors hold the investment for a short interval, we can apply the backward substitution approach. In these cases, we will assume a simple zero-coupon bond is to be evaluated.

Expected Value at the Maturity Date

Using the concepts introduced for a zero bond in Equation 12–2 and dividing both sides by $(1 + r)^T$, we can now summarize the result. If we discount the expected amount by the spot curve, we will be able to calculate the present value, which will be the same as discounting the promised payments by the spot curve together with the spread delta. This argument can be extended to coupon issues. However, one must assume that any interim payments are to be reinvested at the risk-free rate to the maturity date. We can determine the expected dollar amount accumulated on the maturity date. Now that we have the expected dollar amount again, we just apply the same procedure.

In the case of the zero-coupon bond, the interim payment arises when the bond goes bankrupt at any time. The amount received on bankruptcy is reinvested at the risk-free rate to the stated maturity of the bond. The survival rate of the bond determines this interim cash flow. If the survival rate is high so that the default probability is very small, then the cash accumulated by the interim cash flow will be small. Conversely, if the survival rate is low, there will be a significant probability of defaults. In this case, the amount of cash accumulated by the reinvestment would be significant.

Discounting to the Present Value

Using the constant survival rate, we can always calculate the cash flow of expected payments. Take the example of a zero coupon bond. At any future time period, we can calculate the probability of default:

$$(1 - \lambda), \lambda(1 - \lambda), \lambda^2(1 - \lambda), \ldots \quad \text{for periods 1, 2, 3, } \ldots$$

The payment in case of the default is given by our previous assumption. Therefore, we can calculate the expected cash flow of each period.

$$\frac{(1 - \lambda)\alpha}{(1 + r + \Delta)^{T-1}}, \frac{\lambda(1 - \lambda)\alpha}{(1 + r + \Delta)^{T-2}}, \ldots$$

If we discount the expected cash flows by the spot curve, we can calculate the present value of the cash flow, which can be shown by discounting the promised payments by the spot curve with the spread delta.

$$\frac{1}{(1 + r + \Delta)^T} = \frac{(1 - \lambda)\alpha}{(1 + r + \Delta)^{T-1}(1 + r)}$$

$$+ \frac{\lambda(1 - \lambda)\alpha}{(1 + r + \Delta)^{T-2}(1 + r)^2}$$

$$+ \cdots + \frac{\alpha(1 - \lambda)\lambda^{T-1}}{(1 + r)^T}$$

$$+ \frac{\lambda^T}{(1 + r)^T}$$

In simplifying this expression, we get Equation (12–5).

Multiperiod Method

In this pricing methodology, we assume that the investors only want to hold the bond for one period. They would sell the bond one period later and would get the fair return over that period.

To determine the value of the bond at the present time, we need to apply the backward substitution methodology. We start our argument with the beginning of the last period. These investors would hold the bond till maturity. But the bond may default on maturity, so the bond price would be less than that of a default free bond. Now let us move to the beginning of the period before that last period. We repeat the previous arguments and discount the bond price at the end of the period by the market interest rate with the credit spread. We repeat this argument and recursively price the bond period after period until we reach the present value.

THE BINOMIAL LATTICE MODEL

In value attribution, we have identified that the bond value has three components. We have discussed the Treasury equivalent value and the credit premium. The last component is the embedded option value. To determine the embedded option value, we will construct a bond pricing model that can incorporate all the bond features.

The corporate-bond-pricing model is similar to the model of bond options described in Chapter 11. We will use a binomial lattice model that can take the default risk into account. That is, we will use the binomial model described in Chapter 11. The only difference is that during each period, the discount rate is no longer just the prevailing interest rate but the prevailing interest rate together with a spread.

To demonstrate this procedure we can use a simple example. Using the spot discount rates developed in Chapter 11, we can add the spread value of 33 basis points to each rate to reflect the additional compensation for credit/liquidity risk. Table 12–1 shows the spot rates with the additional spread.

This binomial lattice is used to price the callable bond that is subject to default risk. It is important to point out that this procedure captures a number of important economic interpretations. For example, the likelihood of a bond getting called depends on the shape of the yield curve. Since the binomial lattice model takes the shape of the yield curve into account, the probability of the bond getting called is taken into account.

Using the binomial lattice valuation approach discussed in Chapter 11, we can obtain the bond price of $100.50. Then the embedded option value is $7.68 ($108.18 − $100.50), and the spread related to the option value is 71.8 basis points (9.194% − 8.476%). We can see that the option value is quite significant, for it constitutes over 7 percent of the bond value.

The spread delta that we use in this context is called *option-adjusted spread (OAS)*, which refers to the additional return that the bond provides

TABLE 12–1
Spot Discount Rates with Corporate Spread[a]

$t = 0$	$t = 1$	$t = 2$	$t = 3$	$t = 4$
			NODE 3,3 1 6.73	
		NODE 2,2 1 7.26 2 7.26		
	NODE 1,1 1 7.79 2 7.79 3 7.79		NODE 3,2 1 7.80	
NODE 0,0 1 8.33 2 8.33 3 8.33 4 8.33		NODE 2,1 2 8.34 2 8.34		
	NODE 1,0 1 8.88 2 8.88 3 8.88		NODE 3,1 1 8.89	
		NODE 2,0 1 9.44 2 9.44		
			NODE 3,0 1 9.98	

[a] delta spread is 33 bp.

after adjustments for the embedded option value. Note that the option value should account for the time decay of the option and the option convexity. Therefore the OAS is the return that pays for the default and liquidity risks. In the survival rate section, the discussion focuses on the default risk. For this reason, delta is the OAS. But, in general, when the bond price is adjusted for liquidity, the OAS net of the delta credit spread is the liquidity spread.

RELATIVE PRICING AND ESTIMATION OF MARKET PARAMETERS

In the above discussion, we are assuming that we know the interest rate volatilities and that the binomial lattice of interest rates can be determined. But as we have discussed before, interest rate volatilities cannot be observed directly. They are estimated and we will discuss the procedure here.

Also we are assuming that the spread for each rating and sector group is known. In general, these spreads are also very difficult to observe. The major obstacle for determining the spread is that nearly all long-term actively traded bonds have embedded options. For this reason, there is no simple way to determine these spreads.

First, we need to estimate the market parameters indirectly. Once again, we will use the procedure described in Chapter 11. We can construct a bellwether portfolio of corporate bonds and then apply a non-linear estimation technique to determine the market parameters that will best explain the observed bond prices. In this estimation procedure, the spreads and the volatilities are all jointly estimated.

Volatilities here refer to the term structure of volatilities: the volatility of the pure discount bond yield of each maturity across the term structure. Short-rate volatility at any time can be different from the long-rate volatility. These volatilities clearly affect any option pricing, particularly the long-term options. For this reason, the term structure of volatilities is important in the corporate bond market.

The term structure of volatilities can be specified by the binomial lattice. Chapter 11 has described how the binomial lattice can be estimated for the bellwether portfolio of securities prices. For corporate bond pricing, the bellwether portfolio should consist of a sizable sample of corporate bonds across the spectrum of investment grades and sectors. Here we describe how the term structure of volatilities can be calculated from the binomial lattice.

By the construction of the binomial lattice, we have specified the initial spot curve. In addition, we have also specified the spot curves for the two possible states at the end of the first binomial step. The binomial probability has also been assigned. Consider a particular maturity T. We can now determine the yields of the discount bond with maturity T in the two possible states. This way, we have specified the uncertain movement of the T-year yield, and we can then calculate the standard deviation of the T-year rate. Since the length of a period on the binomial lattice is typically one month and not a year, the yield uncertainty obtained thus far refers to the one-period risk.

If the binomial period is one month, we multiply the standard deviation by 12 to annualize the standard deviation. Finally, we divide the annualized standard deviation by the initial T-year yield to obtain the T-year volatility number. If we repeat this procedure for all the maturities, we can specify the term structure of volatilities.

These volatilities are inferred from the observed corporate bond prices. While they measure the yield uncertainties of the Treasury bonds (not corporate bonds), the volatility numbers are not derived from the historical behavior of the Treasury bond yields. Therefore, the term structure of volatilities is implied from the corporate bond prices. They reflect the market perception of the Treasury-bond-yield volatilities via the value of the embedded options in the corporate bonds.

Clearly, the OAS of lower-rated bonds is wider than that of higher-rated bonds. In addition, OAS values are not constant over time since they are determined daily in the market. They may rise or fall in accordance with the market's perception of the probability of a bond's default

EMPIRICAL EVIDENCE ON THE OPTION-ADJUSTED SPREADS AND IMPLIED VOLATILITIES

Using the corporate bonds in the Moody's index as the bellwether portfolio and a sample of actively traded bonds, we can estimate the market parameters of the corporate bonds on a daily basis. Therefore, we can determine the option-adjusted spread for each rating group. Figure 12–2 shows the option-adjusted spreads of each rating group over the two-year period. The fluctuations of the OAS for each rating are very

FIGURE 12–2
Corporate OAS

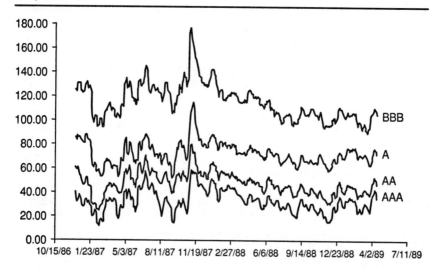

pronounced. They all reach the peak on Black Monday (October 19, 1987). Then they gradually decline.

It is interesting to apply the constant-survival-rate model to determine the probability of default for each rating group. Consider Equation (12–4). The proportion of remaining value of a bond, alpha, is assumed to be 41 percent. This proportion, as mentioned previously, is reported to be reasonable based upon historical experience. Now, we use Equation (12–5) to calculate the probability of default for high, average, and low OAS over the sample period for each rating. The results are displayed in Table 12–2.

We should first note that the OAS for each rating group is rather stable for the year 6/88–6/89. We will use the mean of the OAS for the year to estimate the default probability. The results are very interesting. Similar to the other studies, these probabilities are significantly higher than the historical experience of corporate bond default, as reported in Altman and others. In particular, compared with the mortality table estimated by Altman's study, the implied default probability for each rating group is significantly higher. However, one can argue that the default risk of the corporate bonds outstanding now is much higher than that in past decades. Nevertheless, the methodology that is provided

TABLE 12–2
OAS and Mortality Rate[a]

OAS	1 year	5 years	10 years	20 years	30 years
AAA					
26.33348	.995915[b]	.979741	.959894	.921396	.884442
	.004085[c]	.020258	.040106	.078604	.115557
AA					
39.608238	.993863	.969691	.940300	.884165	.831381
	.006137	.030309	.059700	.115835	.168619
A					
66.121255	.989780	.949935	.902377	.814285	.734792
	.010220	.050065	.097623	.185715	.265218
BBB					
100.95471	.984445	.924611	.854906	.730865	.624821
	.015555	.075389	.145094	.269135	.375179

[a] Mean OAS for each rating group is displayed in OAS column.
[b] The probability of survival (λ^T).
[c] The probability of default ($1 - \lambda^T$).

here enables investors to make a systematic evaluation on the size of the spread.

We must note that there are several factors with which we have concerned ourselves. First, there are the liquidity risk and the liquidity premium. However, even if we assume 10 basis points for the liquidity premium, the calculated default risk is still significantly greater than the historical level.

As in the case of estimating the OAS for each rating and sector type, we can estimate daily the 10-year-rate implied volatility of the corporate bond market. If the market is uncertain about the future outlook of the rates level, the embedded options in bonds would increase. This results in the change in bond prices. In the estimation procedure of the binomial lattice, we will observe a change in the implied volatility. Figure 12–3 shows that the implied volatility of the 10-year rate changes over time. In particular, the volatility was high in late 1986, and had been moving slowly downward. Figure 12–4 also shows that the implied volatility and the historical volatility track each other to a large extent, as is to be expected. Of course, at any time the anticipated rate change need not be the same as the historical rate change.

FIGURE 12–3
Trend Analysis: Implied Volatility

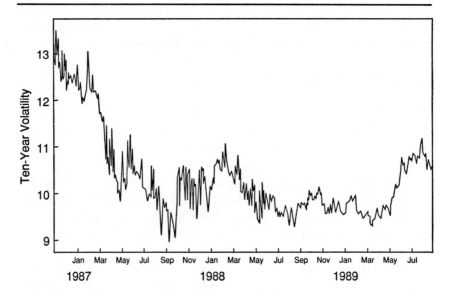

FIGURE 12–4
Trend Analysis: Implied versus Historical Volatility

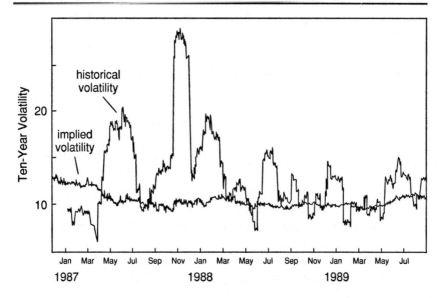

PERFORMANCE PROFILES

In this section, we will examine the performance profiles of different corporate bonds. The purpose of this study is to demonstrate how different bond provisions affect the behavior of the bonds.

Immediately Callable Bond

First, let us consider the bond that is immediately callable. For simplicity, we will say the call price is 104. That means the bond cannot trade above 104. Therefore, as the interest rates drop, the bond value rises. However, the bond value is capped at 104. At some point, the market price of the bond would meet the value 104. At this point, the corporation would call the bond. On the other hand, as the interest rates rise, the bond value will fall. When the bond is selling at a great discount, the option value becomes insignificant, so the callable bond in this case behaves almost like a straight bond.

The interesting result of this analysis is that the callable bond must at some point exhibit negative convexity. As a result of the negative convexity, a callable corporate bond will not be able to participate in the upsided return of a noncallable bond (see Figure 12–5). On the other hand, when rates rise, the callable bond would suffer as much loss as a noncallable. To compensate for this negative convexity behavior, the bond tends to give a higher return when the interest rates do not move significantly. This high return is attributable to the diminishing value of the short option as time passes, Figure 12–6 depicts the performance profile of such a callable bond.

Callable Bond with a Call Protection Period

Next we consider the performance profile of a callable bond with a call protection period. Let us assume that the first call price is 104 and that the call protection period is one year. Unlike the previous example, the call price is not the value that caps the bond value. However, as interest rates drop, the bond is almost certain to be called on the first call date. In this case, the bond should behave much the same way as a one-year bond with a face value of 104. When interest rates rise, the bond value would drop, and the bond would become more like the long-term bond.

The resulting performance profile of this bond is also depicted in Figure 12–6.

A Sinking Fund Bond That Is Accumulated (Private Placement)

The sinking fund bond that is accumulated requires the bond issuer to call the bond at the sinking fund call price to satisfy the sinking fund requirement. In this case the bond resembles a pro rata bond, a package of bonds with different maturities. Thus the performance profile would be similar to a straight bond but with a duration shorter than the bond without the sinking fund provision. This performance profile is depicted in Figure 12–7.

A Sinking Fund Bond with the Sinking Fund Option

When the interest rates are low, the firm is expected to call the sinking funds at the *call price*. Therefore, the bond would be priced as if it were an accumulated sinking fund bond, and its performance profile in this environment would be similar to that of the private placement issue depicted in Figure 12–7. On the other hand, if interest rates are very high, the firm is expected to purchase the bond from the open market to satisfy the sink provision. In this case, the bond would behave like a bond without any sinking fund provision. As a result, the performance profile should be quite steep, mimicking the performance profile of a straight bond under a high interest rate environment. Therefore, combining the two curves we derive the performance profile of the publicly traded sinking fund bond (Figure 12–7).

A Putable Bond

Often a corporate bond has a put option. It is usually a European put option, allowing the investor to put the option to the issuer, and the put price is often par. Even if the interest rates have risen or if the bond's credit rating has fallen, the investor is guaranteed a yield to the put date. This is so because the investor can also receive par by putting the bond to the issuer on the put date.

The put option has more value when interest rates are high. When

FIGURE 12–5
Performance Profile: Reference Security

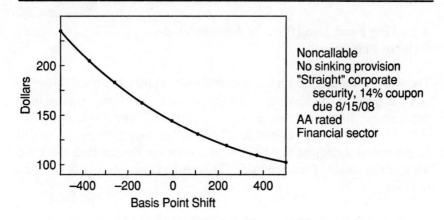

Noncallable
No sinking provision
"Straight" corporate
   security, 14% coupon
   due 8/15/08
AA rated
Financial sector

FIGURE 12–6
Performance Profile: Immediately Callable Bond and Bond Callable after One Year

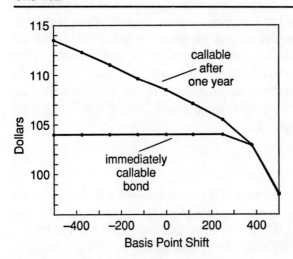

FIGURE 12–7
Performance Profiles: Private Placement (Accumulated Issue) and Sinking Fund Bond with Sinking Fund Option Contrasted with Straight Bond

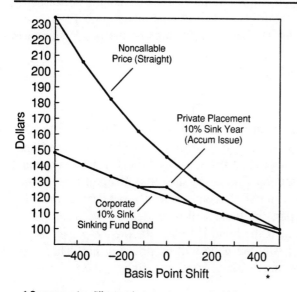

* Compare price difference between issues under high interest rate environment

FIGURE 12–8
Performance Profile: Putable Issue after Six Months Contrasted with Straight Bond

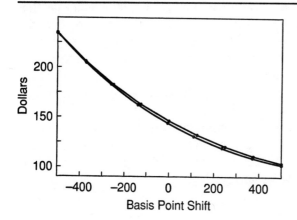

the interest rates are so high that we are sure that the bond would be put, the bond will be valued as a straight bond maturing on the put date. Hence the performance profile would be less steep, like the performance profile of a bond with maturity on the put date (see Figure 12–8).

Table 12–3 summarizes the characteristics of the bonds shown in Figures 12–5 through 12–8.

An Extendable Bond

An extendable bond has both put and call options. The issuer has the right to call the bond, while the investor has the right to put the bond. In a special case, the put price is the same as the call price (say, equal to the par price). And the put date is the same the first call date. In this case, let us consider these possible scenarios for the put date. If the bond price is trading above par, the bond will be called, as we discussed in the optimal call decision. If the bond is trading below the par price, the bond will be put. Either way the bond will be priced at par. Therefore, this bond should behave much like a bond maturing on the put date.

BOND PERFORMANCE PARAMETERS

In this section, we will discuss the parameters that specify the performance of a corporate bond. The values of the parameters are simulated from the model.

The effective duration is simulated by using the pricing model to calculate the percentage change in the bond price with a small parallel shift of the yield curve. The effective duration is influenced by both the OAS and the embedded option. With the OAS widening, the effective duration of a bond would be lowered. This is the result of an increase in the discount rate, which would lead to more emphasis on the nearby cash flow. Hence, the widening of OAS shortens the duration. The embedded call option would also lower the duration.

The convexity of a callable corporate bond can be positive or negative. The bond tends to have positive convexity when the option value is relatively small. On the other hand, if the option value is high, the bond convexity can be negative.

TABLE 12-3
Summary of Bonds

Bond	Description	Size	Price	YTW	Duration	Convexity	Accr.	Total Value
12–6	CS 8/08 14 Callable	10.00	104.00	13.37	0.00	0.0	0.27	10.427
12–6	CS 8/08 Defer 1 Year	10.00	108.46	8.61	0.86	0.0	0.27	10.873
12–5	CS 8/08 Noncallable	10.00	146.06	8.92	8.43	1.1	0.27	14.633
12–7	PP 8/08 14 (accumulated)	10.00	120.69	8.88[a]	3.90	0.2	0.27	12.096
12–7	CS 8/08 14 10% Sink	10.00	120.67	11.33[b]	3.93	0.2	0.27	12.094
12–8	CS 8/08 W/PUT	10.00	146.15	8.91	8.36	1.1	0.27	14.642

[a] Cash flow yield value.
[b] Yield to maturity value.

249

Volatility sensitivity applies only to the option-embedded bonds. For the callable bond, an increase in volatility would increase the option value. As a result, the bond value falls because the callable bond is a Treasury equivalent bond, short a call option. The short position of the option leads to the drop in the bond price.

The time decay of the embedded option also contributes to the performance of the bond. If we hold the bond over a period, the embedded option would lose its time premium. In this case the bond would increase its value. So a bond with significant call option value should provide an expected higher return, assuming all other factors held constant (only time to maturity is changing). Table 12–4 shows some simulated results suggesting the magnitude of these values for a sample of bonds.

SUMMARY

This chapter began with a description of the salient features of corporate bonds. The discussion focused primarily on the investment grade bond,

TABLE 12–4
Performance Parameters for Bonds Callable in One Year

| | | | | | Return Impact[a] | |
| | | | Effective | | Time | |
Bond Type		Price	Duration	Convexity	Decay[b]	Δ Volatility[c]
10-year	9% Noncallable	104.01	6.54	0.6	0	0
	7% Callable	89.74	5.84	−0.3	0	−23
	8% Callable	95.01	4.64	−1.0	0	−32
	9% Callable	98.91	3.04	−1.2	1	−31
	10% Callable	101.22	1.70	−0.5	2	−17
	11% Callable	102.42	0.81	0.	3	− 4
20-year	9% Noncallable	105.64	9.45	1.4	0	0
	7% Callable	84.45	8.07	−0.1	0	−49
	8% Callable	91.88	6.44	−1.1	0	−58
	9% Callable	97.51	4.30	−1.7	1	−54
	10% Callable	100.86	2.19	−1.6	2	−31
	11% Callable	102.35	1.04	−0.5	6	− 9

[a] Basis point return after one week for bonds with embedded short call options.
[b] Time decay: return impact attributable to spot curve equaling forward curve after one week.
[c] Δ volatility: return impact attributable to implied volatility increase of 1 percent.

in that we did not analyze in depth the impact of default risk on the bond. For the investment grade bonds, we discussed how the bond convenants and provisions affect the bond value.

This chapter showed that when the market takes the bond characteristics into the valuation, the bond price behavior can be quite different from the Treasury bonds. To deal with this difference, a framework was developed to analyze these bonds. In particular, a constant mortality model was described to value the default risk. This model led to the discussion of the option-adjusted spreads for a bond. Finally, we incorporated the mortality model into the binomial lattice model to value the default risk and the embedded options in the bonds jointly.

Historical corporate bond prices were used to compare the model results. In particular, we showed how historically the option-adjusted spreads of different rating groups behaved and how the implied volatilities of the corporate bond market tracked the historical volatilities.

In the concluding sections, we demonstrated how the bond models can be used to analyze corporate bonds. They can be used to simulate performance profiles of different types of bonds. These performance profiles are particularly useful in summarizing the bond behavior under interest rate risk. Bond models were also used to determine to performance parameters of an individual bond or portfolio. These performance parameters may be duration, convexity, time decay, and volatility risk.

Later chapters will use the result and the analytical framework described in this chapter to study bond strategies and the other fixed-income portfolio management techniques.

CHAPTER 13

PRICING CONVERTIBLE BONDS

The previous chapter reviewed almost all the major characteristics associated with corporate bonds. This chapter will add another dimension to the discussion of corporate debt instruments. The following sections will introduce and explain the nuances of corporate bonds that include a conversion provision.

INTRODUCTION

The convertible bond market is an important part of the fixed-income sector. The convertible bond offers the holder the option to convert a corporate bond into a specified number of shares of the firm, usually any time up to the maturity of the bond. This feature is in addition to the other features previously discussed in Chapter 12. Briefly restated, these features are:

- The call provision that allows the firm to buy back the bonds at prespecified prices
- The sinking fund requirement that obligates the firm to redeem the bonds over a period of time
- The put option that gives the investor the right to sell the bond back to the firm at a predetermined price

As we had explained, these features often dramatically affect the bond's behavior and value. Although similar to nonconvertible corporate bonds, convertible bonds represent a spectrum of vastly different securities. Because convertibles are hybrids of bonds and stocks, they must inherit all the complexities of the underlying instruments and behave in an often complicated fashion as a mix of two securities. While convertible securities may offer many opportunities for investing and for formulating portfolio strategies, they are also relatively complicated to analyze. Thus, the purpose of this chapter is to provide a basic framework for analyzing these securities given their diverse characteristics. This chapter offers an analytical framework that will enable the bond issuers and investors to deal with these difficulties in a systematic fashion.

We will begin by showing how the complex structure of a convertible may be broken down into five basic components: the underlying bond, the latent warrant, the latent call option, the sinking fund option, and the put option. We will then analyze each component separately. After discussing the value and behavior of each part, we will show how they affect the convertible bond. In so doing, our analytical approach will provide valuable insights into the convertible bond's behavior. We will also demonstrate how the analysis enables us to analyze the fair value of a convertible bond.

THE BASIC FRAMEWORK

This section will describe the basic assumptions of the model. The approach we will take here is the standard framework for studying securities pricing. Since our concern is to derive the fair value of a convertible bond, we will need to consider the determining factors of the bond price in a specific way. As in the previous chapters, we will make the perfect capital market assumptions.

We will ignore all types of transaction costs: the commissions, the bid ask spreads, the issuance costs, and all the explicit costs that are involved in a transaction. The reason is that we are not asking for the price at which an investor can buy or sell a bond. We are asking for the price that the bond should be sold at equilibrium. We, in essence, want to determine the bond price if the market is functioning perfectly (i.e., the fair value).

These assumptions will enable us to focus our discussion on the options aspect of the pricing problem. In this chapter, we will ignore issues such as tax implications of the convertible, marketability of the issues, and corporate strategies. While we recognize that these issues are important to the bond pricing, they are beyond the scope of this chapter.

Our concern is, given the stock price and the investment value, how should a convertible bond be priced in a perfectly functioning market?

In making the above assumptions, we can deal with the main issues most effectively.

An Illustrative Example

There are many terminologies and notations to describe a convertible bond. We will discuss them by examining a particular bond. The example we use is Corroon and Black (CBL), 7.5, June 1, 2005. The bond holder can convert each $100 face value bond into 3.5714 Corroon and Black shares any time up till the maturity. (For the purposes of this chapter, we will use $100 face amount denominations and the associated conversion values instead of the commonly used $1000 denomination). The issuer can call back the bond at 107.5 percent of par in year 1985. The call schedule then decreases linearly to 100 percent in 1994 and remains on that level till maturity. However, the firm cannot call the bonds before June 1, 1987 unless the common stock trades above 140 percent (the call trigger) of the conversion price at the time of call. The bond also has a sinking fund. The firm is obligated to retire 7.5 percent of the amount issued each of the years 1995 through 2004.

On November 15, 1986, the stock was traded at $35/share and the bond was $131. The stock at that time was paying $0.65 dividend/share. The credit risk of the bond is given by the Moody's rating of A2. Now we summarize the information below with the notations of each item given in the first column.

Corroon and Black (CBL)

T	= the bond maturity	6/1/2005
c	= the bond coupon rate	7.5%
k	= the conversion ratio	3.5714
t	= the call trigger	140%
B	= the market bond price	$131
S	= the market stock price	$35
d	= the dividend	$0.65
R	= the rating	Moody's A2

Given this information, we next calculate some other parameters.

$$P = \text{parity (conversion value)}$$

The parity, or conversion value, is the value of the bond if the holder decides to convert. It is, therefore, the equity worth of the convertible bond. The share price per se is not important. More important is the parity. The parity is the product of the conversion ratio and the share price.

$$P = kS \text{ or } (3.5714 \times 35) = \$124.99$$

The conversion price, Cp, is the price of a share such that the parity value is $100. That is,

$$100 = k\text{Cp}$$

In this case, Cp equals $28/share.

The investment value (I) is the value of the bond, ignoring the possibility of converting the bond to equity. The investment value is therefore the underlying bond value given by the present value of the bond cash flow (coupons and principal) adjusted for the credit risk, the sinking fund provision, and other bond related features.

Basics of the Convertible Bond

The convertible offers the investor the upside return when the common stock value increases. This is possible because, when the stock value becomes high, the investor can always convert the bond to equity. But that does not mean that the investor must convert to capture the price appreciation of the equity. When the parity value is high, the convertible would trade like equity, and the convertible bond value would appreciate in step with the stock price.

If the stock value drops, the investor at worst would still receive the coupons and principal. That is, the investor still holds the bond or has the investment value. As a result, the downside risk of the investment is protected.

In short, the convertible offers the upside return and protects the investor from the downside risk. The investor, in essence, is holding a straight bond and a warrant. A warrant is an instrument that provides the holder with the right to purchase a prespecified number of shares of stock at a specific price. Although this is a useful way of thinking about a convertible, it does not accurately describe most of the convertible bonds traded in the U.S. market.

We will show later that, for most bonds, the investors are expected to be forced to convert to stocks in a relatively short time period. For this reason, it is more appropriate to think of the convertible bond as the parity value (the equity value) plus the present value of the coupons net of the present value of the dividends that the investor can receive before being forced to convert. This alternative way of viewing a convertible bond can significantly affect the analysis of the bonds.

The above description of a convertible bond is incomplete because the estimate of the inflow of coupons net of dividends is inadequate to describe the option-like feature of the bond. When the firm decides to force the bondholders to convert the bond to equity, it is the option of the firm, and such an option must be priced. This chapter will deal with the formal analysis of this and other option aspects of the problem.

THE BOND MODELS

In this section, we will present models of the convertible bonds. We begin with the simplest possible model that captures the essential features of the convertible, and we then gradually incorporate other features of the bond until we finally have a model that can adequately describe the bond behavior.

The Latent Warrant

First let us consider the simplified version of the CBL bond. Let us assume that the bond has no call or sinking fund provisions and has no credit risk. For the time being, we will even assume that the bond pays no coupon, and the stock gives no dividends. In this simple case, we would like to determine the fair value of the bond.

The important observation one should make here is that, although the bondholder can convert the bond to stocks any time up till the maturity, there are no economic incentives to do so. The argument is quite simple. If the investor converts the bond, then at maturity time the investor would have the prevailing value of the parity value. On the other hand, if the investor holds the bond till maturity, the bond can always be converted whenever it is beneficial to do so. Indeed when the parity value is above the bond value, the bondholder would convert. That is, the bondholder basically has the stock return but is also guaranteed to have the minimum value of the bond par value (investment value). For this reason, it is always advantageous to hold the bond till maturity because there is value to retain the option of converting. Even if the parity value is high and the convertible bond is traded like equity, the convertible bond still offers the protection of the downside risk. Once the conversion is effected, the downside protection would be eliminated.

Recognizing that there is no value to the early exercise, we can now simply focus our attention on what the investor would optimally do at maturity. As we've discussed, when the parity is above par, the investor would give up the principal and receive the shares. But that is precisely the same as receiving the principal and using the amount to exercise a warrant. In sum, the convertible bond is the same as the basic bond plus a warrant, where the exercise price of the bond is par value and the expiration date is the bond's maturity. This warrant is called the *latent warrant*.

To illustrate the latent warrant, we refer to our example of the CBL bond. It essentially has a warrant that gives the holder the right, but not the obligation, to buy 3.5714 shares on 6/1/2005 for $100. Therefore, the latent warrant is a long-term American option.

Coupon and Dividends

So far, our analysis assumes that there are no coupon and dividends. But that assumption is made for the clarity of exposition, and relaxing the assumption affects little of the analysis. The crux of the argument is to recognize whether or not the warrant would be exercised early. When the bond pays coupons, there would even be less of an incentive to exercise early because, in holding onto the bond, one receives all the coupons in addition to retaining the option to the last minute. We must note that we have ignored the dividends on the stock. In fact, if the investor converts the bond to equity, the investor would receive the stock dividend. But it is clear that as long as the coupons payments are higher than the dividends, the warrant would not be exercised early. Luckily, most convertible bonds pay coupons that yield significantly more than the dividends on the stock. For this reason, our arguments apply for nearly all convertible bonds. For example, in the case of CBL, the annual dividends on the parity is given by the product of the conversion ratio and the dividends ($0.65 \times 3.5714 = $2.3214). As we see, it is significantly less than the $7.50 earned on each $100 par bond. Note that we have ignored the growth rate of the dividend/share for illustrative reasons.

As the investor holds the bond till maturity, the convertible bond value should be equal to the consolidated investment value of the under-

lying bond plus the latent warrant. We will denote the latent warrant by
W. Now we have a simple formula.

$$B = I + W \tag{13-1}$$

It is instructive to represent the convertible bond value diagrammatically.
Such a diagram is called the *value diagram*.

The Value Diagram

The value diagram is a graphic representation of the security's value as
a function of the parity value at any time before the bond's maturity.
In other words, we can show how the underlying bond value, latent
warrant, the convertible bond, and other related instruments change their
values as the parity value varies.

On the value diagram, the *y*-axis is the value of any instrument,
and the unit of measure is in dollars. The *x*-axis is the parity value and
is also in dollars. First, we represent the underlying bond curve. This
curve is the investment value of the bond. When the parity is high (stock
value is high), presumably the bond would have little credit risk, and
for this reason the curve should be flat, taking the value of the present
value of the coupons and principal. However, when the parity is low,
the share value has dropped, reflecting a drop in the firm value. In this
case, the bond credit risk would increase and the bond value would drop.
The bond curve in Figure 13-1 depicts the behavior of this bond. The
45 degree line through the origin is called the *parity line*. It represents
the convertible bond value at the instant that the bond is converted to
equity (conversion value).

Note that the investor always converts when it is advantageous to
do so. Since it is never advantageous for the bondholders to convert
the bond early, the convertible bond fair value must lie above both the
underlying investment value and the parity value. For this reason, the
curve that is the higher of the bond curve and the parity line represents
the formula prices. The formula prices are the lower bound of the values
of the convertible bond. Turining our attention to the latent warrant, the
formula value of the warrant is the higher of the following two lines:
the 45 degree line starting from the exercise price (par value) and the
horizontal line on the *x*-axis from the origin to the par value. The formula
price curve represents the minimum value of the warrant.

FIGURE 13–1
Bond Curve and Parity Line

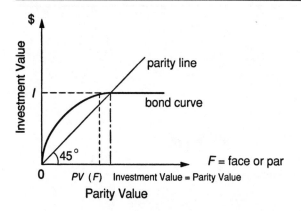

Standard option theory shows that the minimum warrant value is in fact the 45 degree line that intersects the *x*-axis at the present value of the exercise price, or the present value of the par value in our case. Given this argument, we can sketch the warrant curve in Figure 13–2.

Now, the convertible bond is the sum of the bond curve and the warrant curve. It is represented in Figure 13–3, where the curve XY represents the convertible bond value. Figure 13–3 also depicts the composition of the convertible bond value. The line OA is the parity line. However, when the parity value is high, the convertible bond value does not converge to the parity line. Instead the convertible bond value converges to the parallel line of DE. The distance of point D from the *y*-axis (the distance is the same as OB) is the present value of the face value of the bond. Since the bond value, or the investment value, is the sum of the present value of the face value and the coupon value, it follows that the distance between the parity value and the line DE is the present value of the coupon (see shaded area in Figure 13–3). We can conclude that the convertible bond value must exceed the higher of the investment value or the sum of the parity value and the present value of the coupons. The level of excess is the term premium of the latent warrant. This excess is the cost to the convertible bondholder for having a position that participates on any upside return of the stock and is limited on the downside to the investment value of the bond.

FIGURE 13–2
Warrant Curve

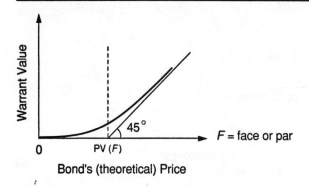

Bond's (theoretical) Price

FIGURE 13–3
Composition of the Convertible Bond Value

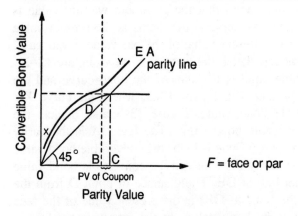

Parity Value

Since the latent warrant is a long-term stock option, this excess value is very sensitive to the estimate of the stock return volatility. Unfortunately, the stock return volatility is not observable (as a price is observable). As a result, the market has to determine the precise value of the term premium, and convertible bond models can only provide relatively rough estimates of fair value.

Thus far, we have ignored any stock dividends. If there is any dividend on the stock, we need only alter the discussion by considering the present value of the coupon net of the dividends, instead of just the coupon. Many analyses of convertible bonds tend to focus on the latent warrant value. Unfortunately, this analysis is far from complete. As in the case of straight corporate bonds, the call provision must be taken into account in analyzing the convertible bond value.

First, we want to estimate the minimal value of the warrant, which can be achieved by assuming that there is no early exercise of the dividend-paying stock. Then the option value is greater than the stock value (parity) net of both the present value of the stock dividends that the option holder will not receive and the present value of the strike price. In the case of the convertible bond in the earlier example, for which we will assume a 7 percent discount rate, the present value of the strike price over 19 years is $27.65. Assuming constant dividends (a conservative estimate) of $2.3214 per year, the present value of all the dividends in the next 19 years is the product of $2.3214 and the present value annuity factor at 7 percent for 19 years. The value is $26.3144. Therefore the warrant value should exceed $71.025 ($124.99 − $27.65 − $26.3144).

Now we can estimate the investment value of the bond. We have shown that the investment value of the bond cannot be greater than the convertible bond traded price net of the lower bound value of the warrant. Hence the investment value cannot exceed $59.975 ($131 − $71.025).

We will now address another aspect of the convertible bond's price, the call feature.

The Call Feature

The call provisions on convertible bonds are quite homogeneous and in many ways similar to industrial corporate bonds' call provisions. The call provision allows the issuer to call back the bonds in part or in whole at the prespecified price, or the call price. The call schedule tends to decline linearly, reaching the lowest call price, or the par value, some time before the maturity. But the similarities between the call provisions in the convertibles and the corporates end here.

Although the convertible bond call provision also has a call protection period, it is implemented differently. Most convertible bonds issued after 1985 have a call trigger price stated typically in percentages (140%, as in the case of CBL). In these cases, the firm cannot call the bond unless the common stock is traded above the product of the call trigger price and the conversion price. This restriction of calling the bonds applies only for a period of time, typically two to three years. After this call protection period, the firm can call the bonds whenever it is advantageous to the issuer. But that does not mean that the firm would call the bonds when traded slightly above the call price.

In fact, for bonds with a coupon rate similar to those of the current new issues, the firms in general would only call the bonds when they are traded 20 to 25 percent above the call price. There are many arguments put forward to explain this observation. For example, when the bond is called, the investor has one month to decide whether to convert the bond into stock or surrender it for cash based on the call price.

If it cannot be sure whether the investors will decide on cash or shares, the firm must prepare to issue the shares as well as to pay cash. This scenario may create administrative complications. However, if the firm waits until the market price of the stock reaches a level that would make it obviously more advantageous to convert rather than to accept cash, then the firm would call its bonds. In line with this reasoning, the firm would have to decide that, over the one month period, there would be a small probability that the stock price would drop to a level causing investors to change their minds and select cash.

Notice here that the calling of the bond is motivated by the rise in the parity value. There is also another reason; it may be an optimal call period. As we discused in Chapter 12, if market interest rates have fallen significantly, then the firm may call the bond to refinance the issue at a lower interest cost. In this case, there is no need to consider the complexities involved in forced conversion. The firm may call the bond because it is economically optimal.

We do not intend to dwell on this issue. But we should note that the convertible bonds are usually called when the bonds are traded significantly above the call price for whatever reason.

When the bond is called, the parity value must be high; otherwise the bond would not be traded at such a high premium. For this reason, the investors would always prefer to convert into equity than to receive that call price. This calling of bonds is called the *forced conversion*, perhaps the most important aspect of the call provision of the convertibles. The provision is used by the firm to force the bondholders to convert the bond into equity.

This forced conversion feature significantly affects the pricing of the convertible. Suppose there is a market consensus that when the convertible bond trades above a price, called the *implicit call price* (ic), the bond would be called. We should also note that the more volatile the stock, the higher this implicit call price would be. So following from our previous discussion, the spread between the implicit call price and the stated call price will depend on the stock return volatility.

No investor would pay a price higher than the implicit call price, no matter how high the parity value rises. If we refer to the value diagram, we see that when the convertible bond rises in step with the higher parity value, it must rise at a slower rate as the value approaches the implicit call price. When the bond value reaches the implicit call price, the bond price must be the parity value because the investor should be indifferent about whether to hold the bond or to convert to equity. Referring to Figures 13–3 and 13–4, we see how the call provision affects the bond values.

In Figure 13–4, we see that the convertible bond value must be capped by the implicit call price. As the parity value rises, the convertible bond value rises in step. But as the convertible bond value approaches the implicit call price, the market will anticipate the firm's calling the bond, and the bondholders would convert the bonds to the parity value. For this reason, the market still trades the bond at the parity value. Figure 13–4 depicts this relationship between the parity value and the convertible bond value.

FIGURE 13-4
Effect of the Implicit Call Price

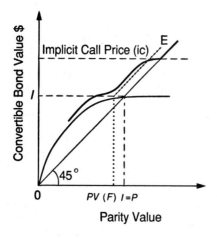

Parity Value

The Latent Call Option

The forced conversion of the bond introduces another option built into the convertible bond. We call this feature the *latent call option*. We will denote this option by C. This time, the issuer decides the optimal exercise of the option. In exercising the option, the issuer forces the bondholders to convert the bond to equity. In so doing, the firm saves the present value of the coupons in the subsequent years. If the convertible bond value does not rise above the implicit call price, the firm would not call the bond, and the call option has little value. Therefore, the latent call option is valuable to the firm for saving the interest costs.

The most striking feature of the latent call option is that the option pricing behavior has to be significantly different than the stock option. The major difference is that no matter how high the underlying asset value (in this case, the convertible bond value), the value of the option is capped. It does not rise unbounded as in the case of the stock option because the latent call option allows the firm to save the interest cost, which has a maximum value.

In the presence of the call provision, the convertible bond has three components. The pricing formula is given below.

$$B = I + W - C \tag{13–2}$$

The impact of the call option on the convertible bond price is best illustrated by the example of the CBL bond again.

From Equation 2, we see that

$$C = I + W - B \tag{13–3}$$

But we have argued earlier that the warrant value must exceed the parity value net of the present value of the dividends and the present value of par. Hence, we have $C > I + P - \mathrm{PV}(d) - \mathrm{PV}(\mathrm{par}) - B$. But by definition, $I = \mathrm{PV}(c) + \mathrm{PV}(\mathrm{par})$. Hence, we get

$$C > P + \mathrm{PV}(c) - \mathrm{PV}(d) - B \tag{13–4}$$

Here, P is the parity value, $\mathrm{PV}(c)$ the present value of the coupons out to the bond maturity, $\mathrm{PV}(d)$ the present value of the dividends out to the bond maturity, and $\mathrm{PV}(\mathrm{par})$ the present value of par.

Now we can estimate the numbers for B, P, c, d, and $\mathrm{PV}(\mathrm{par})$. B is $131. P is $124.99. Let us assume 7 percent discount rate (the prevailing ten-year rate) and a conservative estimate of a constant dividend of \$2.3214 per year. The present value of the annuity of the coupon net of the dividends over nineteen years is \$58.696 (the present value annuity factor is 11.3343). Therefore, using Equation 13–4, the latent call option has a value of more than \$52.686.

In the presence of the call provision, investors no longer believe that they will be able to hold the bond till maturity, as we argued previously. They expect that they will be forced to convert. Therefore, the convertible bond price is not the sum of the parity and the present value of all the coupons. In the presence of the call provision, it will be the sum of the parity and the present value of the coupons up till the time of forced conversion. We can use this line of argument to calculate the expected time that the bond would be forced to convert. Let the time be b years. The present value of the coupons and dividends in b years is PV(coupons) and PV(d). The bond value is B and the parity value is P.

So by the above argument, we see that the following equation must hold.

$$B = P + \text{PV(coupons)} - \text{PV}(d) \qquad (13-5)$$

Using Equation 13–3 and the time b, it is relatively straightforward to calculate that the market expects the bond to be called. Notice that this is precisely the break-even analysis often used by convertible investors. Although this approach seems tractable and useful, we are making several assumptions. Indeed, Equation 13–3 can be derived from Equation 13–2 if several assumptions are made. First, the latent warrant is traded sufficiently in-the-money that its value is approximated by the formula price of P − PV(strike price). Noting that the strike price is the par value, we can write,

$$W = P - \text{PV(par value)} \qquad (13-6)$$

Also if the premium of the latent call option is neglible (the market is quite certain about when the firm will call the bonds), then C (option value) is the present value of the coupons not paid to the investors.

$$C = \text{PV(coupon after } b) \qquad (13-7)$$

Combining Equations 13–3, 13–6, and 13–7, we get Equation 13–5.

The above analysis shows that if we use the break-even analysis to determine the expected time of forced conversion, we must be willing to assume that the warrant is very much in-the-money and the volatility of the latent call option is negligible.

THE PREMIUM DIAGRAM

Let us consider two polar cases. When the stock prices are high so that the parity value is significantly higher than the investment value, the market should anticipate a forced conversion. For this reason, the convertible bond should be traded very near the parity value. On the other hand, when the stock value drops significantly so that the bondholder does not expect to convert the bond to equity, then the convertible bond would trade near its investment value. These two polar cases of the convertible bond's performance are relatively straightforward.

Of course, the important part of pricing the convertible bonds occurs when the parity value is close to the investment .value. In this region, the convertible bond value is greatly influenced by the latent warrant value and the latent call value; therefore the convertible bond value is no longer a simple relationship to the parity and investment value. Pricing the convertible bond value in this case requires the modeling of the warrant value and the call option value.

We can gain much insight into the bond behavior if we analyze the fair value of the bond in the premium diagram, which is derived from the value diagram. While the value diagram is concerned with the absolute value of the bond, the premium diagram is concerned with the parity value and the convertible bond value as percentages to the investment's value (ratio). This way, the premium diagram focuses on the region where the parity value is close to the investment value. Also, by normalizing the convertible bond values around the investment value, we can cross compare different convertible bond pricing behaviors. Figure 13–5 provides a summary depiction.

Specifically, the x axis of the premium diagram is defined as the ratio of the parity value and the investment value. For example, when the x value is unity, the parity value is the same as the investment value. The y axis of the premium diagram is the ratio of the convertible bond value to the investment value. In essence, the premium diagram depicts the relationship between the convertible bond value and the parity value, normalized by the investment value of the bond.

The Intrinsic Value

We can derive the premium diagram from Figure 13–4. The striking result is that the premium seems to represent a call option, as the

FIGURE 13–5
Premium Diagram

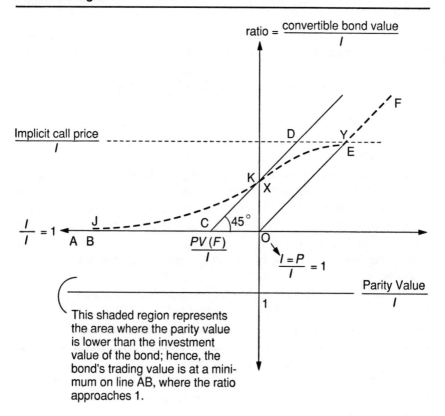

This shaded region represents the area where the parity value is lower than the investment value of the bond; hence, the bond's trading value is at a minimum on line AB, where the ratio approaches 1.

normalized convertible bond value rises monotonically from 0 to a 45 degree line. Perhaps this is the source of confusion in defining the latent warrant because the value curve looks somewhat similar to a warrant value curve. But as the analysis has shown, this curve is really representing two options. And this curve is not specified by the standard option parameters: expiration date, exercise price, volatility.

To illustrate this point, it is instructive to consider a special but somewhat unrealistic case. Assume that there is no stock return uncertainty. And for simplicity, we will assume that the stock does not pay any dividend. To be consistent with the no arbitrage argument, the stock must appreciate at a risk-free rate, which we will also assume to be known with certainty. Now let us construct the premium diagram of the convertible bond.

We can analyze the bond behavior in four regions. First, when the parity value is low, the bond-to-the-investment-value ratio is unity; therefore, the value curve is depicted by AB in Figure 13–5. Point C is the present value of the exercise price of the latent warrant (divided by the investment value). When the parity ratio goes beyond point C, the bondholder is expected to convert the bond to equity at the bond maturity. That is, the convertible bond must now incorporate the intrinsic value of the latent warrant value. For this reason, the value curve must increase along the 45 degree line, depicted by line CD.

As the parity ratio increases, the value curve also increases in step. But the value curve cannot go beyond the implicit call price. Indeed, when the bond value reaches the call price, the bond price would remain at the value even if the parity value continued to increase. This behavior of the bond is depicted by the line DE, which represents the case when the call option has value to the issuer. In this case, the issuer can call back the bonds and thus can eliminate the ability of the bondholder to collect the coupons on the bond and to convert the bond to equity at maturity.

Finally, let us remember that the convertible bond cannot be traded below the parity value. Therefore, when the line DE meets the parity line, the convertible bond would trade at parity. The explanation is quite simple. When the parity value is sufficiently high, the bond would simply be traded at the parity anticipation of a forced conversion. When the firm calls the bond, the bondholder simply converts the bonds to equity without losing any value. For this region, the bond curve is represented by the line EF.

The piecewise linear graph ABCDEF represents the intrinsic value of the convertible bond. To construct the intrinsic-value graph, we need the (estimated) value of the parity, present value of the warrant exercise price, the investment value, and the call price (or implicit call price). The important point is that all these parameters, in principle, can be measured, so the intrinsic-value graph can be constructed without developing complex mathematical models.

The Fair Value

The intrinsic value of the convertible bond is derived by assuming no uncertainty. In the presence of uncertainty, the convertible bond fair-value curve would deviate from this intrinsic-value graph. It would be a smooth curve because it is reasonable to assume that the uncertainty is resolved in a continuous and smooth manner. For this reason, the convertible bond value must relate to the parity value in a smooth fashion.

Such a fair-value curve is depicted in Figure 13–5 by XY. The curve must originate from point F because, under uncertainty, the bond would be called when it reaches the implicit call price; at this point, the bond must be worth only the parity value. As the parity value drops, the bond value must drop because, in the world of uncertainty, the bond value can be at most the implicit call price. Meanwhile, if the parity value drops significantly to the region CD, the bond value will also drop. For this reason, the bond value will have to come down, instead of remaining at the call price as in the certainty case.

On the other hand, consider the region OA. In this instance, the minimum value of the bond is the investment value. But if the parity value increases substantially, the bond will also incorporate the warrant intrinsic value. For this reason, the bond would trade above the investment value. This resulting fair-value curve is depicted by JK. The complete fair-value curve must link curves XY and JK smoothly, as depicted by YJ.

The precise fair-value curve is determined by the level of the stock-return uncertainty: the higher the uncertainty, the smaller the curvature of the fair-value graph. But in any case, the intrinsic-value graph provides a valuable frame of reference for pricing or analyzing a convertible bond. Also, what is clear from this analysis is that the convertible bond fair-value curve is not a simple option-value curve. It is a curve that is perturbed from the graph OF in that it is a combination of the latent warrant and the latent call option. Analysis that focuses on either the warrant value or the call option value (by using the break-even analysis) is misleading. The two aspects of the problem have to be studied together, and the convertible bond intrinsic-value graph provides such a framework.

SUMMARY

This chapter provided a framework for ascertaining a convertible bond's fair value. Here we have shown that, for most convertible bonds traded in the market, the bond value incorporates both the warrant and call option values. We have shown that, by constructing a graph depicting the intrinsic value of the convertible bond under different stock values, we have enhanced our capability of identifying and analyzing the effects of the warrant and call options.

CHAPTER 14

BOND ANALYSES AND STRATEGIES

Evaluating a bond value is central to portfolio management, bond sales, and trading. In previous chapters we have discussed the determinants of a bond value and described the bond-pricing models. This chapter describes a procedure using bond-pricing models to evaluate a bond's component values. We then show how bond-pricing models can be used to analyze bonds from the perspective of a risk-and-return profile that is useful for cross-comparisons.

These basic techniques are then extended to the portfolio context. A model can be used to establish a proper analytical framework: *proper* meaning to identify the range of returns obtainable by the portfolio without violating the risk minimization constraints.

Last, but not least, this chapter will discuss the construction of some portfolio strategies. This section synthesizes many of the techniques described in previous chapters.

ANALYZING A BOND

Analyzing a bond is a two-part process. The first part can be thought of as taking a snapshot of the inherent relative values of each component at a specific point in time and under the present economic environment. The purpose of this part of the procedure is to determine the security's fair, or theoretical, value. Another aspect of this step is establishing the relative significance of each value using the perspective of historical occurrences.

The next part requires submitting the security to horizon analysis, which implicitly requires subjective assessments. Horizon analysis allows one to extract not only the probable range of returns, but also the probable changes in risk exposure.

Component Identification for Assessing the Fair Value of a Bond

The value attribution approach, recognizing that a value is simply the sum of its parts, dissects the market value. We will decompose the bond price into four components: the Treasury equivalent value, the option value, the credit/liquidity premium value, and the cheap/rich value. This approach requires the use of bond models.

Bond models are an integral part of the value attribution process. Specifically, a model derives the implied spot curve, which is subsequently used to discount the promised cash flow of the bond, determining the Treasury equivalent price, denoted by $P(\text{TSY})$. Using the market prices of the bonds in a bellwether portfolio, we can use a pricing model to determine the price of the (equivalent) straight bond with the appropriate credit/liquidity spread, denoted by $P(\text{st})$. Lastly, the bond-pricing model calculates the bond price, taking all the bond features (i.e., embedded options) into account; we call this the fair price, denoted by P.

Using these prices, we can now decompose the observed price, $P(\text{obs})$, into its components. The first component is the cheap/rich value (c/r), defined as the observed price net of the fair price (theoretical price).

$$c/r = P(\text{obs}) - P$$

When the cheap/rich value is positive, the bond is trading above its fair value. Conversely, if the cheap/rich value is negative, the bond is trading below its fair value.

The second component is the credit/liquidity value, c/l, which is defined as the Treasury equivalent value net of the straight bond price.

$$c/l = P(\text{TSY}) - P(\text{st})$$

The third component is the option value, O, which is defined as the straight bond price net of the fair price.

$$O = P(\text{st}) - P$$

From these definitions, we can see that the observed price is in fact the Treasury equivalent price plus the cheap/rich value net of both the credit/liquidity value and the option value.

$$P(\text{obs}) = P(\text{TSY}) - c/l - O + c/r$$

This decomposition enables us to analyze the bond's value by evaluating each of its components. We will start with the cheap/rich value.

Cheap/Rich Analysis

The cheap/rich value is the only component that is bond-specific. It measures how the bond is traded away from the other benchmark bonds that the pricing model uses. When the traded price deviates from the fair price, the discrepancy is not being captured by other market factors that are taken into consideration by the bellwether portfolio. If the cheap/rich value is positive, we say the bond is traded rich; if the value is negative, the bond is traded cheap.

There are two main reasons for a bond to be traded cheap or rich. First, the bond may be "mispriced." At first glance, the concept of a bond being "mispriced" is somewhat curious. After all, the traded price is the only price at which the bond can be traded, so there is no other market or trade that anyone can use to exploit the "mispricing." However, in this context, "the bond is mispriced" has a clear interpretation. If a bond is traded rich, and if one can construct a portfolio of fairly priced bonds such that the portfolio has the attributes identical to the rich bond's, then the portfolio's value should be less than the rich bond's. Price deviations can be caused by any liquidity change or supply/demand imbalance in the market that may be affecting a particular bond.

Bonds trading cheap or rich can highlight the existence of other factors not captured by the bond model. For example, we have seen in Chapter 9 that on-the-run Treasury issues are very often traded rich. The richness is attributable to the fact that the spot-curve-estimation methodology does not take the on-the-run premium into account.

The cheap/rich value should not be used for a simple trading rule: buy when a bond is cheap and sell when the bond is rich. Rather, the cheap/rich value should be used as a guide for screening bonds. When a bond is identified as having a significant cheap/rich level, a two-step analytical procedure should be implemented. The first step should entail investigating whether there are any factors that can explain the price discrepancy. Included in this step is an evaluation of whether the discrepancy will be eliminated over a certain time period. This naturally leads to the second step, preparing a time-trend analysis of cheap/rich values. This step requires a history of quoted prices in order to determine whether the cheapness/richness is an anomaly or falls within a particular pattern.

Suppose the analysis suggests that a bond is cheap and that the price discrepancy will disappear over a holding period of one week. The purchase of the bond does not necessarily ensure a positive excess return over the holding period. The bond will, however, have a higher return than that of a portfolio of fairly priced bonds with attributes that are identical to the bond's.

Credit/Liquidity Value

The credit/liquidity value of the bond measures the portion of the bond's value attributable to the sector's credit risk and liquidity. Treasury bonds, of course, will have no credit/liquidity value. Conversely, a low-rating corporate bond will have significant value. The identification of this value, which is tied into the bond's price, is extremely useful for ascertaining whether the instrument is trading within the bounds of the market price for credit/liquidity risk. If we determine that the credit/liquidity value contributes significantly to the bond value, we have to pursue further the analysis on the market option-adjusted spread (OAS).

A bellwether portfolio is used for estimating the market OAS for a particular sector the bond belongs to. Therefore, we have to analyze the estimated value of the market OAS. Similarly to cheap/rich analysis, a time-trend study of market OAS could be helpful. In a time-trend analysis, narrowing OASs signify higher holding-period returns than originally expected; the security's traded yield spread to the implied spot curve is collapsing. Alternatively, widening OAS values generate lower holding-period returns.

Option Value

Option value represents the dollar value or yield value (in basis points) associated with the embedded option component. For instance, the issuer of callable bonds has the benefit of exercising an option, and this benefit is offset by the extra yield offered to an investor for buying this bond instead of straight bond. For this reason, we must bear in mind that the option value measures the issuer's option value. In the case where the bond has both put and call options, the option value measures the net option value to the issuer.

By the definition of option value, it is unfortunate that the option value can be negative. This is the case when the bond is a putable bond, or more generally when it is the investor's option. If the investor has the option, it is offset by providing the issuer the funds at lower "cost," or lower yield, relative to a straight bond.

The most important factor about the embedded option value is that the value is sensitive to the market interest rate volatility. The value of the embedded option by definition is determined by the implied volatility of the market. Therefore, as discussed in Chapter 12, the option is priced relative to the value of the embedded options in the bellwether portfolio. When such is the case, what do we mean when we say that the options are overpriced or underpriced?

If there are reasons to believe that the implied volatility of the market will rise, option value will rise. If we anticipate this outcome, we should not purchase a bond with significant option value. Similarly, if the implied volatility is expected to fall, the purchase of the bond with high embedded option value is desirable. However, this analysis once again assumes other factors are of no concern to the investor or are held constant. This option value aspect of an analysis should not be overlooked. For example, embedded options affect the bond's duration, so buying and selling option-embedded bonds will lead to changes in the portfolio's duration.

Treasury Equivalent Value
Treasury equivalent value represents the risk-free value of the underlying cash flow, assuming the issue was a single straight bond. In most cases, this is by far the most important component that explains the bond value. Any analysis of this component of bond value is equivalent to the analysis of the spot curve. We shall defer this discussion to Chapter 15, where we introduce and discuss key rate durations.

Sensitivity Analysis for Components

This section will discuss assessing a security based on the aforementioned four aspects of value. We will start by analyzing an AA industrial bond as of August 22, 1989. Here are the relevant characteristics of the issue.

Cusip	Description	Observed Price	YTM	Effective Duration	Convexity
263534AD	Du Pont E I 8.5% 5/01/06	94.875	9.1% [a]	6.085	−.703

Additional Information: The bond's call price changesd linearly over time, ocurring every May 1st. Since 5/1/89, the bond is callable at 104.08. On 5/1/90 the new call price will be 103.740. The call price is finally par starting on 5/1/05. On August 22, 1989, the call-option was far out of the money. Therefore, the bond was trading to its yield to maturity and not to its yield to call.

MacDur = 8.770   Modified MacCaulay Dur = 8.389

[a] On August 22, 1989, the call option was far out-of-the money. Therefore, the bond was trading to its yield to maturity and not its yield to call.

The analytical system we used suggested the bond had the following cheap/rich characteristics.

Observed Price	Cheap/Rich ($)	Optional Value ($)	Credit Spread ($)	Treasury Equivalent Price
94.88	0.40	−3.25	−2.96	100.69

We first review the historical OASs of a bellwether portfolio of AA bonds in order to determine the magnitude of previous changes. Figure 14–1 depicts the OAS for AA industrial securities since December 1988 as well a 15-day moving average.

Similarly, for the embedded option, we review the historical record of the implied volatilities of the spot curve. The current implied volatility is associated with the existing bond's option value. We can compare this volatility level to a prior period's or to a current view of the appropriate volatility level. Figure 14–2 shows the implied volatility of the 10-year spot rate as estimated from the bellwether portfolio of corporate bonds.

FIGURE 14–1
OAS for Industrial Securities, December 1988 to August 1989, 15-Day
Moving Average

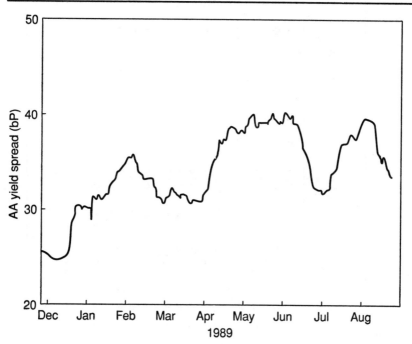

If we wanted to formalize the relative value relationships, we could construct 90 percent confidence levels to ensure that there were a sufficient number of historical observations for determining whether the current OAS or implied volatility value is beyond two standard deviations from its mean value.

Finally, all of the above analyses could be represented as a series of yield value equivalents for the various components. Table 14–1 shows how an existing YTM can be constructed from the Treasury equivalent yield, the option value yield component, the option-adjusted spread component, and the cheap/rich component. Various bonds are analyzed accordingly as of August 22, 1989. You may note that the issues with deep in-the-money option values are traded as if they will be called on their first call date; their YTW will be significantly different than their YTM.

TABLE 14–1
Option-adjusted Spread Attribution Report for Example Bond

No.	CUSIP	Description	Maturity Date	Coupon	Sect	Qual.	Price	YTW	Obsrvd = YTM%	Chp/ Rch + (bp)	Opt Val + (bp)	Cred Sprd + (bp)	Tsy Eq YTM (%)	Size	Mkt Val
1	912794TH	TL 12/14/90 0%	12/14/89	0.000	TSY	TSY	97.52	8.14	8.14	-13.25	0.00	0.00	8.27	10.00	9.752
2	912827SZ	TN 2/91 9.125%	02/15/91	9.125	TSY	TSY	100.78	8.55	8.55	5.83	0.00	0.00	8.49	2.00	2.019
3	912827ME	TN 8/91 14.875%	08/15/91	14.875	TSY	TSY	112.44	7.96	7.96	-49.17	0.00	0.00	8.45	15.00	16.908
4	912810BU	TC 5/05 8.250%	05/15/05	8.250	TSY	TSY	98.75	8.39	8.39	-4.02	1.16	0.00	8.42	3.00	3.029
5	912810ED	TB 8/19 8.125%	08/15/19	8.125	TSY	TSY	98.15	8.29	8.29	0.00	0.00	0.00	8.29	10.00	9.831
6	011830RF	ALASKA ST HSG F	06/01/99	16.250	INDL	A	104.00	13.60	15.43	0.00	629.16	77.98	8.36	30.00	32.297
7	025818BK	American Expres	04/15/91	8.125	FINL	AA	98.71	8.97	8.97	0.00	0.00	51.48	8.46	15.00	15.236
8	030177AU	AMERICAN TEL &	05/01/99	4.375	TELE	AA	70.79	8.94	8.94	0.00	0.00	54.20	8.40	60.00	43.281
9	031904AB	AMOCO CO	06/01/91	14.000	OIL	AAA	100.00	13.96	13.96	0.00	550.11	17.96	8.28	10.00	10.315
10	078167AU	BELL TEL CO PA	01/15/19	9.250	TELE	AA	100.00	9.25	9.25	-24.02	63.73	54.05	8.31	25.00	25.238
11	121897WM	Burlington Nort	08/15/15	11.625	INDL	BBB	110.23	10.30	10.47	0.00	87.80	122.63	8.37	20.00	22.092
12	149123AW	Caterpillar	06/01/19	9.750	INDL	A-	100.93	9.64	9.65	0.00	42.33	92.41	8.30	5.00	5.156
13	171205CH	Chrysler Financ	01/15/93	8.750	FINL	BBB	97.48	9.63	9.63	0.00	0.00	121.95	8.41	0.00	0.000
14	173034AG	CITICORP	07/01/07	8.125 TSY	FINL	AA	90.25	9.25	9.25	3.14	28.64	50.94	8.42	30.00	27.420
15	263634AD	DU PONT E I DE	05/01/06	8.500 TSY	INDL	AA	94.88	9.10	9.10[a]	-4.92	39.01[b]	33.90[c]	8.42	100.0	97.496

[a]9.10 percent = (842 + 3390 + 39.01 − 4.92)/100.
[b]This number was obtained from the AR model, which requires the input of the volatility number shown in Figure 14–2.
[c]From Figure 14–1.

FIGURE 14–2
Implied Volatility of 10-Year Spot Rate from Bellwether Portfolio

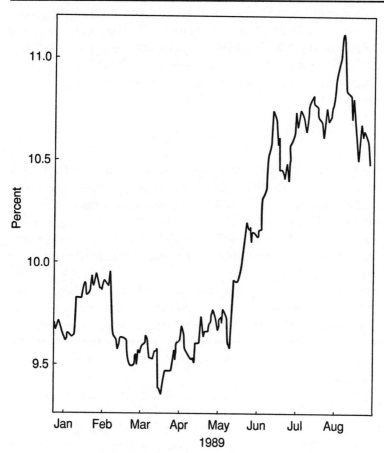

Interest Rate Risk Evaluation

The previous section formalized the process of analyzing a particular security's attributes at a point in time. This section extends the analysis into the consideration of a time dimension, the future holding period.

   In evaluating a particular security's interest rate risk exposure, we can simulate the bond's value under different interest rate levels and note the percentage change in price. If the bond has embedded options, the percentage change in bond price can be dramatically different between an increase in the interest rates and a decrease in interest rates. The indication of an embedded option would be immediately revealed in a security's performance profile. An extensive discussion of these interest-rate-change effects was presented in Chapter 12.

The change in interest rates is a major variable affecting the investment in a particular bond. The importance of this variable is assessed by consolidating all prior analyses and focusing on a particular time dimension. This procedure, which isolates a particular holding period for deriving a summary measure used in cross comparisons, is called horizon analysis.

Horizon Analysis

In most cases, portfolio managers who consider holding a bond over a period of time want to investigate the possible returns of the bond. However, there are several measures of return. *Total return* is defined as the bond's return over a specific period of time under the prevailing interest rates. Note that for this definition to be meaningful, we have to account for a refinancing, or reinvestment, rate at which all coupons or other cash receipts can be reinvested.

Since we know that the yield curve scenario is not certain, we determine the best scenario and the worst scenario. Accordingly, we can specify optimistic and pessimistic bond return scenarios. Finally, we can assign a probability to each scenario and calculate a bond's expected return for the horizon period. This expected return can be compared to the total return.

For option-embedded bonds, this exercise generates particularly interesting results. The negative convexity of these bonds hinders the upside returns and reduces the expected return. The higher the projected interest rate volatility, the larger the difference between the expected return and the total return.

For straight bonds, when there is no embedded option to affect the bond's convexity, the total return should not deviate too far from the expected return. Continuing with our example from earlier in the chapter, we are going to use a portfolio holding of not only the Dupont 8.5 percent 5/1/06 callable bond, but also a couple of theoretical straight bonds. One bond (bond 2 in Figure 14–3) will be theoretically identical except that it will not have the call option. The other bond will have the same coupon and maturity, but no call option or credit spread (bond 3 in Figure 14–3). This second one would be the theoretical risk-free equivalent issue (it also provides the Treasury equivalent yield value shown in Table 14–1).

FIGURE 14–3

(a) Sample Bond and Two Theoretical Bonds; (b) Change in Yield Curve; (c) Return Measures

	Basecase Statistics								Tue Aug 22, 1989
Bond	Description	Size	Price	YTW	Ch/Ri	Dura	Convx	Accr	TotValue
1	DU PONT E I DE	10.00	94.88	9.10	0.40	6.11	−0.7	2.62	9.750
2	THEOR 5/06 8.5	10.00	97.73	8.76	0.00	8.52	1.1	2.62	10.035
3	USTr 5/06 8.5	10.00	100.67	8.42	0.00	8.63	1.1	2.61	10.328

(a)

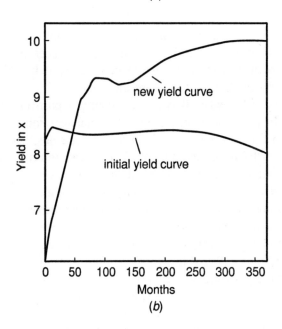

(b)

	Basecase: 8/22/89					Scenario: 8/22/90				
Itm	Description	Return	HiRet	ExpRet	LoRet	Sdev	Min%	Max%	Opt%	TotVal
1	DU PONT E I DE	3.87	10.49	3.90	−2.60	4.49	0.00	100.0	32.38	9.75
2	THEORET NO CALL	1.45	9.18	1.63	−5.41	4.99	0.00	100.0	33.32	10.03
3	THEOR TSY EQUIV	1.01	8.83	1.20	−5.92	5.05	0.00	100.0	34.30	10.33

(c)

Horizon analysis provides a couple of summary statistics that are extremely useful for judging the relative advantages of holding one issue over another. However, when a portfolio manager must rapidly assess the net risk exposure associated with hundreds of bonds, portfolio statistics should be used as the guiding criteria. The next section will elaborate on this aspect of fixed-income management.

ANALYZING A PORTFOLIO

The basic ideas in analyzing a portfolio are, in many ways, similar to those in analyzing a bond. After all, in both instances the portfolio manager seeks to maximize return while controlling risks. The risks, discussed in the preceeding sections, are the same.

But there are differences between analyzing a portfolio and analyzing a bond. In portfolio management, the manager must adhere to defined portfolio objectives or stated portfolio strategies. Under these constraints, the portfolio has to maintain a certain risk/return profile. For example, some managers cannot expose their portfolios to more interest rate risk than that embodied by the Treasury index. Some portfolios are structured to maintain a steady stream of coupon income or to support a specific pattern of cash outflows.

Another difference is simply a function of size (number of securities and total market value). When the portfolio manager wants to increase the convexity of the portfolio, she cannot just swap the present portfolio out and buy another portfolio with a higher convexity. Taking a number of constraints and factors into account, the manager must properly analyze the portfolio and decide on the optimal approach for changing the portfolio's convexity. Typical constraints are transaction costs and the availability of the types of bonds. Factors that must be taken into consideration include how to change the convexity while maintaining the duration, credit risk exposure, and other portfolio attributes.

Portfolio Composition

Students majoring in finance in business schools embrace the problem of "analyzing a firm." They can implement many techniques to analyze the data from financial statements to determine whether the firm is operating profitably according to certain guidelines and stated objectives. After all, the "analyzing a firm" procedure is a standard course in finance.

We must recognize that a firm is a far more complex entity than a bond portfolio. In fact, "analyzing a bond portfolio" is a special case of "analyzing a firm." The reason is simple: The firm's liabilities, collectively, constitute a bond portfolio. Similarly, analyzing a thrift institution is analogous to analyzing a bond portfolio.

Using these analogies, we can apply some of the techniques taught in a basic corporate finance course to analyze a portfolio. Specifically, we can use procedures that resemble the construction of financial ratios for discerning a portfolio's composition. We will use ratios that normalize the size of the individual components of the portfolio. The ratios can then be compared against those representing a market index portfolio.

Determining which ratios to construct in order to extract additional insight on the portfolio's structure is not a simple task. In addition, one cannot reach an inference or conclusion guided solely by making comparisons and defining some simple decision rules. The interpretation of the comparisons is part of the analysis. Portfolio ratios are simply tools that can be used to provide us with information. Creative use of these ratios is the core of portfolio analysis. The following section suggests one type of ratio construction.

Sector Ratios

A portfolio is composed of many bond sectors. The primary sectors are the Treasuries, Government agencies, corporates, mortgage-backed securities, and options/futures. Each sector may then be further divided into subsectors. For example, the corporate sector is composed of the financial, industrials, utilities, and transportation subsectors.

A *sector ratio* is the ratio of market value of each sector or subsector to the total portfolio value. Therefore, these ratios provide information about the composition of the portfolio. They are especially useful for formulating a comparison between these ratios and those of some benchmark index. In this context, we are interested in seeing how the portfolio is different from some "norm."

For example, the Treasury ratio is the ratio of the market value of all the Treasury securities to the total market value of the portfolio. If this ratio is high, we can infer that a large part of the portfolio's assets are sufficiently liquid and have minimal exposure to credit or call risk. Note that the ratio can shift quickly, depending on the portfolio manager's view and the constraints imposed on the portfolio management. If the portfolio manager later is convinced that the corporate sectors can potentially offer higher return, he or she may reduce the Treasury ratio to a negligible level and increase the holdings in corporate bonds. The use of these portfolio ratios will document the change and can provide guidance as to how much the ratios should be changed.

There is little need to point out that these ratios should be calculated on the market value basis and not the par value basis, unless the ratios are used for some accounting purposes or tax purposes. For example, the U.S. STRIP ratio in market value terms can be greatly different from the par or even book value terms. Since market values represent the present value of the bonds, they generally provide more appropriate information.

Most bonds do not have market prices in the sense that they are not actively traded. Therefore, these ratios have to be constructed using marking-to-market procedures integrated with a bond model. Can these ratios still be useful when there is no "actual" market price for these bonds? Yes; the use of market values enables us to investigate the composition of the portfolio in present value terms. They correctly take the option values, the market discount rate, and reinvestment rate into account. Therefore, the use of market value is not confined to the case of an observed trade. In fact, the prevalent use of market ratios in corporate finance is evidence of the unrestricted nature of assigning market value. In using market ratios, few financial analysts really believe they can sell the whole firm's equities at the current stock price or that they can eliminate all the liabilities at the fair price. Yet the debt ratios based on market values are used for estimating the composition of debt in the firm's capital structure.

Value Attribution

In the previous section of this chapter, we discussed the value attribution approach, which decomposes a bond's market value (or YTM). Specifically, an observed bond price can be decomposed into the Treasury equivalent value, credit/liquidity value, option value, and the cheap/rich value. In the case where there is no observed price, the fair price is used and the cheap/rich value is then zero. All values can be similarly represented on a yield basis. An option-adjusted spread attribution report can provide this type of information for every bond in a portfolio.

For a portfolio of numerous issues, we can prepare a value attribution summary, analogous to the attribution approach for individual bonds, for each subdivision within the portfolio. However, instead of one bond, we are working with a number of issues, so we must prepare dollar value *ratios* for representing each of the component values (Treasury equivalent, cheap/rich, option, credit/liquidity). We will highlight the construction of the component ratios by focusing on a particular subdivision, rating.

Bond holdings are first segregated according to their S&P ratings. Then, within a particular group (e.g., AAA) each bond position's market value (the product of the bond invoice price and par amount of holding) is decomposed into its component dollar values. For a particular component (e.g., credit/liquidity), we add all the component values together to get the sum for the AAA group. Lastly, we form a ratio of the group's component value to the total portfolio's market value.

Now we will focus on the type of information these ratios provide, starting with the Treasury equivalent ratio.

The Treasury equivalent ratio is the ratio of the Treasury equivalent value to the total portfolio value. In other words, if all the risky issues in a sector were stripped of their OAS spread and embedded options, and then the cash flows were discounted using the implied spot curve, the resulting Treasury equivalent market value of this sector would be much higher than its current market value. In fact, as a ratio, it could be 1.5 times greater (150%). Therefore, in dollar terms, you are *paying less* for the same cash flow stream a Treasury portfolio would generate. Inherent in paying less, and if you don't lose on a widening OAS or an increasing option value, you will realize an incremental return over risk-free securities. The size of the incremental return will be determined by the *size of the decrease* in the OAS spread and option values. The incremental return, by definition, has a maximum point. The increment's limit is the implicit divergence in market values. In this example, the incremental return over a riskless portfolio is capped at 50 percent. This means that the credit spreads and the option values would have to disappear overnight to transform the portfolio into a riskless portfolio. The associated increase in market value would be 50 percent.

It is interesting to note that this Treasury equivalent ratio will usually exceed unity when securities other than Treasury securities are in the portfolio. In other words, the portfolio value is actually the Treasury equivalent value net of the option value to the issuers and the credit risk premium. Indeed, a Treasury equivalent ratio close to unity would indicate that the portfolio is almost a Treasury portfolio. On the other hand, if the Treasury equivalent ratio is as large as 1.5, we can infer that the portfolio is significantly discounted by the credit and option value.

Given the large upside potential associated with a ratio of for example, 1.5, we can also expose substantial downside risk. The downside exposure counteracts the upside and establishes the risk and return trade-off reflected in the market prices used in calculating these ratios.

The next part of the analysis is identifying the individual sources of this amalgamated upsided return number. We can show that the Treasury equivalent market value (ratio) can be adjusted by risk component values (ratio) to arrive at the observed market value. By this process, we can visualize the market's value for each risk/return trade-off. We will start by considering the option ratio and then discuss the credit/liquidity and cheap/rich components.

Option ratio is the ratio of the embedded option value in the portfolio to the total market value of the portfolio. Option ratio is useful because it quantifies the issuer's option value as a proportion in the portfolio. The option ratio increases as more is invested in option-embedded corporate bonds. One generally expects the ratio to be less than unity. It is important to note that if the option ratio is 10 percent we cannot say that the portfolio has 10 percent option value. This is so because these options are not the investor's options, and it is therefore inappropriate to infer paying 10 percent for the options in the portfolio. Instead, the option ratio represents the potential return to the investors if the issuers lose all the option value to the investors. Note that the ratio can change quite rapidly even if the portfolio manager effects no trades, because the option values depend very much on the interest rate level. For example, if the portfolio has many callable bonds and if the interest rates rise to a sufficiently high level so that most bonds are priced at a discount, the option value would fall substantially.

Credit/liquidity ratio is defined as the ratio of the credit/liquidity value to the total portfolio value. The interpretation of this ratio is similar to that of the option ratio. The main difference is that the credit/liquidity ratio represents the upside return of the credit/liquidity bet. For an investment grade portfolio, this ratio is rather small, or even negligible. However, for a junk bond portfolio the ratio can be as high as 30 percent.

Assume we have a ratio indicating that the credit value for a certain sector (e.g., industrials) represents 5 percent of the total portfolio. This could be depicted as follows.

SECT	Observed %Market Value		Chp/Rch %MktVal		OptVal %MktVal		Credit %MktVal		TsyEquiv %MktVal
INDL	100	=	0.0	+	0.0	+	–5.0	+	105.0

There are no embedded option or price discrepancy risks in this portfolio, only credit risks that can at most provide 5 percent incremental returns above a similar Treasury portfolio (same cash flow composition). Note that we are not using a yield-to-maturity concept; we cannot state that this portfolio has a yield spread of 500 basis points. This 5 percent is a return accrued over the life of the bonds.

Cheap/rich ratio is defined as the ratio of the cheap/rich value to the total portfolio value. This ratio can be positive or negative. For a large portfolio, this ratio is expected to be very small, simply because of the construct and the interpretation of the bond-pricing models. Bond-pricing models are based on the relative pricing concept, and it is rather unlikely that there are many bonds in the market significantly underpriced or overpriced relative to a broad spectrum of bellwether bonds. For this reason, the ratio is less important in a portfolio context.

Tables 14–2 and 14–3 show value attribution summary reports for a government corporate index and a fixed income portfolio, respectively.

We have just defined some of the tools for investigating a portfolio's composition. However, these tools (i.e., the ratios) are helpful only if one has a defined objective.

PORTFOLIO CONSTRAINTS AND ADJUSTMENTS

Although we have the tools, we must define what we are trying to achieve. Once again, we can draw an analogy to corporate finance. Financial ratios themselves are not solutions to the "analysis of a firm." Students in finance courses learn that they have to use these ratios for in-depth analysis of a firm, particularly in their case studies. Problems posed in their case studies vary greatly in nature, even though there may be some generic types. The same is true in analyzing a bond portfolio. The purpose of the analysis can present itself in so many ways and the procedure to analyze them can be so varied that it would be futile to develop a general procedure for analysis. It would be as futile to develop

TABLE 14–2a
Value Attribution Summary for Government/Corporate Index

Printed on Wed Oct 25, 1989

Priced as of Thu Oct 19, 1989

	Average Maturity	Avg Coupon	Observed %Mkt Val	= Chp/Rch %Mkt	+ OptVal %Mkt	+ Credit %Mkt	+ TSY Equiv %MktVal
Treasury Bonds	03/17/99	9.463	65.58	-0.03	-0.14	0.00	65.752
US Agency Bonds	11/23/94	8.761	10.96	0.01	0.00	0.00	10.947
AAA Corporates	04/17/04	8.586	2.10	0.00	-0.08	-0.05	2.229
AA Corporates	06/16/01	8.705	9.66	0.01	-0.23	-0.35	10.228
A Corporates	05/10/04	9.427	7.44	-0.00	-0.21	-0.43	8.080
BBB Corporates	08/25/04	10.059	4.26	-0.02	-0.13	-0.37	4.777
Treasury Bonds	03/17/99	9.463	65.58	-0.03	-0.14	0.00	65.752
US Agency Bonds	11/23/94	8.761	10.96	0.01	0.00	0.00	10.947
INDL Corporates	12/02/03	9.451	6.79	-0.02	-0.18	-0.42	7.406
FINL Corporates	08/09/96	8.972	7.95	0.00	-0.08	-0.24	8.274
UTIL Corporates	05/22/09	9.832	2.46	-0.00	-0.12	-0.18	2.771
TELE Corporates	11/05/11	8.553	3.54	0.01	-0.19	-0.21	3.936
OIL Corporates	12/04/03	9.246	2.71	-0.00	-0.07	-0.15	2.928

TABLE 14-2b
Value Attribution Summary for Government/Corporate Index

Printed on Wed Oct 25, 1989

Priced as of Thu Oct 19, 198

	Average Maturity	Avg Coupon	Observed %Mkt Val	= Chp/Rch %Mkt	+ OptVal %Mkt	+ Credit %Mkt	+ TSY Equ %MktVal
Coupon 0.0 to 2.0	04/23/07	0.000	0.22	-0.01	0.00	-0.00	0.232
Coupon 4.0 to 6.0	05/21/98	5.150	0.40	0.00	-0.00	-0.01	0.408
Coupon 6.0 to 8.0	12/31/96	7.342	18.32	0.01	-0.02	-0.11	18.441
Coupon 8.0 to 10.0	05/03/99	8.852	54.07	0.03	-0.32	-0.70	55.067
Coupon 10.0 to 12.0	02/27/02	11.018	17.69	-0.03	-0.30	-0.29	18.308
Coupon 12.0 to 14.0	05/29/02	12.826	7.94	-0.03	-0.13	-0.08	8.177
Coupon 14.0 to 16.0	12/15/99	14.480	1.37	0.00	-0.02	-0.00	1.381
Maturity 0.0 to 4.0	01/20/92	9.007	39.68	0.00	-0.01	-0.09	39.778
Maturity 4.0 to 8.0	07/15/95	9.170	22.05	0.00	-0.03	-0.15	22.235
Maturity 8.0 to 12.0	03/24/99	9.040	8.58	0.02	-0.04	-0.14	8.740
Maturity 12.0 to 16.0	04/26/04	10.941	5.55	-0.00	-0.05	-0.09	5.697
Maturity 16.0 to 20.0	10/17/07	8.628	2.93	0.01	-0.05	-0.11	3.085
Maturity 20.0 to 24.0	01/28/12	11.215	4.91	-0.03	-0.18	-0.12	5.244
Maturity 24.0 to 28.0	03/21/16	9.487	10.84	-0.01	-0.22	-0.29	11.372
Maturity 28.0 to 32.0	11/30/18	9.164	4.91	-0.01	-0.12	-0.16	5.197
Maturity 32.0 to 36.0	08/23/23	10.255	0.54	0.00	-0.08	-0.04	0.666
Total Portfolio	09/03/99	9.317	100.00	-0.03	-0.79	-1.20	102.014

TABLE 14–3a
Value Attribution Summary for Portfolio

Printed on Wed Oct 25, 1989

Priced as of Thu Oct 19, 1989

	Average Maturity	Avg Coupon	Observed %Mkt Val	= Chp/Rch %Mkt	+ OptVal %Mkt	+ Credit %Mkt	+ TSY Equiv %MktVal
Treasury Bonds	02/25/97	7.420	23.47	0.08	-0.00	0.00	23.397
AAA Corporates	06/01/91	14.000	4.36	0.00	-0.36	-0.02	4.738
AA Corporates	09/25/04	6.900	46.87	0.00	-1.13	-2.21	50.208
A Corporates	03/12/02	15.347	15.88	0.00	-5.46	-1.11	22.450
BBB Corporates	08/15/15	11.625	9.42	0.00	-0.83	-1.35	11.593
Treasury Bonds	02/25/97	7.420	23.47	0.08	-0.00	0.00	23.397
INDL Corporates	03/11/07	13.962	25.30	0.00	-6.29	-2.46	34.042
FINL Corporates	11/28/01	8.125	17.90	0.00	-0.34	-0.70	18.947
TELE Corporates	06/25/06	6.144	28.97	0.00	-0.78	-1.51	31.260
OIL Corporates	06/01/91	14.000	4.36	0.00	-0.36	-0.02	4.738

TABLE 14–3b
Value Attribution Summary for Portfolio

Printed on Wed Oct 25, 1989   *Priced as of Thu Oct 19, 1989*

	Average Maturity	Avg Coupon	Observed %Mkt Val	= Chp/Rch %Mkt	+ OptVal %Mkt	+ Credit %Mkt	+ TSY Equiv %MktVal
Coupon 0.0 to 2.0	11/26/89	0.000	8.21	0.00	0.00	0.00	8.205
Coupon 4.0 to 6.0	05/01/99	4.375	18.46	0.00	0.00	-0.79	19.246
Coupon 8.0 to 10.0	02/11/09	8.571	38.73	0.01	-1.24	-1.67	41.629
Coupon 10.0 to 12.0	08/15/15	11.625	9.42	0.00	-0.83	-1.35	11.593
Coupon 14.0 to 16.0	07/18/91	14.544	11.51	0.07	-0.36	-0.02	11.816
Coupon 16.0 to 18.0	06/01/99	16.250	13.68	0.00	-5.35	-0.87	19.897
Maturity 0.0 to 4.0	12/20/90	8.426	26.73	0.07	-0.36	-0.07	27.094
Maturity 4.0 to 8.0	10/15/95	8.625	1.70	-0.00	0.00	0.00	1.703
Maturity 8.0 to 12.0	05/14/99	9.429	32.13	0.00	-5.35	-1.66	39.142
Maturity 12.0 to 16.0	05/15/05	8.250	1.30	0.00	-0.00	0.00	1.298
Maturity 16.0 to 20.0	07/01/07	8.125	11.73	0.00	-0.34	-0.65	12.727
Maturity 24.0 to 28.0	08/15/15	11.625	9.42	0.00	-0.83	-1.35	11.593
Maturity 28.0 to 32.0	03/27/19	9.032	16.98	0.00	-0.89	-0.96	18.829
Total Portfolio	12/30/02	9.118	100.00	0.08	-7.78	-4.68	112.386

a recipe for analyzing a firm. The prescription of a process would be the equivalent of advocating that creative input is unimportant in financial analysis. This is never the case!

For this reason, we will only suggest some of the motivations for prompting an analysis of a bond portfolio. Most such analyses are prompted by portfolio managers who need to adjust the portfolio to satisfy the portfolio objectives or to position the return profile of the portfolio in a manner consistent with their view of future changes in the market. Here are some examples.

Evaluating and Adjusting Risk Exposure

A portfolio faces different sources of risks: default risk, interest rate risk, credit risk, call risk, and others. For a number of reasons, the portfolio manager may need to evaluate the risk exposure and take steps to make adjustments.

When there are many corporate bonds in the portfolio with low credit ratings, the portfolio will be exposed to credit risk. Credit/liquidity ratio can suggest the severity of the risk exposure in value attribution, but there are other issues. The credit risk could be even more significant if the default risk is not well diversified away. The portfolio manager has to ensure that a substantial portion of the portfolio's bonds cannot be tied to a single issuer. Furthermore, the portfolio's holdings should be diversified among the corporate bond sectors.

If the objective is to provide a steady stream of cash flows to investors, the portfolio manager will have to evaluate the call risk. The option ratio can provide a measure of the uncertainty of the cash flow derived from the portfolio. Further, the level of call risk of each bond can be determined. Selling bonds with high call risk and swapping into bonds with lower call risk would be consistent with this type of objective.

Anticipating Shifts of the Yield Curve

A portfolio manager who anticipates a shift in the yield curve wants to analyze the portfolio in order to adjust the portfolio to best exploit the yield curve shift. The simplest method is adjusting the portfolio duration. If one seeks to lengthen the duration in anticipation of a drop in rates, then one needs to determine the appropriate short duration bond to swap out in exchange for a long duration issue. In general, it is not feasible or desirable to swap out of the shortest duration bond. Other factors are involved: the level of convexity, the types of embedded options, and so on. Analysis is needed to determine the optimal restructure of the portfolio.

Lengthening the duration need not be the optimal strategy for a particular portfolio. Maybe it is more advisable to structure a barbell portfolio or employ other ways to increase the convexity without lengthening the portfolio's duration (particularly for more conservative portfolios). Implicit in this strategy is, of course, some assumption about the type of shifts of the yield curve, whether the shift is parallel or not.

These are some of the examples of motivations behind analyzing a bond portfolio. Clearly there are many other examples, and there are just as many ways to analyze the portfolio. In any case, the use of bond-pricing models and the use of such bond performance measures as duration and convexity to analyze a bond portfolio are very recent subjects of investigation. The next chapter will elaborate on an even more recent development that extends the duration concept. As more research effort is devoted to analyzing bond portfolios, we will better master the techniques. In the meantime, we hope that analyzing bond portfolios will unearth opportunities for improving expected performance without significantly increasing the portfolio's risk exposure. The next section will discuss some applicable strategies.

BOND STRATEGY

Previous sections discussed the analysis of a bond or a portfolio. This section discusses the actions that may follow from an analysis.

Bond Swap

A bond swap refers to buying a bond and at the same time selling a different bond. Bond swaps may be motivated by different intents. The simplest reason is that a portfolio manager has identified a rich bond that can be replaced with a bond that is trading cheap. The analysis involved in this type of situation is straightforward. The portfolio manager, using the techniques discussed earlier in the chapter, has identified one bond value that is above the high range and another whose value is below the low range. If the manager believes that the bonds will soon return to their fair value, he or she would consider buying the cheap bond and selling the rich bond. This type of swap, although easy to describe, is hard to identify and subsequently make a judgment call as to whether the cheap/rich values are an anomaly or represent fundamental structural changes in the market. In addition to this plain vanilla type swap, there are a host of others.

Rate Anticipation Swap

In this case the portfolio manager may have a certain view about an imminent shift in the yield curve; for example, that a forthcoming downward shift will cause the resulting curve to lie below its current implied forward curve. Therefore, the manager would sell a short-duration issue and buy a long-duration bond. Conversely, if the prediction is for an increase in rates, then the manager can implement the reverse strategy: buy short duration and sell long duration. If there is a specific holding period in mind, the manager could review a horizon analysis table to determine the precise difference in expected returns over a simulated yield curve environment.

Duration-Hedged Swap

Swapping out of a rich bond and buying a cheap bond may also affect the portfolio's duration. Unfortunately, this would be equivalent to simultaneously making an interest rate bet. In an effort to hold the duration constant, we could execute the swap using three issues instead of two. We can maintain duration if we are willing to buy one bond and sell two bonds or sell one bond and buy two bonds such that the market value and combined duration of the bonds sold are the same as the value and duration of the bonds bought. It should be noted that portfolios of bonds to sell and to buy can always be constructed. However, because of transaction constraints, a portfolio manager can often execute trades using only round lot positions. There will usually be net proceeds. Assuming that the net proceeds go into the cash position, we generally cannot exactly match the dollar durations of the buys and the sells. In this case, we need to pick the best bond candidates.

Cross-Sector Swap

Thus far we have not focused on any swap strategies that deal with any mispricing of bonds across sector. What do we mean by swapping a cheap bond in the industrial sector against the Treasury sector? In this problem there are two levels of analysis. First we have to analyze the relative values of the two sectors. For example, we are comparing the Treasury market with the AA industrial bond markets. We have to decide whether the industrial sector is cheap or rich first. This can be achieved by analyzing the trend of the OAS. If the OAS is very narrow but is expected to widen again, the sector is considered rich. If the OAS is historically wide and is expected to tighten, it is considered cheap. When the sector is identified as cheap, the cheap bonds in that sector are considered for purchase.

Stripping Embedded Options in Corporate Bonds

Suppose we are convinced that the embedded call option in a corporate bond is mispriced relative to similar embedded options in similar instruments. In order to realize a higher return by capitalizing on the mispricing, it is first necessary to decompose the corporate bond into the call option component and the cash-flow component. This technique, which allows us to hedge the component risks more accurately, is called *stripping the embedded option*.

The procedure has two steps. First we must isolate the embedded option. This can be achieved by constructing a corresponding straight bond with the same stated maturity and coupon. The cash flows are discounted using the same OAS spread to the spot curve as the corporate bond's. Holding a long position in the callable corporate bond is the equivalent of holding a long position in this corresponding straight bond and a short position in the embedded option.

The second step involves constructing a riskless arbitrage. We must hedge the option position in order to realize a riskless profit associated with the mispricing. We must replicate the embedded option with exchange-traded options. Note that exchange-traded options have very short lives and are therefore quite different from a long-term option, such as the embedded option in the corporate bond. It is therefore impossible to find an exchange-traded option that would be appropriate for hedging the embedded option. To tackle this problem we should use a portfolio of options instead.

The portfolio of options has to be constructed such that the duration and the convexity of the embedded option are the same as those of the portfolio. If we are willing to assume the shape of the yield curve, volatility level, and other market parameters on a horizon date, we can also set up the portfolio such that it has duration and convexity equal to those of the embedded option under the predicted scenario. In other words, we will have base case duration and convexity values and scenario duration and convexity values.

Considering we require these constraints on the portfolio of options, and that there are altogether four constraints, we would require in general four options. The cost of the portfolio of options need not be the same as the embedded option value. The pricing discrepancy can be exploited in this type of strategy. For example, if the embedded option has a higher relative value (it is rich), then we should buy the corporate bond, buy the option portfolio, and sell the corresponding straight bond. This way, the proceeds from the sale of the straight bond should exceed the cost of buying both the corporate bond and the option portfolio. As a result of these maneuvers, as the short option approached fair value, the long callable bond's price would increase and the combined investment position should realize a riskless excess return. Tables 14–4 and 14–5 depict the steps of this analysis.

Table 14–4a shows the portfolio's characteristics as of the basecase date and the scenario date. The bottom section of the table, total portfolio, depicts the characteristics of the net holdings of the portfolio. In this case, the effective duration and convexity values are the attributes of the the long position in the embedded option. There are generally many options on futures available for use in hedging. Table 14–4b is a partial list of these securities.

Table 14–5 shows a hedging position composed of four of these contingent claim securities that mitigate the embedded option's effects. In other words, the combination of these four securities mirrors the embedded option's characteristics, and the new (target) performance profile for the portfolio would therefore be a horizontal line.

Results
Essentially, by solving for the positions of four contingent claim securities that provide the same attributes as the embedded option, we have duplicated the option using over-the-counter securities. However, in addition to transaction costs and security specific liquidity concerns, there is another important component that should be considered when determining what combination of portfolio holdings should be established: the implied volatilities of the corporate bellwether portfolio and of the traded options. For instance, if one believes that the corporate implied volatilities have been unusually high and will soon trend lower, then one would want to be short the embedded options and hedge

TABLE 14-4

(a) Initial Portfolio

Bond	Description	Size	Rate	Coup	YTW	Matur	McDur	EffDur	Conv	Basecase: 10/19/89 Price	Duration	Convexity	Scenario: 12/19/89 Price	Duration	Convexity
1	DUPONT E I DE	-10.0	AA	8.50	-3.21	16.53	12.81	106.31	74.40	96.61	5.81	-0.89	96.63	5.93	-0.96
2	CS[a] 5/06 8.500	10.0	AA	8.50	-2.93	16.36	12.71	107.08	76.08	99.31	8.44	1.08	99.31	8.64	1.10

Total Portfolio	Total Par	Market Val
Basecase	0.000	0.271[b]
Scenario	0.000	0.268[b]

[a] CS: Corporate security with same maturity, coupon rate, and sector OAS as DuPont.
[b] Net market value of portfolio, which reveals value of embedded option (market values in 100s).

(b) Partial List of Existing Interest Rate Options

CC	Description	Size	Basecase: 10/19/89 Price	Duration	Convexity	Scenario: 12/19/89 Price	Duration	Convexity
5	MAR90 TBND 94C	0.0	5.13	137.1	80.5	5.09	152.2	77.7
6	MAR90 TBND 96P	0.0	1.05	-264.0	433.7	0.47	-483.8	1179.8
7	MAR90 TBND 96C	0.0	3.58	168.3	139.7	3.37	196.7	175.8
8	MAR90 TBND 98P	0.0	1.77	-219.0	288.2	1.07	-339.9	645.3
9	MAR90 TBND 98C	0.0	2.41	203.7	226.6	2.03	258.7	356.5
10	MAR90 TBND 100P	0.0	2.83	-176.9	179.2	2.09	-244.3	332.5
11	MAR90 TBND 100C	0.0	1.53	246.3	348.5	1.08	350.2	666.4

TABLE 14–5

Composition of Hedging Position to Offset Embedded Option

Portfolio's Scenario Profile–Before Hedging (12/19/89)

BP Shift	Total Value	Duration	Convexity
−50	0.437		
+0	0.268	107.25	76.1
+50	0.150		

Target Duration: 0.000   Target Convexity: 0.000

Hedging Instruments

Description	Price	Size	Total Value (00's)
MAR90 TBND 96P	1.047	−12.123	−0.1269
MAR90 TBOND FUT	98.656	11.193	0.0000
MAR90 TBND 100C	1.531	−17.653	−0.2703
MAR90 TBND 98P	1.766	24.653	0.4353
			+0.0381[a]

Portfolio's Scenario Profile–After Hedging

BP Shift	Total Value	Duration	Convexity
−50	0.281		
+0	0.281[b]	0.00	−0.0
+50	0.281		

[a] Cash needed for establishing option positions that duplicate convexity and effective duration of embedded option.

[b] Difference of .013 from original scenario is attributable to variation margin associated with futures contract.

the position with market-traded options. Of course, when using traded options to offset an embedded option's performance profile, or even to capitalize on a projected market adjustment, the investor is explicitly making bets on the implied volatilities in two different markets.

Hedging with Futures

Treasury notes and bond futures are effective hedging instruments. They have very active markets and they incur relatively small transaction costs. We shall now analyze a scenario where we want to immunize a bond portfolio such that any shift of interest rates would not affect the bond portfolio's value.

Recall that the duration of a futures contract is defined as

$$D_F = -\frac{\Delta F / \Delta r}{F} \qquad (14\text{--}1)$$

where D_F is the futures duration, and F is the futures value. (See Chapter 10 for additional information.) And the portfolio duration is defined as

$$D_V = -\frac{\Delta V / \Delta r}{V} \qquad (14\text{--}2)$$

where V is the portfolio value.

Let the number of contracts that the hedge requires be x. If the dollar value of the profit (loss) of the portfolio is offset by the dollar value of the results from the futures hedge, then the portfolio would be insensitive to the shift in the spot curve. Therefore, we require

$$\Delta V + x \Delta F = 0 \qquad (14\text{--}3)$$

Solving for the required number of contracts, we have the solution:

$$x F D_F + V D_V = 0$$

It must be pointed out that if the portfolio has many embedded options so that the portfolio has very high absolute convexity value, the futures position alone would not be adequate for immunizing the interest rate risk. Changes in the volatility level would affect the underlying portfolio value without affecting the futures value. For this reason, a futures position would not be able to hedge against the volatility risk.

Use of futures on hedging often requires dynamic strategies; that is, the hedge position has to be adjusted or revised. Portfolio duration changes over time. The change may be a result of the change in the interest rate level or in the investments within the portfolio (e.g., portfolio now has a shorter maturity). In any case these changes are often not the same as the changes in the future's duration. Fortunately, the transaction costs of revising a futures position is not too costly, so a dynamic hedging strategy is possible.

Hedging with Options

As discussed previously, in the case where the underlying portfolio has embedded options, a futures contract may not provide adequate hedging against a significant change in the spot curve or a change in interest rate volatility. In hedging such risks, it is important to combine the use of futures and options. Here we will use the combination of futures and options such that the portfolio duration and convexity are hedged.

Unlike the previous case, we now need to consider the price sensitivity of the futures, options, and the portfolio to the interest rate changes in terms of both duration and convexity. Recall that we have the following equations. For futures we have[*]

$$\Delta F = -D_F F \Delta r + 50 C_F F (\Delta r)^2$$

For options we have

$$\Delta O = -D_o O \Delta r + 50\ C_O O (\Delta r)^2$$

For the portfolio we have

$$\Delta V = -D_V V \Delta r + 50\ C_V V (\Delta r)^2$$

Since we need to pay for an option, we need also cash (A) for constructing the hedge. If we need x futures contracts and y options, then hedging such that both duration and convexity are zero, we derive the following equations.

$$\Delta V + y \Delta O + x \Delta F = 0$$

$$V D_V + y O D_O + x F D_F = 0$$

$$V C_V + y O C_O + x F C_F = 0$$

Through these two equations, we can solve for x and y:

$$x = \frac{-V D_V O C_O + O D_O V C_D}{O D_O F C_F - F D_F O C_v}$$

$$y = \frac{F D_F V C_v - F C_F V D_v}{O D_O F C_F - F D_F O C_O}$$

An option that has a high convexity should also be sensitive to the change of volatility (see Chapter 11). Therefore, if we have hedged the convexity, we will have hedged the volatility risk of the portfolio to a large extent.

We must note that the use of futures and options is not confined to the simple immunization we have discussed thus far. Indeed, we can

---

[*] By convention, convexity is commonly derived as $[(d^2p/dr^2)/100]$. Therefore, in actual usage, convexity value is multiplied by 50, rather than divided by 2.

think of such immunization as a special case. We have discussed in Chapter 5 the concept of using target performance profiles and strategic profiles for constructing bond strategies. For the above special cases, our target performance profiles are horizontal lines where the target duration and convexities are zero. The strategic performance profile is derived from the optimal futures, option, and cash mix. As we can see from the derivation of the hedging strategy, we can always solve for the hedging positions given the target duration and convexity values.

The previous chapters on options, futures, and bonds have discussed the behavior of these securities under interest rate risks. The pricing models enable us to derive the duration and convexity value. These analyses are therefore central to developing bond strategies. The construction of the target performance profiles, duration, and convexity of a bond or a portfolio requires simulation of the security value under different scenarios. The pricing models are often indispensible for simulating these results. More often than not, there is no simple formula for determining the duration and convexity values of a security, as there is in the case of a zero-coupon bond (see Chapter 6).

PORTFOLIO STRATEGIES

Unlike bond strategies, portfolio strategy is concerned not with single or several securities trading but with broader issues. The actual implementation of the portfolio strategy may involve a sequence of actions in bond strategies, but the objective of a portfolio strategy is distinctly different. Here are some examples.

Target Duration (Single-Period Immunization)

For some portfolios, the portfolio manager is required to maximize the portfolio return and minimize the risk of the portfolio value on a future date. For example, the portfolio is used to cover a promised payment, a liability, sometime in the future. Of course, the simplest approach is to hold a zero-coupon bond with the same maturity as the promised payment date, but in practice it is generally very difficult to purchase a significant amount of zero-coupon bonds. Therefore, one has to form a strategy to realize the portfolio objective.

The portfolio strategy is a dynamic simulation of a zero-coupon bond that matures on the promised payment date. To do so, we can actively manage the portfolio such that the effective duration of the portfolio is the same as that of the zero-coupon bond. However, this condition may not suffice. Suppose the portfolio has many callable corporate bonds and therefore many embedded options. We can adjust that portfolio's duration to be the target duration, but clearly the portfolio is far from the same as a zero-coupon bond. Even over a short period of time or over a small change in interest rates, the portfolio would not behave like a zero-coupon bond. For example, there is a time-decay element with the options, and the embedded options give a higher return than the risk-free rate in a stable interest rate regime. However, the option also affects the convexity of the portfolio. For this reason, to replicate the zero-coupon bond correctly, we should target both the duration and the convexity of the portfolio to the zero-coupon bond.

The portfolio has to be revised quite frequently so that the portfolio will always equal the target duration and convexity. If the portfolio manager then seeks to buy cheap bonds while maintaining these constraints, then the portfolio can in principle realize an even higher return than the risk-free return. This strategy is often called immunization. Table 14–6 illustrates this portfolio strategy.

Dedication

Dedication is a procedure of constructing the assets to match the cash flows of a liability schedule. The liability schedule can be generated from a variety of activities. They may have been constructed by the actuaries in an insurance company to reflect their estimates of the cash outflows of a pension pool. The liability schedule can be the estimated capital outlay for a construction project. For these examples, a bond dedication takes the liability schedule as given, even though the cash flow is often an estimate.

The purpose of a dedication is to ensure that there is an asset investment to pay off the liabilities over the course of time, under a wide range of interest rate scenarios. In the case of a pension plan, dedication procedure will take part of the insurance premium received to invest in assets such that the cash flows generated from the assets can be ensured to pay off the pension liabilities. Similarly, in dedicating the cash outflow in a construction project, the financing of the project can be

TABLE 14–6a
Illustration of Target Duration

Bond	Description	Basecase Portfolio		Thu Oct 19, 1989					
		Size	Price	YTW	Ch/Ri	Dura	Convx	Accr	TotValue
1	TL 11/09/89 0%	10.00	99.59	7.16	0.03	0.05	0.0	0.00	9.959
2	TL 12/14/89 0%	10.00	98.83	7.72	-0.00	0.15	0.0	0.00	9.883
3	TN 2/91 9.125	2.00	101.31	8.04	-0.05	1.21	0.0	1.61	2.058
4	TN 8/91 14.875	15.00	112.63	7.33	1.15	1.56	0.0	2.63	17.288
5	TN 10/95 8.625	4.00	102.81	8.02	-0.02	4.63	0.3	0.09	4.116
6	TC 5/05 8.250	3.00	101.31	8.06	0.30	7.43	-1.9	3.52	3.145
7	TB 8/19 8.125	10.00	101.69	7.97	0.07	11.26	2.2	1.44	10.312
8	ALASK 6/99 16.3	30.00	104.00	13.38	0.00	0.00	0.0	6.23	33.069
9	Ameri 4/91 8.1	15.00	99.37	8.58	0.00	1.38	0.0	0.09	14.919
10	AMERI 5/99 4.4	60.00	72.35	8.70	0.00	7.07	0.6	2.04	44.635
11	AMOCO 6/91 14.0	10.00	100.00	13.97	0.00	0.00	0.0	5.37	10.537
12	BELL 1/19 9.3	25.00	99.25	9.32	0.00	5.72	-1.4	2.42	25.417
13	Burli 8/15 11.6	20.00	111.79	10.11	0.00	5.43	-0.2	2.07	22.772
14	Cater 6/19 9.8	5.00	102.95	9.42	0.00	7.54	0.5	3.74	5.334
15	Chrys 1/93 8.8	0.00	98.39	9.33	0.00	2.72	0.1	2.28	0.000
16	CITIC 7/07 8.1	30.00	92.09	9.03	0.00	6.70	-0.5	2.44	28.360
17	TN 10/99 0.000	0.00	45.13	8.12^*	0.00	9.61^*	1.0^*	0.00	0.000

Total Portfolio	Rate	Coup	YTW	Matur	McDur	EffDur	Conv	Total Par	Market Val
Basecase	AA+	9.12	9.56	13.20	6.23	4.24	-0.03	249.000	241.805

*Zero bond characteristics that set constraints for a single-period immunization.

303

TABLE 14–6b
Portfolio Restructured

Itm	Description	Coupon	Price	Duratn	Conv	Yield	Min%	Max%	Opt%	TotPos
				Basecase: 10/19/89						
1	TL 11/09/89 0%	0.00	99.59	0.05	0.00	7.16	0.05	85.00	0.05	0.12
2	TL 12/14/89 0%	0.00	98.83	0.15	0.00	7.72	0.05	85.00	0.05	0.12
3	TN 2/91 0%	9.13	101.31	1.21	0.02	8.04	0.05	85.00	0.05	0.12
4	TN 8/91 0%	14.88	112.63	1.56	0.03	7.33	0.05	85.00	0.05	0.12
5	TN 10/95 0%	8.63	102.81	4.63	0.27	8.02	0.05	85.00	0.05	0.12
6	TC 5/05 0%	8.25	101.31	7.43	-1.91	8.06	0.05	85.00	0.05	0.12
7	TB 8/19 0%	8.13	101.69	11.26	2.15	7.97	0.05	85.00	85.00	205.53
8	ALASKA ST HSG F	16.25	104.00	0.00	0.00	13.38	0.05	85.00	0.05	0.12
9	American Express	8.13	99.37	1.38	0.03	8.58	0.05	85.00	0.05	0.12
10	AMERICAN TEL &	4.38	72.35	7.07	0.63	8.70	0.05	85.00	0.05	0.12
11	AMOCO CO	14.00	100.00	0.00	0.00	13.97	0.05	85.00	14.19	34.30
12	BELL TEL CO PA	9.25	99.25	5.72	-1.43	9.32	0.05	85.00	14.19	0.12
13	Burlington Nort	11.63	111.79	5.43	-0.22	10.11	0.05	85.00	14.19	0.12
14	Caterpillar	9.75	102.95	7.54	0.46	9.42	0.05	85.00	0.11	0.28
15	Chrysler Financ	8.75	98.39	2.72	0.09	9.33	0.05	85.00	0.05	0.12
16	CITICORP	8.13	92.09	6.70	-0.50	9.03	0.05	85.00	0.05	0.12
17	TN 10/99 0.00	0.00	45.13	9.61	0.97	8.12	0.05	85.00	0.05	0.12
Portfolio				9.61	1.83	8.83	0.85	1445.00	100.00	241.80

Minimum Convexity 1.000000
Maximum Convexity 4.000000
Minimum Effective Duration 9.610000
Maximum Effective Duration 9.650000

invested at the initial stage of the project such that the asset investment can be ensured to cover a certain portion of the project's operating costs.

Bond dedication in managing assets and liabilities has a number of advantages over less structured investment strategies. First, bond dedication is a systematic procedure to generate the asset cash inflow to cover the cash outflow. For this reason, we can better evaluate the risk that the cash inflow will not be able to cover the liabilities. In contrast, if we take the total return approach to managing the assets, the ability to meet the liability obligation depends greatly on the manager's performance.

Dedication Procedure

We will now specify the dedication procedure more precisely. A liability schedule is the starting point. The schedule is a cash flow stating the cash outflow on a specified date. A pension liability schedule typically has a specified amount on a monthly basis, which then declines to a less frequent interval, say annually. The schedule may extend to 50 years. The annual amount of cash outflow also declines over time.

The construction of the asset portfolio to meet the liability obligation in a bond dedication has to satisfy the following conditions:

1. There is no requirement to sell or buy any assets and liabilities after setting up the asset portfolio.
2. There is a reinvestment rate specified such that all the cash surplus can be reinvested at that rate. To be conservative in ensuring that the asset portfolio meet the liability payment, we can assume a low reinvestment rate. In such a case, the dedication procedure would automatically understate the ability for any surplus to generate future revenue.
3. At any time, there is enough cash in the surplus to pay off any liability cash flow stated in the liability schedule.
4. The cost of the asset portfolio must be minimized subject to all these constraints.
5. The universe of assets that can be selected may be subject to a number of constraints. We will discuss this issue later. For the time being, we will assume that only noncallable Treasuries are used.

Determining a Solution Using Linear Programming

The above problem can be stated as a linear programming problem. Let the ith bond in the universe of the noncallable Treasuries have price P_i. The cash flow of this bond is denoted by $(x_{i1}, x_{i2}, \ldots, x_{in})$ where x_{ij} represents the cash-flow payment of the ith bond on the jth month. For simplicity, we shall assume that all payments are given at the end of each month. Some of the x_{ij} may have zero value. Let the liability schedule be given by $(y_1, \ldots, y_n)$, where y_j is the payment on the jth month. Let the number of bonds that we want to hold in bond i be a_i. Then the objective function is given by

$$\text{minimizing } a_i \times P_i$$

with the constraints imposed on each month's net cash flow and the further constraint that the surplus (s_n), which is the accumulated surplus form previous months together with the net cash flow of the assets and liabilities, is always positive. That is,

$$S_1 = \sum a_j x_j - L_1 \geq 0$$
$$S_2 = S_1(1 + r) + \sum a_j x_{j2} - L_2 \geq 0$$
$$\vdots$$
$$S_n = S_{n-1}(1 + r) + \sum a_j x_{jn} - L_n \geq 0 \qquad (14\text{--}4a)$$

The holdings of the bonds must also be positive. That is,

$$a_i \geq 0 \qquad (14\text{--}4b)$$

This procedure is called linear programming because the objective function and all the constraints are linear equations. There are many methodologies for solving this particular mathematical problem, but this chapter will not be concerned with them.

Other Constraints and Generalizations

As pointed out earlier, the projected reinvestment rate can be conservatively low. Then the linear programming solution will focus on matching the cash flows at the expense of lowering the total portfolio value. If it is possible to match the cash flows perfectly such that there is no surplus at the end of each month, and if the Treasury bonds are correctly priced with no arbitrage possibility, then the dedication procedure will take the perfectly matched solution as the optimal solution. In any case, the surplus of the last month should always be zero for the optimal solution.

Suppose we discount the liability schedule by the spot curve to determine the market value of the liability. Then we can analyze the asset and liability in terms of market valuation analysis. We should observe the following behavior. If the Treasury bond prices do not differ significantly from the theoretical prices estimated from the spot curve (which is often the case), the asset value should exceed the liability value. This is attributable to the fact that the reinvestment rate is often set below the market level. Second, the duration of the asset portfolio should be shorter than the liability cash flow. This is an outcome associated with an optimization procedure seeking to ensure a sufficient number of early cash flows in order to generate a positive surplus. According to these observations, if we consider the asset and liability together as a portfolio position, the performance profile of the net position should have a positive value and a negative duration as depicted in Figure 14–4. That is, if interest rates rise, then the net position would have increased value because the surpluses can be reinvested at a higher rate.

The bond dedication procedure requires the bonds in the asset portfolio to have a cash flow that is certain, not probable. For this reason it is inappropriate to incorporate callable bonds. But in many dedications, corporate bonds are preferred because some bonds are "cheap" and the

FIGURE 14–4
Performance Profile of Net Asset Value

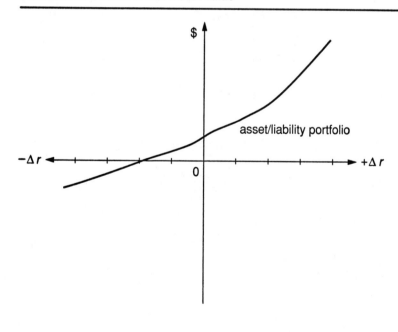

firm may be willing to take the call risk in order to maximize the return. In this case, deep discount corporate bonds are preferred so that the traded price is significantly below the call price; this way, we can minimize the call risk. Another constraint may be the percentage of the portfolio represented by a single issuer. Often a portfolio manager wants to avoid buying too many bonds from a single bond issuer as a means of diversifying the default risk. In line with this objective, we may have to constrain the optimization so as to avoid the selection of too many low-rated bonds (lower than BBB +). These are only a few of the constraints a bond dedication procedure is typically subjected to.

If corporate bonds are used in the asset portfolio and we discount the liabilities by the spot curve, the performance profile would be similar to that depicted in Figure 14–5. We see that the absolute asset portfolio value will be less than the absolute liability value; therefore the net asset value is negative. In addition, the call option value will further lower the net value if interest rates drop. This analysis clearly depicts the incursion of call risk and default risk as one seeks to lower the cost of the asset portfolio funding the liabilities.

FIGURE 14–5
Performance Profiles: Assets, Liabilities, and Net Value

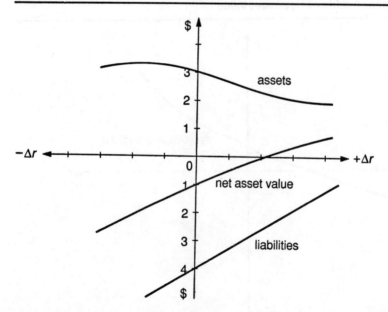

Contingent Immunization

In contingent immunization, the portfolio has a guaranteed return as of the initial date when the portfolio is funded. This return, termed the *floor rate*, is used to calculate the target floor value of the portfolio as of a horizon date.

Now the problem of maximizing returns subject to the constraint of meeting the target portfolio value is the same as that of ensuring that the portfolio value at any time is not less than the equivalent zero-coupon bond value. The reference zero-coupon bond has a maturity equal to the horizon date, and the par value is the same as the target portfolio value. The floor rate is often below the market rate of return over the same horizon time period. Of course, the portfolio manager is expected to realize a portfolio return that exceeds the return.

The performance profile of the zero-coupon bond establishes the floor values of the portfolio. Therefore, if the portfolio value is above the floor value, the portfolio manager can be aggressive in seeking higher returns by taking on more interest rate risk. However, if the portfolio value is not significantly above the floor value, the portfolio manager should not take on much interest rate risk. In the extreme case, if the portfolio value falls to the floor value, the portfolio should be liquidated, if possible, and the proceeds used to purchase the zero-coupon bond with a maturity equal to the horizon date. Figure 14–6 gives an illustrated example of this strategy.

Principal Preservation

Sometimes the portfolio has a stated requirement that the principal of the portfolio must be preserved. If the original endowment is X and the horizon of the investment is N years, the portfolio manager is required to maximize the return of the portfolio over this period of time while ensuring that the portfolio has a value at the terminal date that exceeds the original endowment. Here we are dealing with a specific case of a single-period immunization or contingent immunization strategy problem. The unique characteristic of this problem is that there is no minimum guaranteed rate of return; the floor rate of return is zero. If we again consider using the simplest approach of investing in a zero-coupon bond, the bond's maturity should be N and the face (par) amount should be equal to X.

FIGURE 14–6
Contingent Immunization Analysis

Initial value	241.805	Current value	241.805
Original date	10/19/89	Market rate	8.005
Horizon date	10/19/90	Immun. terminal value	261.548
Target rate	7.5%	Total Return	8.165
Target value	260.280	Presual Reserve	1.172
		Annual Return	8.005

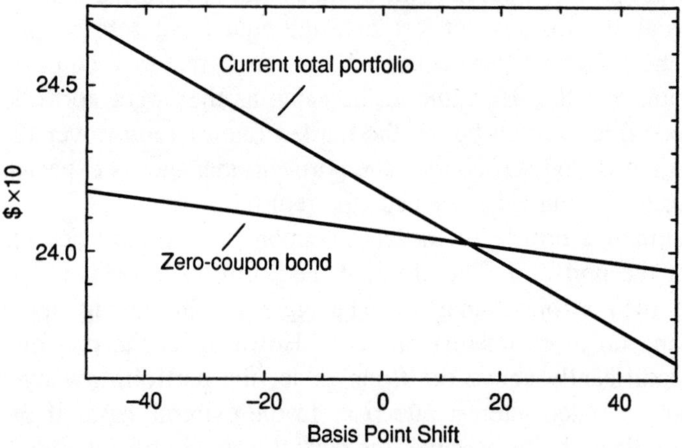

Asset and Liability Management

Before we investigate asset and liability management, we need a discussion of the performance profile of a liability. In the previous chapters we have been more concerned with the performance profiles of a security. In these cases, it is convenient to study the relationship between price and interest rates. In this chapter, we are more concerned with portfolio strategy, hence the portfolio value. Therefore, we are more interested in the relationship between the portfolio value and the level of interest rates.

Now we can extend this argument to include the consideration of liabilities. For example, we can analyze the interest rate risk exposure of a bank by combining the interest rate risk exposure of the bank's assets as well as the liabilities. In many asset and liability problems, we need to analyze the interest rate risk exposure of the liability as well.

Liability can be considered an asset portfolio with negative value. For example, a zero-coupon bond held in a long position would have a performance profile given by AB in Figure 14–7. However, if the bond

FIGURE 14–7
Performance Profiles: Long and Short Zero

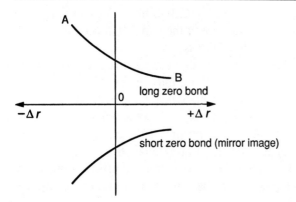

is held in a short position, the performance profile is the mirror image of the line AB reflected along the *x* axis. Therefore, with a rise of interest rates, the negative bond value will drop (becomes less negative); the portfolio value will increase. Alternatively, if the bond is held as an asset, the portfolio value will drop.

After constructing the performance profiles of the assets and the liabilities, we can study the combined effect. The performance profile of an asset and a liability can be constructed by considering the difference between the asset and the liability. We can illustrate this with a few simple examples. Suppose we borrow cash to purchase a ten-year zero-coupon bond. Then the asset portfolio is the ten-year zero, and the liability is the borrowed cash. The performance profile of the asset and that of the liability are shown in Figure 14–8. The combined effect

FIGURE 14–8
Combined Effect of Assets and Liabilities

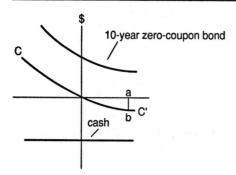

is given by the curve CC'. If the interest rates rise to point a, the profit of the position is given by line ab.

Consider a bank with both assets and liabilities. It is important to determine the interest rate risk exposure of the bank. In this case, we first construct the performance profile of the assets and then the performance profile of the liabilities. We may expect that asset value exceeds liability value. The net value, of course, is the equity value of the firm. By using the previous argument, we can construct the performance profile that represents the net interest rate risk exposure of assets and liabilities. That represents the interest rate risk exposure of the equity of the bank. Therefore, if the performance profile is horizontal, the equity does not face any interest rate risks. In this case, the combined effect of the assets and liabilities of the bank portfolio is the same as that of a money market fund.

Multiperiod Immunization

In single-period immunization, we try to match the duration of the assets to that of the liabilities. The single-period immunization strategy would work if the yield curve made a parallel shift, but often the yield curve makes nonparallel shifts. One may, however, apply the multiperiod immunization technique.

The basic idea is quite simple. First we define several regions in the maturity range. For example, the first region is any time up to 5 years, the second is between the 5 and 10, and the third is any time beyond 10. Now we can break up the liability schedule, creating the cash flow up to 5 years, the cash flow between 5 and 10 years, and finally all the cash flows beyond 10 years.

We can calculate the present value of cash flows in each region, and we can also calculate their duration values. We can also apply this procedure to all the bonds, then carry out the immunization procedure in each region. This way we can create a portfolio that can satisfy the conditions that the cash flow of the asset portfolio in each region have the same present value as that of the liabilities in that region and that they match in duration value. This procedure is somewhat similar to the horizon immunization procedure in that the solutions to the immunizations to all the regions are jointly determined. Consider the situation whereby we decide to dedicate the liability cash flow up to five years and immunize the remaining cash flows. Suppose that in this ideal world all the bonds in the asset universe either have cash flows up to five years or have no cash flows in the first five years. Then the horizon immunization is quite simple. We dedicate the first-five-year liability schedule to all the bonds with maturity less than five years. Then we immunize the remaining liability schedule for the bonds with no cash flow in the first five years. That is, we can separate the problem into two parts.

The complication is, of course, that we cannot separate the two problems: dedication and immunization. If a bond is a good candidate for immunization, the coupon payments prior to the horizon date would be used for dedication. If a bond has maturity longer than the horizon date, a portion of that bond would be used for immunization. In other words, the bond dedication and immunization solutions have to be jointly determined.

The Horizon Immunization Procedure

For each bond, we have to create two bonds: The first bond consists of all the cash flow up to the horizon date, and the remaining cash flow forms the second bond. Let the bond price of the ith bond be P_i, and the holding in that bond be a_i. Then our objective function is to minimize the cost: Minimize $a_i \times P_i$, with the same constraints of Equations (14–4). In addition to those equations, we need the conditions for immunization. Let v_i and d_i be the present value and duration of the cash flow beyond the horizon date for bond i, respectively. Let L and D be the present value and the duration of the cash flow of the liability schedule beyond the horizon date, respectively. Then the conditions are

$$\sum a_i v_i = L \qquad (14\text{–}5a)$$

$$\sum a_i d_i = LD \qquad (14\text{–}5b)$$

This system of equations is linear; therefore, we can solve the horizon immunization problem using linear programming procedures.

Horizon immunization has provided a methodology to ensure a closer duration match between the assets and liabilities. Also, the value of the asset portfolio is often lower. However, immunization procedure requires revisions to ensure that the durations are matched. Therefore, horizon immunization may require more portfolio revision than the standard bond dedication.

We have completed our brief description of various portfolio strategies. In the next section, we will look at one particular insurance product, guaranteed investment contracts, and see how a bond strategy can be applied.

GUARANTEED INVESTMENT CONTRACTS

A guaranteed investment contract (GIC) is often a loan agreement made between an insurance company and a corporation. The loan contract can be arranged in many ways. Usually, no money changes hands at the time of the GIC agreement, but the insurer has guaranted a specific loan rate. Therefore, there is a brief time period after the insurer's commitment date during which the insurer actually receives funds from the corporation to put the GIC into effect. This time period is called the window period. The GIC has a guaranteed investment rate. Anyone who invests in the corporation's GIC realizes principal increases at this rate, but does not typically receive any coupons or interest payouts. The investment increases in line with an accrual schedule.

A GIC normally has a fixed term, typically three to five years. During this term, investors may withdraw the cash, but since an early withdrawal may incur penalties, we may not expect too many withdrawals. However, they do occur, for a number of reasons. For instance, people sometimes want to withdraw simply because they need the money. But there are also other reasons. For example, interest rates may get so high that it is worth incurring the penalty in order to reinvest at higher rates. Another reason deals with expectations. If investors perceive that the stock market can provide a much higher return, they may allocate money from the GIC account to the equity account. There are thus two major reasons for withdrawing money: an interest-rate-sensitive reason and a noninterest-rate-sensitive reason.

We can now analyze a GIC agreement from the insurance company's perspective. Consider the simple case where there is no early withdrawal of the GIC participation as a result of interest rate changes. From the insurance company's point of view, the payout occurs at the end of the term. This payout is the liability to the firm. On the other hand, the corporation pays the insurance company over the window period. Therefore, this cash-flow stream is an asset to the insurance company. The important point is that the liability has a much higher duration than the asset. In addition, the value of the GIC agreement is the asset value net of the liability value. If both the asset and the liability are fairly priced (priced completely by the market parameters as discussed previously), the asset value would equal the liability value, and the GIC agreement would therefore have no value. However, the GIC agreement remains interest rate sensitive. When interest rates rise, the investment received can be reinvested at a higher rate to cover the liability. For this reason, the GIC value would increase. On the other hand, if interest rates fall, the investment has to be invested at a lower rate, so the GIC would have less value. In sum, when an insurance company enters into a GIC agreement, it is essentially holding a short position in a forward contract. Recall the discussions on forward contracts, where we argue that shorting a forward contract is equivalent to buying a short-term bond and selling a long-term bond. This basic idea applies to the analysis of a GIC contract.

SUMMARY

This chapter is a consolidated presentation of all the concepts introduced in the previous chapters. Actual trading and portfolio management techniques are used not only to present examples, but to reinforce the importance of recognizing the multiple types of decisions that go into structuring a strategy. Many of these decisions rely on a bond model that integrates representative values.

The integrated approach is extremely useful for understanding the problems of managing fixed-income securities. Recent trends in the market are the quantification of nonparallel yield curve shift effects. Since our previous discussions on effective duration and convexity addressed only parallel shifts, we will in the next chapter present a discussion of how one can identify the impact of nonparallel shifts. The topic in the next chapter, which is a very recent development, requires an understanding of all the material presented thus far.

CHAPTER 15

FACTORIZATION AND ITS APPLICATION IN THE FIXED-INCOME MARKET

This chapter will present a new fixed-income portfolio management tool called Factorization. Factorization is an approach that decomposes a bond or portfolio's total return into components using the bond-pricing models. The components are return effects attributable to the interplay of market factors and a security's specific characteristics. The first half of this chapter begins with an in-depth explanation of Factorization. In this discussion, we introduce a new duration concept, *key rate duration*, which is the core of the Factorization process. Lastly, we introduce the other components of the Factorization technique. The end result of this technique is the identification of each source of a bond's or portfolio's total return and risks.

The second half of this chapter addresses how this new approach can enhance a fixed income manager's ability to manage the risks embodied in the instruments he/she invested in. We explain how the technique can be used in any of the following three areas:

- *Active management:* We discuss applications pertaining to swap analysis as well as structuring portfolio strategies.
- *Structured management:* Specific areas of interest are enhanced indexation, immunization, and dedications.
- *Return attribution:* We use the results of the analysis of a real investment company's portfolio to highlight the application of Factorization in a Performance Measurement context.

In sum, Factorization has many broad applications that the chapter will convey in a systematic manner.

FACTORIZATION: A DECOMPOSITION OF BOND RETURNS

Only a few market factors are needed to explain the holding period returns of typical fixed-income securities. This apparent simplicity contrasts sharply with the complexities and uncertainties of the equity market, where a large component of a stock's return cannot be explained by any market factor other than those specific to the security itself.

The primary bond market pricing factors are embodied in a spot-rate term structure. The change in price of default-free bonds, such as U.S. Treasury securities, can be fully explained by movements of spot rates. Change in the rate of discount to time t will influence the price of any security with a cash flow at t. In this sense, the spot rate associated with each cash flow of a security is a factor of bond return.

It is elementary to define the price sensitivity of a straight Treasury bond directly in terms of spot rate movements. For callable bonds and bonds with credit risk, a model of contingent claims pricing allows direct extension of the concept. By modeling arbitrage-free rate movements, any security's price and its change in price due to rate changes can be identified, both ex-post and ex-ante. The model will identify more factors that influence return, such as those factors that are associated with equilibrium prices for contingent features and the price of credit risk.

Generally, security factor models postulate that the excess return on a security or portfolio can be expressed as a linear combination of systematic sources of price change. Moreover, these factors are usually specified or determined so as to be independent of each other. This is a mathematical—as opposed to economic—constraint, and often produces models that entail *unobservable* factors.

This chapter introduces an alternative process that decomposes fixed-income security returns. *In our method we assert the fundamental identifiability of a set of factors*. The components of total return are specified by economic effects a priori. Both alternative views of the process of Factorization result in models with linear expressions of systematic effects on return. Nonetheless, the identifiability of the factors forms an important distinction.

This procedure identifies each risk source and then models how it will affect a bond or portfolio return. Factorization identifies the *sources of risk* to be the unanticipated changes in

- key rates (points along a yield curve)
- volatilities of interest rates
- option-adjusted spreads

The portfolio sensitivity to each of these risk factors is called an attribute. These attributes can be estimated by bond-pricing models. In addition, we can identify the fundamental *sources of returns*. They are

- risk-free return
- option-adjusted spread
- time decay of embedded options
- change in cheap/rich level

The following sections will first explain how this process has *a subtle, but important, difference from existing return attribution methodologies* and then highlight its applicability and contrast those methodologies.

Factors of Return in Securities with Certain Cash Flows

Arguably the most basic and most familiar equilibrium model for risky assets is Sharpe's Capital Asset Pricing Model (CAPM). This model asserts that the return of any risky asset is linearly related to the market portfolio return. More precisely, we have

$$r = r_f + \text{beta} \times (r_m - r_f) + e$$

where r is the return of the risky assets; r_f is the riskfree rate; beta is an attribute of the security; r_m is the market return; and e is some random noise. The term $(r_m - r_f)$ is referred to as the "market factor," and beta is termed the "market attribute" of the security.

Consider a default-free coupon Treasury bond. Typically, the CAPM is not directly applied to such a security. However, a factor model with exactly the same form can be developed for fixed-income securities.

To develop a fixed-income factor model in CAPM form, we first define the spot discount function, and associated spot rate function for t_0, $R_0(T)$. The forward rate function, $F_0(T)$, at t_1 is the "pure expectations" view of rate curve that will exist at t_1. Now say that the ex-post spot curve at t_1 is precisely the forward curve found at t_0. In this case, it is easy to verify that every fixed-income security would return the one-period riskless rate. Necessarily, this rate must be the one-period return on a Treasury bill. This proof is given in Chapter 3.

When the spot curve at t_1 is different from the forward curve, the rates of return of fixed-income securities will in general be different from each other. Let the ex-post rate at t_1 differ from the forward rate $F_0(T)$ by a small amount ΔR_1 for any term T:

$$R_1(T) = F_0(T) + \Delta R_1 \qquad (15\text{--}1)$$

This defines a parallel shift from the forward curve. The sensitivity of the rate of return of a fixed-income security, i, with respect to dR_1 is given by the effective duration *with respect to the forward function*.

$$D_i = \frac{-\Delta P_i / \Delta R_1}{P_i} \qquad (15\text{--}2)$$

where P_i is the price or discount factor on the forward curve. Effective duration is usually expressed in terms of a parallel shift from the *spot function*, not from the forward function. The former concept provides a measure of sensitivity of total return; here, we analogously define sensitivity of excess return.

Effective duration relative to the forward function implies a single-factor model for fixed-income securities that is analogous in form to the CAPM. Referring to the CAPM equation, we see that beta can be placed by D_i of Equation (15–2); and the "market factor" is interpreted as a parallel deviation from the "expected" spot curve; that is, a deviation from the implied forward curve. Hence, we have

$$R_i = {}^*r_f - D_i \times \Delta R_1 + e \qquad (15\text{--}3)$$

More recently, multifactor models of risky return have been presented. The general form of multifactor return models may be given as

$$r = r_f + \text{beta}_1 \times f_1 + \text{beta}_2 \times f_2 + \cdots + \text{beta}_n \times f_n + e \quad (15\text{--}4)$$

Here, the beta_i terms are factor attributes or weights for security i, the f_i are the factors that determine the returns and the products are the factor effects on the asset return.

There is great latitude in economic interpretation of multifactor models for returns. One taxonomy of factors extends from the market

---

* r_f is determined by the one-period rate specified by the spot curve.

factor to sector and industry and size factors, for example. For default-free bonds, the major source of risk remains interest rate risk. We note that (15–3) is defined in terms of a parallel shift from the forward curve. Extension of the single-factor model, then, will proceed from a generalization of effective duration. Therefore, the effect on asset returns from "nonparallel" rate shifts can be identified.

Effective duration is the derivative of bond return with respect to a single rate factor that represents movement over the entire spot rate range. We define *key rate duration* of an asset as the partial derivative of asset return with respect to a rate of a specified term, or key rate. The development is described in the next section.

Nonparallel Rate Movements and Key Rate Duration

Effective duration is a standard measure of the interest rate risk exposure of a bond or a portfolio that has come to have many applications in managing interest rate risk. Two main assumptions underlie the definition of duration. Effective duration measures price sensitivity to a shift of the yield if:

- The shift is instantaneous, which implies an instantaneous investment horizon; and
- The yield curve shift is parallel and sufficiently small.

If either assumption is relaxed, effective duration will misstate return sensitivity. Yet both assumptions are quite unrealistic. Money managers typically take positions with an investment horizon implicit in their bond strategy. In actuality, the manager may not hold the bond for the intended horizon period because strategy can be revised continually. Nevertheless, a manager may wish to evaluate the interest rate risk exposure over time and not the instantaneous risk.

The second assumption is equally restrictive. Parallel shifts of the spot curve can capture much of the nature of term structure movements. However, the returns to two securities with the same effective duration can be significantly different if the yield curve undergoes nonparallel shifts, such as "rotations" or "inversions."

Key rate durations define the risk of the changing shape of the spot curve.* Formally, the kth key rate duration for the ith security is denoted

---

*For purposes of exposition, the spot curve will automatically mean the spot curve expected on the horizon date (the implied forward curve at the initial date).

$_iD_k$. Associated with each duration is a spot rate of specified term, for example, the five-year spot rate. Then the k-year rate defines the kth spot rate epoch. Within the epoch, the relative shift away from the forward curve is linear from either end, rising to the unit change at the center. The following diagram illustrates two epochs.

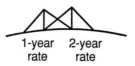

1-year   2-year
rate   rate

In effect this means that the rate change from the forward curve describes a triangle with the key rate at the peak. The key rate duration thus defines the effect, expressed in basis points, of a unit basis point change in the neighborhood of the kth spot rate.

Key rate durations are not a single measure as is effective duration. As a set, the key rate durations define return over the entire range of possible movements of the yield curve. In the special case where the risk of parallel shifts is to be considered, the combined use of the key rate durations becomes identical to the use of effective duration.

When there is no investment horizon, the concept of controlling the yield curve movements needs elaboration. If the yield curve at the horizon date is the implied forward yield curve, then all the default-free liquid bonds will have the same total return, and the return is the risk-free return. From this analysis, we can then conclude that the appropriate yield curve shift should be measured by the shift of the yield curve from the forward curve on the horizon date.

Let $h(K)$ denote the spot rate prevailing on the horizon date, which gives the yield on a default-free pure discount bond maturing at time K, and let $H(T)$ denote the spot discount function defined for all T. Consider a set of epochs $\{K_j\}$, and choose the elements such that a linear combination of $h(K_l)$ and $h(K_{l+1})$ is a sufficiently high-order approximation to $h(t)$ on the interval $[K_1, K_{l+1}]$. In effect, this assumption implies that any yield curve on the horizon date may be represented accurately by piecewise linear interpolation between a finite (and, optimally, small) set of term rates.

For example, we consider a set of 11 key rate epochs of three months and 1, 2, 3, 5, 7, 10, 15, 20, 25, and 30 years. Other sets could be defined that differ in both number and the term of the key rates.

Further, key rate durations are additive. That is, the key rate durations for 5, 7, and 10 years can be combined as one attribute to describe movement over this 5-year region of the spot curve. In the limit, of course, adding all the key rate durations together yields effective duration.

Now say that there is an autonomous shift of 1 basis point (bp) in one specific key rate. This will induce a price change in every security that has a cash flow at that epoch. Likewise, by assumption, an autonomous shift of 1 bp in a rate with a term between two key rate epochs can be approximated by appropriate shifts of the neighboring key rates.

Initially, consider a default-free straight bond that pays no coupon during the horizon period. Let the bond price on the base date be P_0. Also let the bond price plus any accrued interest or cash payments on the horizon date with the forward curve prevailing be P_f. That price will induce a holding period return identical to the riskless rate for all securities. Assume an autonomous shift in $h(K_i)$, $dh(K_i)$, and denote the new bond price on the horizon date as P_1. This bond then has its ith key rate duration, D_i, defined as

$$D_i = \frac{P_f - P_1}{P_0 \times \Delta h(K_i)} \tag{15-5}$$

Equation (15-5) defines the ith key rate duration as the (negative) change in bond price (including accrued interest) per dollar invested at the beginning of the period, as a result of a small unit shift of the ith key rate.

Key rate durations constitute in fact a linear decomposition of effective duration. By definition, the sum of any set of key rate durations equals effective duration, up to the accuracy of the linear approximation of the spot yield curve. This result can be seen quite readily in the case of straight bonds. Suppose each key rate drops 1 bp. By interpolation, this is equivalent to a 1 bp drop everywhere along the curve, the differential of which defines effective duration. Therefore, the sum of the key rate durations must equal effective duration.

Since effective duration measures only parallel movement, one can say that effective duration is an attribute of the *parallel shift factor*. This is the interpretation used in Equation (15-2) above. In this sense, a shift of n key rates yields an n-factor model, and every default-free security's return has n factor attributes: the respective key rate durations.

Key rate epochs are constructed to model the shifts of the spot curve. The linear combination of these key rate movements can approximate most yield curve shifts.

TABLE 15–1
Key Rate Durations

	D_1	D_2	D_3	Effective Duration
		Securities		
2-year zero	2.0	0.0	0.0	2.0
16-year zero	0.0	16.0	0.0	16.0
30-year zero	0.0	0.0	30.0	30.0
		Portfolios		
I	1.0	0.0	15.0	16.0
II	0.0	16.0	0.0	16.0

A Numerical Example

We begin a simplified example by assuming that change in the spot curve over the holding period can be defined by a set of key rates with terms of 2 years, 16 years, and 30 years. For simplicity, the rate function $H(t)$ is measured in terms of continuous compounding. In this case, it is well-known that the effective duration of any zero-coupon bond is equal to its maturity.

Consider two portfolios: At the beginning of the period, Portfolio I is composed of $50 market value of 2-year pure discount bonds, and $50 of 30-year per discount bonds. Portfolio II consists of $100 market value of 16-year discount bonds.

The key rate durations of the two portfolios are the value-weighted average of the key rate durations of the component securities, which are shown in Table 15–1.

Assume that the yield curve is flat at 8 percent. Then $H(T) = .08$, for all T, since a constant spot rate function implies that the forward function is likewise constant at the same level.

A one-factor model, as in Equation (15–3), will have the same factor attribute for both portfolios, which implies both portfolios have the same return sensitivity. For a 1 bp (parallel) shift from the forward curve (and in this case the spot curve equivalently) the model "predicts" a 16 bp change in portfolio value, in addition to the riskless return over the period.

Using the three key rate shifts as the factors produces an expression like that in Equation (15–4). The return of the ith security or portfolio is now expressed as

$$_iR = r_i - [_iD_1 \times dH(2)] - [_iD_2 \times dH(16)]$$
$$- [_iD_3 \times dH(3)] + e \qquad (15\text{–}6)$$

Note that the signs on the factor terms in (15–6) are all negative, reflecting the normal inverse relationship between bond price and yield and the convention that effective duration is quoted as a positive value.

We take the holding period to be one week. Then the riskless rate of return over the period is

$$.08/\text{yr} \times 10,000 \times (7/365)\text{yr} = 15 \text{ basis points}$$

Consider three alternative scenarios for the horizon date. In the first scenario, the spot curve shifts down 10 bp at all three key rate epochs. In the second scenario, the 2-year rate rises by 10 bp, and the 30-year rate falls by 10 bp; and the third scenario has reverse shifts for the rates. The latter two scenarios are "rotations" around the 16-year rate. The respective scenario returns over the holding period for the two portfolios are given in Table 15–2, with the values obtained by direct substitution into Equation (15–6).

TABLE 15–2
Scenarios

Portfolio	First	Second	Third
I	175 bp	155 bp	−135 bp
II	175 bp	15 bp	15 bp

Table 15–2 shows why effective duration cannot explain returns in cases of nonparallel spot curve shifts, and why key rate duration is much more powerful. Both portfolios have the same effective duration. In the first scenario, the spot curve shift was parallel, and both effective duration attribution and Factorization indicated that the return of both portfolios should be identical. In the latter two scenarios, effective duration cannot be defined unambiguously. Any definition that relies on

a single-factor specification for the complex sport curve's change cannot identify the difference in the returns of the two portfolios.

Key Rate Durations and Alternative Schemes

Other factor models of bond returns have been proposed. One widely known model identifies three factors of return as "level," "steepness," and "curvature." However, the process started with the assumption that there is a set of factors that determines bond returns historically. After the factor analysis was completed on historical data, three empirical factors were found, and then each was named to reflect the nature of its effects over the term structure.

A consequence of that empirical development is that the model is essentially normative; the factors are not identified by algebraic specification. Nonetheless, it is readily shown that three-factor immunization can outperform single-factor immunization (duration matching). We will now discuss how one could re-specify a key rate factor model to entail the same information as a "level, steepness, curvature" factor model.

The factors in (15–6) were autonomous shifts in the three key rates. Instead, one could define factors arbitrarily in terms of *forms* of shift. For example, a unit "level" shift could be described as {1, 1, 1}, a "steepness" shift as {−1, 0, 1}, and a "curvature" shift as {1, 0, 1}, where {x, y, z} represents the proportional shift relative to the 30-year key rate shift. Then, for example, the third scenario in the previous example would now be termed "10 bp steepness shift." Now key rate durations are no longer the relevant attributes of a security; instead, shift attributes would be now defined as the linear combinations of the key rate durations.

If the three key rate shifts are themselves independent, then it can be proven that the shifts defined are also independent. Moreover, the approximation provided by linear interpolation of a continuous yield curve shift is not changed by the redefinition.

In both cases, it is true that the specification of factors is not unique. This is sometimes a source of difficulty in empirical factorization approaches. However, for the model based on key rate durations, the ability to recast the factor specification is arguably an advantage, from the standpoint of infusing heuristic meaning into the model.

The Link between Key Rate Duration and Term Structure Modeling

Throughout this introduction we have concentrated on bonds with certain and default-free cash flows. To have practical application, the concept must be applicable to any fixed-income instrument, including futures, options, bonds with embedded bonds, and bonds with default risk.

Pricing of interest-rate-contingent features of securities requires a model of term structure movements, and a number of models for term structure movements have been proposed. A common underpinning of all currently accepted models is that they entail changes in spot rates over time that result in arbitrage-free price movements for all securities in the market.

The AR model of Ho and Lee (see Chapter 11) directly specifies subsequent arbitrage-free rate movements relative to any initial spot discount function. Key rate durations are defined in terms of perturbations of the forward function, which is an entire function of the initial spot curve. For this reason, the specification of key rate durations for contingent claims depends on the initial spot function parametrically.

Therefore, it appears that the AR model is capable of specifying key rate durations for bonds with embedded options. With the AR model, it can be shown that the decomposition of effective duration into key rate durations is valid for contingent cash flows as well as for specified cash flows.

Using the AR model to evaluate contingent claims, the concepts introduced in this chapter can be extended to include other relevant factors, such as changes in embedded option values and the effects of rate volatility. The analysis can be extended to securities with credit risk as well. The development of such an extended factor model is the subject of the next section of this chapter.

Extending Key Rate Duration Factorization

The usefulness of effective duration as a linear single-factor model is limited. Furthermore any algebraic specification of duration necessarily restricts its application to fixed-income securities with certain cash flows. In contrast, for bonds with certain cash flows, key rate duration makes the factor approach more robust for actual nonparallel spot curve movements. In fact, the majority of fixed-income securities have embedded contingency features. Timing, amount, and receipt of cash flows are then determined by future levels of the term structure. Closed-form specifications of effective duration or key rate duration cannot incorporate this type of uncertainty.

Comprehensive application of key rate duration to portfolio problems must therefore rely on a model of term structure movements for inference of the price and return characteristics of securities that have embedded options. Changes in the value of options embedded in fixed-income securities typically depend on movements of the spot rate. Durations can then be measured with the derivative, or numerical differential, of price with respect to a change in the spot rate function. For analyzing security returns based on key rate duration, the model of term structure movement must be consistent with an arbitrary initial spot function because key rate durations are defined with respect to differentials in current forward rates.

The AR model of term structure movements was the first to specify arbitrage-free future rate movements explicitly in terms of an observed spot curve. Values for all fixed-income securities can be inferred from the model. Further, the model entails the size of relative price changes with respect to instantaneous changes in the spot function.

When the AR model is used to value embedded options, key rate durations extend to encompass securities with those options. Moreover, application of the model explicitly identifies and measures additional return attributes associated with the option component of the security.

Price change of an option is known to arise from a number of identifiable factors. For options dependent on movements of the spot curve, the most important determinants of price change are the change in the *probability of exercise* due to the change of the spot curve (that is, the amount "in-" or "out-of-the money"), change in the *volatility of the spot curve's movements*, and the *time decay* of the value of the option.

The probability of exercise is embodied in the estimation of key rate duration of an option. The last two are factors that can be explicitly defined in the Factorization of the security's return.

Volatility Attribute

This factor is defined in the units of volatility. Although the concept of volatility is familiar and straightforward, its application for the spot curve has a semantic tangle. The spot rate is usually expressed in *return* percent per year. The tendency for the rates to change—their volatility—

is expressed in terms of *relative* change in the level of the spot rate. Therefore, to say, for example, that "spot rate volatility is 10 percent" means that the standard deviation of the annual change in the *level* of the spot rate is 10 percent of its value at the beginning of the year. In this case, for example, a one standard deviation change of an 8 percent spot rate implies the same term spot rate would be 8.8 percent next year. Recall the discussion of volatility in Chapter 12.

An attribute can now be defined for change in volatility for security *i* that incorporates this convention:

- $_iv$ is defined as the basis point return induced by an immediate *1 percent relative change in the volatility of spot rates.*

Obviously, a security without any embedded option characteristics will have $v = 0$. The value of v for securities with embedded options, such as callable bonds, can be determined from the AR option pricing model.

Time Decay Attribute

All options lose time premium as expiration approaches. For the holder of an option-embedded bond, return is earned from the passage of time. The amount of premium "captured" is dependent on the terms of the option and the time elapsed. We define the time premium decay attribute factor for security *i*:

- $_ip$ is defined as the basis point return that accrues from option premium lost over one week *when the spot curve at the end of the week equals the forward curve* implied by the initial spot curve.

Option-Adjusted Spread Attribute

Option-adjusted spread (OAS) refers to the additional yield required by the market to hold securities that have risk of default. As perceptions of the riskiness of a security change, the OAS changes accordingly. In the AR model, the OAS of a security is defined by a parallel displacement of the default-free spot curve. Thus, the return attribute associated with a change in OAS is equivalent to effective duration, since both are defined analagously. We define the attribute of change in OAS for security *i*:

- $_io$ is defined as the return (in basis points) from a 1 bp change in *option-adjusted spread*. $_io$ is equal to the effective duration of security *i*.

The Factorization of Bond Return

In the model presented here, we employ four key rate durations, defined for the epochs of 1 year, 5 years, 15 years, and 25 years, respectively, and, in addition, the factors just defined.

The factorization of the return of security i is given explicitly as

$$r_i = r_f + OAS +_i p_{-i} D_1 dr_1 -_i D_2 dr_2 -_i D_3 dr_3 -_i D_4 dr_4 \\ -_{io} dOAS -_i pd_f -_i vdv + e$$

(15-7)

The AR model determines the attributes of any security's return and will determine the values of all the coefficients of equation (15-7).

A Factorization Example

Factorization serves to highlight the differences in the nature of returns between different securities, as is shown in Table 15-3. Three sets of

TABLE 15-3
Factorization Table for Callable Bonds (All bonds are callable at par after 1 year)

Bond Type	Price	D_1	D_2	D_3	D_4	o	p	v
10-year 9% No call	102.97	0.2	1.7	4.5	0.0	6.4	0	0
10-year 7% Call	88.81	0.3	2.1	3.5	0.0	5.8	0	23
10-year 8% Call	94.21	0.4	2.0	2.3	0.0	4.7	0	32
10-year 9% Call	98.40	0.6	1.6	1.2	0.0	3.4	1	31
10-year 10% Call	100.98	0.9	0.7	0.3	0.0	1.9	2	17
10-year 11% Call	102.41	0.8	0.2	0.1	0.0	1.2	3	4
20-year 9% No call	104.38	0.3	1.7	7.2	0.0	9.1	0	0
20-year 7% Call	83.49	0.3	2.0	5.7	0.0	7.9	0	49
20-year 8% Call	90.99	0.4	2.1	4.0	0.0	6.5	0	58
20-year 9% Call	96.84	0.6	1.8	2.3	0.0	4.6	1	54
20-year 10% Call	100.49	0.8	0.6	0.9	0.0	2.3	2	31
20-year 11% Call	102.31	0.7	0.3	0.2	0.0	1.2	6	9
28-year 9% No call	105.45	0.3	1.6	4.5	3.8	10.3	0	0
28-year 7% Call	81.82	0.3	2.0	4.1	2.3	8.6	0	61
28-year 8% Call	90.03	0.4	2.1	3.2	1.3	6.9	0	70
28-year 9% Call	96.41	0.6	1.7	1.9	0.6	4.9	1	63
28-year 10% Call	100.32	0.7	0.8	0.7	0.2	2.3	9	34
28-year 11% Call	102.25	1.2	0.0	0.0	0.0	1.1	4	9

hypothetical bonds are shown. The sets differ by maturity. Among each set, the bonds differ by coupon and the presence of embedded calls. Specifically, in this example, every callable bond has the same call schedule: callable at par after approximately a year.

Several points deserve note. clearly maturity is not a good indicator of risks in holding callable bonds. For high-coupon callable issues, the expected life of the bonds is shortened by the high probability that the bond will be called as soon as possible; in this case, in one year. This can be seen by examination of the key rate durations. The high-coupon bonds are quite unaffected by changes in the longer key rate durations, because it is not expected that the bonds will exist very long after the call date.

The OAS attribute, again, is equal to effective duration. Note also that the key rate durations sum to effective duration and perforce agree, with for rounding, to the o attribute for each bond.

The volatility attribute v measures the change in return for a unit percentage change in volatility of the spot curve. Consider the 10-year, 8 percent callable bond in Table 15–3. There, v is given as 32. This means that an instantaneous increase in spot rate volatility of 1 percent would reduce the return on the bond by 32 basis points. The reason is easy to see: Higher spot rate volatility implies a higher probability that the spot curve can fall to a level where the bond would be called. As this would be disadvantageous to the holder, the price will fall.

USING FACTORIZATION

Factorization can be a powerful engine of analysis for fixed income securities. The component risks of holding a particular bond, liability stream, or income participation can be examined and compared to the risks associated with alternative securities.

A number of activities can be augmented by application of Factorization. Through the matching of attributes, immunization strategies can take on enhanced value and minimize risk. Time series of Factorizations for portfolios permit analysis of the ways in which the portfolio changed value. These applications are termed *return attributions*.

Chapter 14 highlighted some active and structured portfolio management strategies that relied on effective duration measures. Key rate durations can be easily incorporated into all of these discussions. We simply substitute a set of key rate durations for a single duration measure.

Factorization can be easily adapted for horizon analysis. That is, bond returns can be simulated using scenario yield curves. Once the simulation processing is completed, we have the bond's return effects (the product of the attributes and the factors). These return effects now become the basis of analysis. We can cross-compare the return effects between two candidates in a swap, or we can structure a hedging strategy to offset the specific, undesirable, interest rate risk exposure. This use of Factorization in horizon analysis applies to both active and structured management strategies. The difference in how each manager handles the information would be in the approach. An active manager may seek to increase exposure on a certain region, whereas another manager may want to nullify the exposure. The mitigation would be accomplished by obtaining an instrument whose return effects would complete-offset the first instrument's.

For instance, in analyzing a bond swap, we can now better identify whether we would be exposed to a different section of the yield curve if we executed the trade. A swap based simply on matching effective duration and maturity would not reveal whether the envisaged incremental yield advantage would be obtained at the expense of an increased exposure in a certain region of the yield curve. For example, using key rate durations, we may now see *what* and *where* our interest rate risks will be if we swap from a noncallable into a callable security.

Central to implementing dynamic strategies in fixed income management is the control of risk factors. For such structured management, the asset mix has to be altered in different market scenarios. Bonds with embedded options change their sensitivity to each key rate depending on the level of rates. As a result, Factorization enables managers more accurately to implement dynamic portfolio strategies that use option-embedded bonds. The return attribution system, used for either ex-post or scenario reviewing, provides immediate feedback on the effectiveness of the strategy to the portfolio's management.

In another type of structured management, portfolios are often subject to certain risk exposure. This new return attribution system can be used for continually monitoring the portfolio's risk exposure. The risk exposure may be interest rate risk, credit risk, or option risk. We would be able to plot, on a weekly basis, the return effect attributable to a specific risk. This type of information would not only enable us to structure a more informative monitoring program, but also to respond rapidly to any deviations from a desired range.

In sum, the applications of this return attribution go beyond the traditional portfolio performance analysis; standard return attribution methodologies used dynamically with Factorization can enhance many active or structured management strategies. Lastly, Factorization is the only method that helps not only in structuring strategies, but also in analyzing strategies that have been implemented in the past.

In this context, this procedure can be used for providing a synopsis of a fixed income manager's investment performance during a period of time. The following sections will first outline the types of benefits associated with this application and then provide a detailed overview of a specific portfolio's return attribution.

RETURN ATTRIBUTION

Return Attribution (RA) is the process of breaking down the total return of a portfolio. RA uses the Factorization methodology in this process. Factorization *uses various relevant bond* models, which are consistent within an (arbitrage-free) framework, to decompose the returns of commands or bond portfolios. Factorization takes the modeling approach. By way of contrast, other commonly used return attribution systems take the statistical approach, whereby the common factors and sector factors are estimated from historical returns over the review period.

Technical Advantages

Using Factorization to analyze information on returns, transactions, and market movements, this return attribution procedure can provide more precise detail pertaining to the source of portfolio returns than can return attribution methodologies using statistical procedures. The return attribution procedure, at least the basic part, can be described briefly as follows. Given the initial portfolio bond positions (the bond issue's descriptions and holding sizes) and all the transactions during the period (which may be as short as one week), RA can determine how the portfolio return over that period (that week) is attributable to such interest-rate-sensitive factors as the set of observable key rates (the shifts of key rates), and convexity. In addition, non–interest-rate-sensitive factors are included; these are changes in OAS, theta (time decay of options),* and volatility. Lastly, we identify non-factor impacts on return such as cheap/rich changes, trading profit/loss, and the expected risk-free rate of return for the period. The balance of return, not explained by the model, is the residual. RA has been found to be significantly robust in its ability to explain a holding period return. For example, even for option-embedded bonds such as corporate issues, RA can explain over 90 percent of the observed return over a given period.

Traditionally, return attribution systems' primary use has been to evaluate the performance of a portfolio manager. For this application, a return attribution procedure utilizing the Factorization approach can process all the transactions of a portfolio over a period of time, say two to five years, and decompose the portfolio returns over this period on a weekly basis. This way, the analysis can be more precese in spotting a portfolio manager's market-timing skill or expertise in implementing portfolio strategies. Observation of this type of information enables portfolio managers to evaluate their performance against that of an index to determine the specific impact or side effects of implemented strategies. Moreover, exploiting the accuracy of the performance measurements, the system can provide testimony of portfolio management skills using significantly shorter time periods for compiling a track record. In sum, this RA approach can be used to demonstrate more clearly the strengths of a portfolio manager's skill or the underlying philosophy of a particular fund relative to another fund.

Qualitative Aspects

Total return can be viewed in an overall risk/reward setting. The overall success accruing to active management is shown relative to the results of the passive management of an indexed portfolio.

The attribution analysis made possible by the key rate framework shows the manager at work. A unique window allows one to view both the sector and rate anticipation allocations made within the portfolio. Evidence of successful rate anticipation strategies can be seen in before-the-fact increases in key rate duration in the yield curve regions that subsequently moved favorably from the manager's perspective.

---

* For convenience, p was used to represent time decay in Table 15-3 and the discussion preceding it.

The workings and the effectiveness of this return attribution procedure can be best explained by way of an illustration. Although the illustration focuses on analyzing a portfolio manager's performance, it also demonstrates the breadth of information generated in this process.

An Illustration

Throughout this section we will analyze a particular portfolio. We will analyze the portfolio returns historically and show how the returns of the portfolio are dynamically factorized into the sources of returns. In analyzing the performance we first study the portfolio returns in the standard procedure, and then we show how this return attribution model can provide more relevant information on the portfolio manager's performance.

The data are obtained from an investment company. We have the initial portfolio holding as of 12/13/86 and every transaction up through 6/31/89. Since we have recorded every trade, including cash outflows and inflows, we can determine the portfolio's holding for any point in time.

The objective of the fund's manager is to maximize the portfolio's return. The portfolio's performance is not benchmarked against any index. The portfolio at the beginning of the study, 12/31/86, had a market value of about $167.8 million. Its initial composition was as follows:

Types of Issues	Percentage of Market Value
Treasury and Agency Issues	51.9
Corporate Issues	40.5
Private Placements	7.6
Total	100.0

Maturity Range Proportions	Percentage of Market Value
0 to 2 years	0.3
2 to 3 years	42.4
5 to 10 years	57.3
Over 10 years	0.0
Total	100.0

At any point in time, the number of securities ranged, on average, from 18 to 25 different issues.

Return Attribution Using Some Standard Measures

We calculated both time-weighted and dollar-weighted returns. However, the dollar-weighted return information was superfluous since there were no cash allocation strategies implemented. If there had been allocation strategies (that is, if there was some control over how much to allocate into noncash assets or how much money to take out or add to the fund), then we would have focused on the dollar-weighted return measures. Almost all of the major cash changes were attributable to redemptions or principal additions. In other words, in order for the dollar-weighted measure to be appropriate, all the inflow or outflow of funds had to be outside the asset portfolio. For example, if the portfolio received the coupon payments and the cash was reinvested to buy some long bond, then there was no cash inflow or outflow. However, if cash accumulated from the coupon income was distributed to investors, this was considered a cash outflow.

Figure 15–1 shows the time-weighted return of the portfolio against that of the index for a one-year period. The index is a Treasury index, consisting of all the Treasury notes and bonds with maturities over

FIGURE 15–1
Time-Weighted Portfolio Returns versus Treasury Index

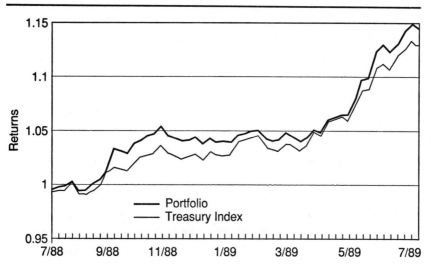

one year. Figure 15–1 depicts four quarterly performances where the
returns are measured on a weekly basis. It shows that the portfolio
in the first quarter outperformed the index. However, in the next two
quarters the portfolio somewhat underperformed the index, and then,
as the market rallied in the last quarter, the portfolio outperformed the
index significantly. The portfolio ended the year with a 120 basis point
return in excess of the market.

Measures of Risks.   In a bond portfolio, we have to be concerned
with different sources of risks: interest rate risks, credit risks, option-
adjusted spread risk, volatility sensitivity, and others. For interest rate
risks, we can use the portfolio's effective duration as a measure of
interest rate risk exposure. However, we must note that the portfolio
duration varies over time, partly due to the active management and partly
due to the changing market environment affecting the duration value. For
this reason, we calculate the average duration of the portfolio over each
quarter. When the duration is higher than the index's, we can interpret
this as signifying that the manager decided to take on more interest rate
risk. In addition to obtaining a trend of the duration measures, we also
computed the 30-day return volatilities for both the portfolio and the
index.

Figures 15–2 and 15–3 show that the portfolio's risk was lower than
that of the index, measured in terms of both duration and volatility, most
of the time during this period, except for the last quarter. However, the
risk exposure differential is quite small.

Market Timing.   Because the portfolio manager's strategies
focused on market-timing the interest rate changes, we directed our attention to identifying the impact of such market timing on the portfolio's
returns.

In market timing, the portfolio manager structures the portfolio to
benefit from an anticipated interest rate increase or decrease; this way the
portfolio can outperform the index. If the yield curve is expected to drop
in a parallel fashion, the manager extends the duration to increase the
return. If the yield curve moves up, and if the portfolio manager cannot
use any futures and options to effect a negative duration portfolio, the
portfolio must often bear a loss. At best the manager can shorten the
duration. Let us define excess return as the observed return less the risk-
free return during the holding period. If we plot the excess returns of the

FIGURE 15–2
Quarterly Average Durations

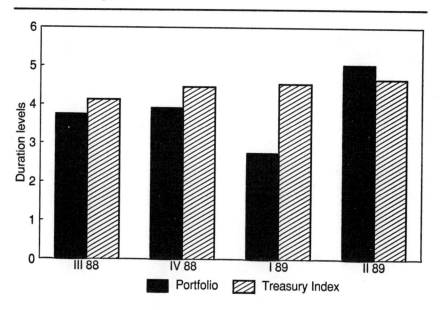

FIGURE 15–3
Quarterly Return Volatility

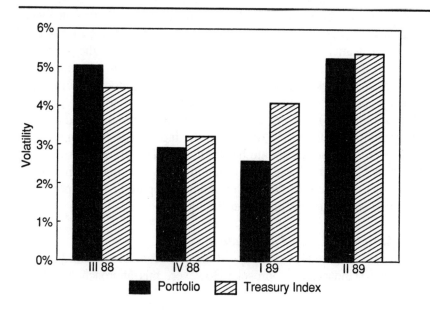

FIGURE 15–4
Comparison of Earned Excess Returns

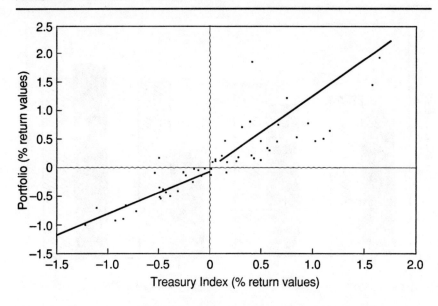

portfolio against the index's excess return and run a regression analysis, we can construct a characteristic line, as depicted in Figure 15–4.

We will now briefly discuss the information that is being conveyed through a characteristic line. The slope of the curve that best fits the points in the scatter plot represents the timing capability of the portfolio manager. If the portfolio manager has market timing skill, the portfolio should, in an up market, have a higher return than the index, resulting in a steeper slope than 45 degrees (i.e., greater than 1). For a bear market (an increase in rates), the portfolio manager should reduce the duration and thus minimize his losses relative to the index. The resulting slope in this lower left quadrant should be less than 1. This argument suggests that the fitted lines in the scatter plot should result in a curve. Figure 15–4 shows that curvature in the plotted points, supporting the hypothesis that there is some success in market timing.

Return Attribution Using Factorization
Thus far we have analyzed the portfolio's performance according to a somewhat standardized approach. However, this approach failed to

depict the performance on a trade-by-trade basis. In other words, we could not isolate particular actions that were responsible for the excess returns. After all, if we wish to analyze a manager, we should be able to give credit for particular actions that distinguish her from someone who may have made a couple of random lucky moves or who adheres to no particular philosophy.

The analysis thus far shows that the portfolio has a risk profile similar to the index and that the portfolio manager, applying market-timing skill, beat the market somewhat successfully. But this procedure does not say when and how the portfolio manager applied the market-timing strategies. Moreover, the concept of market timing is somewhat imprecise. As we discussed earlier, the yield curve can shift in many ways, and effective duration is inadequate to measure the success of the specific bond strategies that the portfolio manager implemented. We will show that the portfolio manager did in fact structure some complex strategies with mixed results. This was accomplished by applying the Return Attribution technique to both the portfolio and the index for a one-year period. We can now analyze the manager's actions and their impacts on the portfolio return over a time period.

As an example of our process, Table 15–4 shows the output from the factorization process for one week beginning June 14, 1989. The key rate durations highlight the portfolio's interest rate risk structure in that week. In general, the portfolio consisted of mostly government issues, with the majority of the corporate issues having maturities ranging from three to six years. The option-related impacts on the total portfolio were negligible; the time decay and the volatility sensitivity of the options were consistently small over time as measured by our procedure. We were also able to determine that there was minimal impact from the nonfactor returns: the change of the cheap/rich value of the portfolio, trading profit, and the residual (returns not explained by the model). In fact, this was the case generally for all the weeks in this sample period (54 weeks). This result confirms the robustness of the factorization procedure in an empirical test.

In summary, the results showed that the effects from the OAS factor and the option factor were negligible, suggesting that the portfolio manager takes on little credit risk. The cheap/rich factor and the trading components were also small. These findings confirmed that the analysis should focus on the manager's market-timing strategies. Given that credit risk and sector allocations were not significant, the use of a Treasury

TABLE 15–4
Factors and Return Effects in Basis Points (Week of June 14, 1989)

	(A) Attributes	(B) Factors	(C) = (A) × (B) Return Effects
Factors sensitive to interest rates			
Key rate 1	.767	+18.8	−14.4
Key rate 2	1.356	+18.7	−25.3
Key rate 3	1.902	+16.4	−31.1
Key rate 4	1.714	+13.0	−22.3
Convexity			0.0
Factors not sensitive to interest rates			
OAS			+2.6
Volatility			0.0
Nonfactor return			
Cheap/rich (securities within portfolio)			+1.0
Trading return			+5.9
Risk-free return			+15.8
Residual			−6.0
TOTAL RETURN			−73.8

index was sufficient for cross comparisons since we decided to focus solely on the manager's ability to time the market. The question then becomes whether one is better off with this manager than simply holding an indexed fund of U.S. Treasury securities? The following results will show that the response may be yes.

Performance Analysis
The weekly Factorization can be used to analyze the market timing on a week-by-week basis. In doing so, we compare the key rate movement to the change in key rate durations of the portfolio on a week-by-week basis. Figure 15–5a depicts the weekly key rate movements over the time period. Figure 15–5b is a consolidated view of the key rate movements and the portfolio's key rate duration composition over the 54-week period. The sum of the key rate durations, or the height of each

FIGURE 15–5(a)

Weekly Key Rate Movements; (b) Portfolio's Key Rate Duration Composition

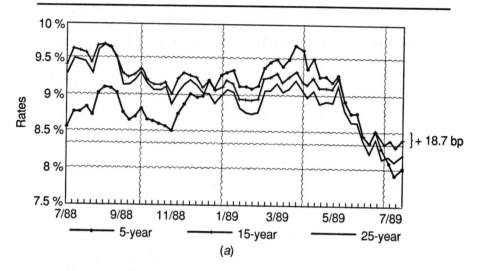

(a)

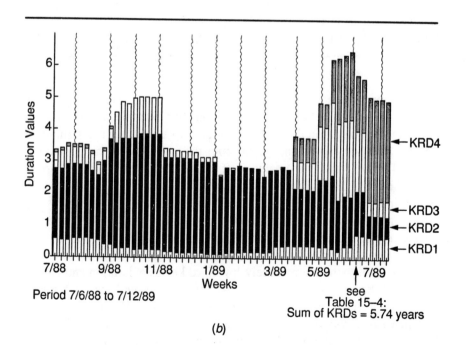

Period 7/6/88 to 7/12/89

see
Table 15–4:
Sum of KRDs = 5.74 years

(b)

bar in Figure 15–5*b*, is the portfolio's effective duration at the beginning of that week.

Since the composition and characteristics of an index are designed to be constant, the key rate durations of the index are somewhat constant. For instance, during May 1989, the index's KRDs had negligible changes. The first key rate duration is 0.59, the second 1.89, the third 1.65, and the fourth 0.44. That is to say, for this Treasury index, for example, if the 25-year rate drops 10 basis points, the index would realize 4.4 basis points of return above the risk-free return. These key rate durations (KRD) represent the sensitivity of the portfolio value to each key rate change.

The following chart shows the key rate duration values for the investment portfolio on May 10 and May 17, 1989 and the KRDs of the index.

Region	0–2 years KRD1	2–7 years KRD2	7–20 years KRD3	20–30 years KRD4	Effective
5/10/89	0.388	2.059	1.640	0.738	4.83
5/17/89	0.330	2.284	2.290	1.320	6.22
Treasury index	0.590	1.890	1.650	0.440	4.57

Each factor can be interpreted directly as a leverage factor on a basis point shift in the yield curve in that region. For example, in the week of 5/10, and 10 bp shift in the 7–20-year region would induce approximately 16 (10 × 1.640) bp of change on both the index's and the portfolio's value. The next week, the same shift in that region of the curve would induce about a 23 bp change in the portfolio's return and only about 16 on the index's.

Comparing the trends of the key rates, in Figure 15–5*b*, and the positioning of the key rate durations for the first quarter, we see that the portfolio was positioned mainly for the second key rate movements (5-year). Indeed, there is a relatively low third key rate duration and hardly any fourth key rate duration value. Any change in the longer rates will have no significant impact on the portfolio's returns. However, we note that there is a two-week period where the rates dropped significantly. During this same period, the portfolio had an increase in its share in the third key rate duration. This clearly depicts the manager's market timing.

For the next two quarters, the portfolio's effective duration was kept short—in fact, over one year shorter than the index's duration. During this period, the longer end of the yield curve drifted lower while the short end (up to 10 years) rose. The yield curve became inverted. Seemingly, the portfolio manager was correct in shortening the duration in this bearish market. Unfortunately, the portfolio's duration was shortened in such a way that the portfolio was very sensitive to the 5-year key rate but totally insensitive to the longer key rates. Although the portfolio's effective duration was still less than the index's, the portfolio still underperformed the index. This outcome was attributable to the fact that the index always has some third and fourth key rate duration values. Since the longer end of the yield curve went down slightly the index picked up some additional returns relative to the portfolio.

Indeed, from the beginning of November 1988 to the end of March 1989, the 5-year key rate rose 125 basis points. During this period, the 5-year key rate duration of the portfolio remained fairly constant at around 2.5 years. Therefore, in allocating the risk exposure to the 5-year key rate, the portfolio lost approximately 312.5 (125×2.5) bp to this rise of the key rate. In contrast, if the risk exposure had been allocated to the other, longer key rates without necessarily changing the effective duration (i.e., creating a barbell position, as evidenced by the portfolio composition as of the end of June 1989), the portfolio would not have suffered the loss. This analysis shows the important distinction between key rate durations and effective duration as risk measures. This analysis also explains why the portfolio underperformed the index. The index is more sensitive to the longer key rates and less sensitive to the 5-year rate, even though the index has a slightly higher effective duration. A manager who knew only that his or her effective duration was shorter than the index's would have a difficult time ascertaining why the portfolio under performed.

The last quarter saw the protracted bond market rally. Here the portfolio manager increased the portfolio's effective duration by allocating funds to longer maturity issues that were sensitive to the long end of the yield. This portfolio transformation is depicted by the increase in the third and fourth key rate durations. In the last few weeks, most of the rate bets were in first and fourth key rates, with an insignificant number in the second and third sections of the yield curve This resulted in a barbell position. The increase in the fourth key rate duration clearly contributed to the portfolio's high return relative to the index, as shown in Figure 15–1, for the period beginning in May 1989. In fact, as shown in Figure 15–5b, the portfolio's effective duration was one year higher than the index's. However, the effectiveness of the barbell strategy was less apparent. With a barbell strategy, in principle, as rates fall the portfolio's duration will increase. As the rates fall further, the portfolio will naturally realize higher returns because of higher, effective duration. However, in this case, the portfolio manager was actively shortening the effective duration and thus mitigating the convexity effect of the barbell portfolio position. Indeed, the drop of the 5-year rate by more than 50 bp during the month of June added little to the portfolio's return as the 5-year key rate duration (KRD2) is only half a year.

From the results, we can clearly conclude that the portfolio manager actively pursued market timing. Although the general strategy was to keep the portfolio insensitive to the change in long rates, the portfolio manager was willing to invest aggressively in bonds sensitive to the long rates in the last quarter, where a bull market was correctly anticipated.

We will now depict the type of report that can be constructed. The sample period is the week 4/10/89 to 4/17/89. Figure 15–6 is a comparison of the distribution of maturities between the index and the portfolio on 4/10/89. Table 15–5 constrasts each source of observed return between the index and the portfolio. Finally, Figure 15–7 is a graphical depiction of the information contained in Table 15–5. The observed return for the week is denoted by the triangular marks.

By evaluating the portfolio returns on a weekly basis, we can gain much insight into the performance of a portfolio. With the precision of a return attribution process utilizing Factorization, we do not have to rely on such notations as "on average, the portfolio beats the index." Instead, we can say "the portfolio can time the market within two weeks in five out of seven major key rate moves."

SUMMARY

The purpose of this chapter was to provide an overview of Factorization and its application in the return attribution system. We have shown how this methodology provides comprehensive information, surpassing that available solely from the standard return attribution approach. We used

TABLE 15–5
Return Attribution: Treasury Index versus Portfolio

		Four Key Rate Returns								
Observed Return	Risk Free	KEY 1 (3mo:2yr)	KEY 2 (2+:7)	KEY 3 (7+:20)	KEY 4 (20+:30)	Contingent Factors[a]	Convexity	Delta R/C	Residual	% Explained
Treasury Index										
0.529	0.161	0.084	0.202	0.081	0.013	0.002	0.001	−0.019	.003	99.4%
Institution's Portfolio										
0.658	0.161	0.039	0.234	0.167	0.033	0.000	0.001	0.008	.017	97.7%

[a] Volatility and time decay

FIGURE 15–6
Observed Returns: Treasury Index versus Portfolio

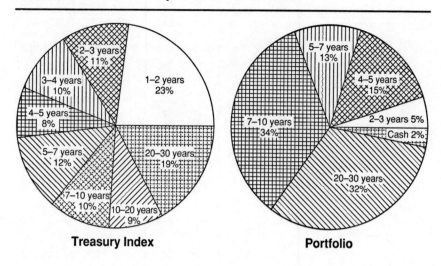

Treasury Index   **Portfolio**

FIGURE 15–7
Distribution of Maturities: Treasury Index versus Portfolio

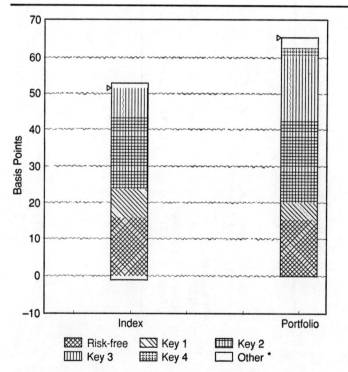

*Other is the sum of contingent, convex, delta rich/cheap, and residual

346

an empirical study conducted on an ongoing portfolio to illustrate some of the capabilities of this new technique.

Of course, portfolio managers vary in purposes and management styles. Therefore, the example was not intended to present a procedure for analyzing a portfolio's performance. Instead it is used simply to illustrate how this type of return attribution approach may be used for some cases.

More appropriately this return attribution procedure can be used as a tool for providing timely feedback on the effectiveness of the portfolio strategies in active or structured management. Effectiveness of a barbell position, of increasing the duration on each key rate, and of sector rotation, to name a few, can all be analyzed (ex-ante) by Factorization and then monitored (ex-post) by return attribution. Such combined use of factorization and return attribution analysis cannot be achieved by the traditional return attribution approaches.

CHAPTER 16

SUMMARY

In the past decade, perhaps one of the most important developments in the fixed-income market has been the widespread use of bond-pricing models. Most students of finance have studied the Black-Scholes option model. To these students, the Black-Scholes model is important because the mathematical formulation works. Looking back over a decade, however, the most important contributions of the model to the financial markets go beyond the fact that the model "works." To research, the Black-Scholes model introduced the concept of relative pricing. To the financial markets, it has legitimized modeling as a trading and investment tool; it has raised the quantification approach to trading and investment to a higher level.

This book has presented the description of the models and their applications. The basic models are relative pricing models in that securities are priced relative to each other in an arbitrage-free fashion, in much the same spirit as that of the Black-Scholes model. These models also have many applications to investments, sales, and trading. The models seemingly are very naturally developed, and the applications follow equally naturally. We often forget the long road that we have taken to come this far; these models and their applications have taken much time to evolve to this stage. Many ideas have been tried, and all the surviving ideas tend to build on top of others. It is only appropriate in this summary chapter to review historically how different ideas have built upon each other and how bond analytics have become popularized.

The focal point of the book is the concept of Factorization. Several lines of thought converge on this concept. They are the spot curve estimation technique, the pricing modeling of option-embedded bonds, specification of the credit premium, and the duration measures. We will summarize these lines of thought in this chapter and show how they are used for Factorization. Meanwhile, Factorization as a tool finds application in a number of areas of portfolio management. For active management, Factorization can be used for identifying the value or relative returns of the bonds. Indeed, Factorization provides a systematic approach to horizon analysis. For structured management, Factorization can implement precise portfolio strategies such as enhanced indexation, immunization, or sector rotation. Finally, Factorization can be used for performance attribution, providing details of the performance both for the track record and for immediate feedback to any portfolio strategies.

Figure 16–1 depicts the flow from theories to applications. Theories are concerned with how bonds should be priced and how bond returns should be analyzed. These theories are then combined together in Factorization of bond or portfolio returns. Such Factorization can then find many applications. Now we will describe this flow of theories to applications in more detail.

THEORIES

This book describe four basic parts of theory. Surely, there are other major parts that this book has not covered. In particular, we have not dealt with the path-dependent models of mortgage-backed securities, or with any detailed modeling of high-yield bonds (junk bonds), or macroeconomic determinants of the spot yield curve. Such a complete discussion would be most worthwhile, but is beyond the scope of this book. Nevertheless, the four basic parts should provide us a useful overview of the interrelationships of theory and application.

The Spot Yield Curve

The book begins with bond arithmetics. Central to bond arithmetics are the concepts of yield and the time value of money. We have argued that the time value of money at any instant of time should be estimated from the Treasury securities prices. Such estimated time value of money, expressed in yields, is the spot curve.

Much research has been concerned with estimating the spot curve. McCulloch was first to propose the methodology for estimating the spot curve using cubic spline estimation. Since then many researchers have proposed various statistical methodologies, including the use of

FIGURE 16–1
The Flow of Theories to Applications

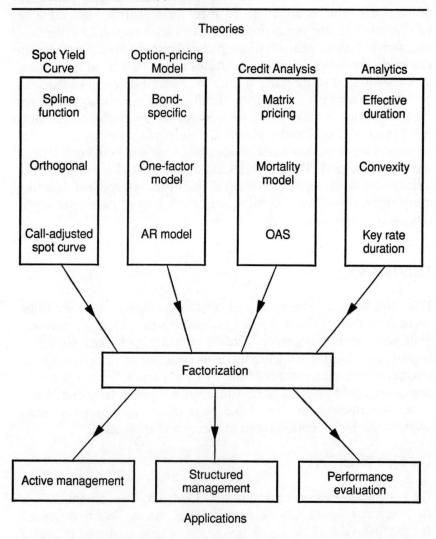

Theories

Spot Yield Curve	Option-pricing Model	Credit Analysis	Analytics
Spline function	Bond-specific	Matrix pricing	Effective duration
Orthogonal	One-factor model	Mortality model	Convexity
Call-adjusted spot curve	AR model	OAS	Key rate duration

Factorization

Active management	Structured management	Performance evaluation

Applications

exponential splines and other polynomial functions. However, research results suggest that these extensions have limited success. The success of these methodologies is constrained by two problems: multicollinearity of the estimation procedures and the pricing of the callable Treasury bonds.

Schaefer recognized the severity of the problem of multicollinearity in these estimation procedures. When the procedure suffers a serious multicollinearity problem, the estimated results are very sensitive to any error in the observations. That is, if some of the observed bond prices are incorrect, the estimated spot curve may be grossly misspecified. This problem is particularly important in estimating the spot curve because there are many callable Treasury bonds with similar maturities. The theoretical pricing of these bonds is more complicated, often resulting in errors. These errors, compounded with the multicollinearity problem, result in a serious misspecification of the spot curve. Alternative estimation procedure can mitigate such problems; Schaefer proposed using orthogonal polynomials in the estimation.

Finally, callable Treasury bonds can be priced by combining the orthogonal polynomial estimation procedure with the binomial lattice model for pricing the embedded options. The resulting iterative procedure was described in Chapter 9.

We have shown the importance of an accurate estimation of the spot curve. The spot curve, a benchmark for the time value of money, provides the foundation for pricing not only straight, default-free bonds, but also other fixed-income securities. The call-adjusted estimated spot curve provides the capability to price securities that have embedded options and/or are subject to default risk. The discussion in the book progresses from an explanation of the spot curve to the development of a bond option-pricing model.

Option-pricing Model

In pricing option-embedded bonds, option models are used. The procedure of discounting a cash flow using a spot curve or a yield curve adjusted from the spot curve is no longer applicable. In Chapter 11, we discussed how various option models have been proposed to extend the Black-Scholes model. These models adjust for the differences between stock options and bond options. We have discussed how the Schaefer and Schwartz model can adjust for the time-dependent variance of a bond option.

Then there are bond models that are formulated assuming a stochastic process for the interest rates rather than the bond price. Models using only the short rate movement are used to price a variety of option-embedded bonds. Such models can be extended to a two-factor model, whereby both the short rate and the long rate movements are modeled by stochastic processes.

Binomial lattice, or the AR model, adds another extension. This approach takes the spot curve as given and generates the movement of the yield curve. This way, the bond options are priced relative to the observed spot curve, and at the same time arbitrage-free conditions are ensured. There are many extensions of this model. Research has extended this framework to continuous time modeling. Another direction of research has extended the model to multifactors.

Credit Analysis

The binomial lattice model incorporates the pricing of options to the spot yield curve. Hence, we can model option-embedded bonds. However, we still need to take the credit risk into account.

Perhaps the most influential paper in this area of the yield spread analysis is Lawrence Fisher's paper on the corporate bond-pricing model. This paper established the foundation for the matrix-pricing approach to a fixed-income pricing model. This approach seeks to specify the determinants of the yield spread. The explanatory factors are mostly related to the creditworthiness of the bonds, and they are empirically estimated, not derived from pricing models.

Altman introduced the mortality model to price junk bonds. Chapter 12 shows how mortality tables of corporate bonds can be estimated empirically. With the estimate of the expected life of a bond, we can calculate the expected return of the bond. This way, we have some comparison of the fair value of a bond to the traded price. In other words, Altman's approach directly models the cost of the expected bond default to the investors and then decides whether the bond is fairly priced. In contrast, matrix pricing is simply a statistical approach for estimating the yield spread.

However, we must integrate the embedded-option models to the mortality model. The link is the specification of the option-adjusted spread (OAS). Chapter 12 shows that the OAS can be estimated for a bellwether portfolio of corporate bonds that have the same rating. OAS represents the excess return to compensate for a certain level of the credit risk. By comparing the mortality rate of a bond in a specific bond rating group to the OAS, we can gain insight into the value of the bond relative to the Treasury market, as represented by the spot curve. Empirical results of such comparisons are provided in Chapter 12.

When compared with the Black-Scholes model, bond pricing models are much more complicated. Yet in many ways their applications are similar. The Black-Scholes model can determine the hedge ratio, gamma, and other analytics; by the same token, bond models are used to derive many important risk measures and other analytics of bonds.

Analytics

The progress made in developing models led to a new development of bond analytics. Models were used as tools to analyze the bond return performance.

For example, people have for years used Macaulay duration as a measure of interest rate risk exposure of a bond. This measure, using the average life of a bond as a measure of interest rate risk exposure, is inadequate. Such is the case particularly for option-embedded bonds. Hence, effective duration was introduced. Chapter 6 discusses the merits of this measure in detail. Briefly, it is a measure of the price sensitivity to the change of interest rates. For option-embedded bonds, there is no simple specification of the effective duration of a bond. More generally, a bond model is used to calculate the duration measure.

Effective duration as a risk measure is confined to a small parallel shift of the yield curve. But this basic idea can be generalized to other, nonparallel shifts of the yield curve. One can clearly define other duration measures that deal with the price sensitivity of the bond to types of shifts of the spot curve other than the small parallel yield curve.

To measure the bond return performance for a larger parallel shift of the yield curve, we introduced the convexity measure. Convexity is discussed in Chapter 7. We showed how convexity is related to the option value embedded in bonds.

But the yield curve can shift in a parallel way or a nonparallel way. In the case when we cannot specify ahead of time what type of shifts the spot curve will make, then the duration measures may not be adequate. We need some new duration measures that can specify the price sensitivities to several types of shifts. One line of research to deal with this problem is the development of key rate durations.

The methodology of the key rate duration is borrowed from the portfolio theory in equity. Arbitrage pricing theory (APT) is a stock return model that stipulates that a stock return is specified by a finite number of factors. These factors are estimated from the historical returns of the bonds. This is a statistical approach. In a way, it is similar to the matrix pricing methodology. However, in factor models we are concerned only with historical returns. Also, unlike the matrix pricing model, information on a sample of bonds over a period of time is used.

In contrast with this statistical approach, this book introduces key rate durations in Chapter 15. Key rate durations measure the price sensitivity of the bond to each key rate change. This way the yield curve can change its shape in many ways, and the risk exposure of the bond can still be properly measured. Moreover, the key rate durations are derived from the bond-pricing models, not empirically estimated.

Factorization

Key rate durations have specified at least in principle most of the interest rate risk exposure of a bond, but they do not fully specify all the relevant factors that determine the bond return. Factorization seeks to determine all the factors that affect a bond return, whether the bond be a simple straight bond or an option-embedded bond with credit risk.

Factorization is presented along with key rate durations in Chapter 15. This procedure of decomposing the bond return can be viewed as a synthesis of research in the estimation of the spot curve, the use of the AR model, credit analysis, and bond analytics. The precision of the decomposition of a bond return crucially depends on the robustness of the model and the accurate representation of the interest rate risk on bonds by the key rate durations.

Bond models, via Factorization, show how each market factor affects the bond returns. When we can identify precisely the factors affecting a bond return or a portfolio return, we can implement a variety of fixed-income investment strategies. In sum, Factorization can be viewed as the focal point. Theories are melded under the Factorization process and then applied in managing various forms of risk (such as interest rate, credit, or volatility risks). At the same time, Factorization finds many applications.

APPLICATIONS

Chapter 14 presented many bond strategies. These strategies can be broadly classified as following either active management or structured management. Factorization is an important tool for both categories. In active management, Factorization can identify the bonds that provide high returns given the anticipated market scenarios. Indeed, Factorization is a systematic approach to the horizon analysis of bond valuation in active management. In structured management, where controlling and measuring risk exposures are central, Factorization also provides the necessary information to develop strategies.

This book also demonstrates how Factorization can be used for performance evaluation. Effectiveness of a bond strategy or of a portfolio manager's market-timing skill can be analyzed in detail. The process involves implementing a return attribution approach that uses Factorization. The application is also discussed in Chapter 15.

The development of bond-pricing models is rather recent. Indeed, most of the models that this book has described were developed in the past four years. As a result, the use of models for portfolio management is in its infancy. In the volatile bond market of today, portfolio management can seek higher returns by market timing and valuation. Portfolio management can also seek customized risk and return profiles that address the needs of the sponsors. No doubt future research will develop bond-pricing models with broader and deeper applications in portfolio management.

APPENDIX A

EARLY EXERCISE OF
AN OPTION

The possibility of exercising an option early can be shown by constructing the option-value diagrams for both call and put options (see Figure A–1). Let us first consider the put option.

First, consider the European put option. If the European put option is deep in the money, that means the underlying stock has little value. Therefore, holding the option is almost equivalent to realizing the exercise price on the expiration date. For this reason, the option should be worth the present value of the exercise price. Indeed, the option value should approach the line that represents the present value of the exercise price, net the stock price, as the stock price approaches zero.

Now we ask if it is possible to price the American put option as if it were a European option. The answer is no. This is because if it were priced like a European option, the option value would be below the intrinsic value when the option is sufficiently deep in the money. We have shown that in such a case, there is an arbitrage opportunity. Indeed, the option price must lie above the intrinsic-value line (*XB* in Figure A–1*b*). If the American option price exceeds the European option price, at some point, it would be optimal to exercise the option early.

Similar arguments can be extended to options on futures. The analysis can show that there are times when it is optimal to early exercise an American option on futures. The American option can be either a call or a put option.

First consider a European call option on futures. Once again, suppose the option is very much in the money. That is, the option is very

FIGURE A–1
Option-Value Diagrams: (*a*) Call Option; (*b*) Put Option

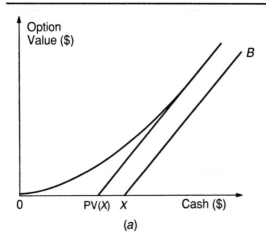

(a)

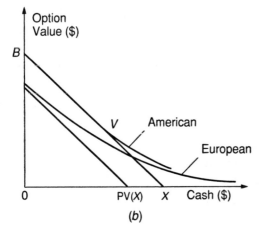

(b)

likely to be exercised on the expiration date. In this case, holding to option is almost guaranteed a return of $(F - X)$ (the futures price net the exercise price) on the expiration date. For this reason, the option is priced as the present value of this return. Line XA in Figure A–2*a* depicts the present value of $(F - X)$ as the futures price F increases. This analysis shows that the value of a European call option on futures must be asymptotic to line XA as the futures price increases.

FIGURE A–2
Early Exercise of American versus European Futures Options: (a) Call; (b) Put

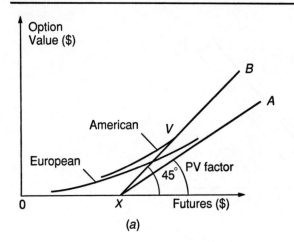

(a)

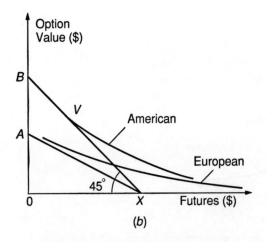

(b)

Now consider the American call option on futures. For an American call option, the value cannot fall below the formula price line *XB*; otherwise, an early exercise would lead to arbitrage opportunity. Therefore, as the option becomes more in the money as the futures price rises, the American call option value must rise above the European call option price. At some point, the option value equals the formula price and at this point (*V* in Figure A–2a) optimal early exercise of the option occurs.

An analogous argument applies to the put option on futures. Consider a European put option on futures. If the futures price falls to a negligible level, the put option offers a return of the exercise price net the futures price on the expiration date. For this reason, the option value is the present value of this payoff. Line *XA* in Figure A–2*b* depicts the value of the present value of the exercise price net the futures price as the futures price falls. Once again, the European put option value must asymptotically approach line *XA* as the futures price falls. For the American put option case, the option price cannot fall below the formula price, so if the option is sufficiently in the money, optimal early exercise of the option would take place.

FURTHER READING

Altman, Edward I. "Measuring Corporate Bond Mortality and Performance." Salomon Brothers, June 1988.

Altman, Edward I., and Scott A. Nammacher. "The Default Rate Experience on High Yield Corporate Debt." Morgan Stanley, March 1985.

Ball, C. B., and W. N. Torous. "Bond Price Dynamics and Options." *Journal of Financial and Quantitative Analysis*, Vol. 18 (1983), pp. 517–531.

Bierwag, G. O. "Immunization, Duration, and the Term Structure of Interest Rates." *Journal of Financial and Quantitative Analysis*, Vol. 12 (1977), pp. 725–741.

Bierwag, G. O., G. C. Kaufman, and C. Khang. "Duration and Bond Portfolio Analysis: An Overview." *Jouranl of Financial and Quantitative Analysis*, Vol. 13 (1978), pp. 671–685.

Black, Fischer, Emanuel Derman, and William Toy. "A One-Factor Model of Interest Rates and Its Application to Treasury Bond Options." Goldman, Sachs, June 1988.

Black, F., and M. Scholes. "The Pricing of Options and Corporate Labilities." *Journal of Political Economy*, Vol. 81 (1973), pp. 637–654.

Bookstaber, R., D. P. Jacob, and J. A. Langsam. "Pitfalls in Debt Option Models." Morgan Stanley, February 1986.

Boyce, William M., Webster Hughes, Peter S. A. Niculescu, and Michael Waldman. "The Implied Volatility of Fixed-Income Markets." Salomon Brothers Research Department, January 1988.

Boyce, W., M. Koenigsberg, A. H. Taterossian, and M. H. Yampol. "Effective Duration of Callable Bonds: The Salomon Brothers Term Structure–Based Option Pricing Model." Salomon Brothers Research Department, April 1987.

Brennan, M. J., and E. S. Schwartz. "Alternative Methods for Valuing Debt Options." *Finance*, Vol. 4 (1983), pp. 119–137.

Brennan, M. J., and E. S. Schwartz. "A Continuous-Time Approach to the Pricing of Bonds." *Journal of Banking and Finance*, Vol. 3 (July 1979), pp. 135–155.

Carleton, W. T., and I. A. Cooper. "Estimation and Uses of the Term Structure of Interest Rates." *Journal of Finance*, Vol. 31 (1976), pp. 1067–1083.

Carverhill, Andrew. "The Ho and Lee Term Structure Theory: A Continuous Time Version." Financial Options research Centre, University of Warwick, May 1988.

Chambers, D. R., W. T. Carleton, and D. Waldman. "A New Approach to Estimation of the Term Structure of Interest Rates." *Journal of Financial and Quantitative Analysis*, Vol. 19 (1984), pp. 233–252.

Courtadon, George. "The Pricing of Options on Default-Free Bonds." *Journal of Financial and Quantitative Analysis*, Vol. 17 (March 1982), pp. 75–100.

Cox, J. C., J. E. Ingersoll, and S. A. Ross. "A Theory of the Term Structure of Interest Rates." *Econometrica*, Vol. 53 (1985), pp. 385–407.

Diller, S. "Parametric Analysis of Fixed Income Securities." Goldman, Sachs, June 1984.

Dothan, L. U. "On the Term Structure of Interest Rates." *Journal of Financial Economics*, Vol. 6 (March 1978), pp. 59–69.

Dyer, L. J., and D. P. Jacob. "A Practitioner's Guide to Fixed Income Options Models." Morgan Stanley, August 1988.

Fisher, Irving. *The Theory of Interest*. New York: MacMillan, 1930.

Fisher, Lawrence. "Determinants of Risk Premiums on Corporate Bonds." *Journal of Political Economy*, Vol. 67 (June 1959), pp. 217–237.

Fisher, L., and R. L. Weil. "Coping with the Risk of Interest Rate Fluctuations: Returns to Bondholders from Naive and Optimal Strategies." *Journal of Business*, Vol. 44 (1971), pp. 408–431.

Fixed Income Group. "Application of Duration and Convexity to the Analysis of Callable Bonds." Kidder, Peabody, 1987.

Fons, Jerome S. "The Default Premium and corporate Bond Experience." *Journal of Finance*, Vol. 43 (March 1987), pp. 81–97.

Gadkavia, V., and C. Thum. "A Note on Duration and Volatility in International Fixed Income Markets." Salomon Brothers, April 1988.

Gultekin, B., and R. Rogalski. "Alternative Duration Specifications and the Measurement of Basis Risk: Empirical Tests. *Journal of Business*, Vo. 57 (April 1984), pp. 241–264.

Heath, D., R. Jarrow, and A. Morton. "Bond Pricing and the Term Structure of Interest Rates: A New Methodology." Unpublished manuscript, Cornell University, 1988.

Ho, T. S., and S. B. Lee. "Term Structure Movements and Pricing Interest Rate Contingent Claims." *Journal of Finance*, Vol. 42 (1986), pp. 1129–1142.

Ingersoll J. E. Jr., J. Skelton, and R. L. Weil. "Duration—40 Years Later." *Journal of Financial and Quantitative Analysis*, Vol. 13 (1978), pp. 627–650.

Jacob, D. P., G. Lord, and J. Tilley. "Price, Duration, and Convexity of a Stream of Interest-Sensitive Cash Flows." Morgan Stanley, April 1986.

Jacob, D. P., and A. L. Toevs. "An Analysis of the New Valuation, Duration and Convexity Models for Mortgage-Backed Securities." Morgan Stanley, January 1987.

Jamshidian, Farshid. "Closed-Form Solution for American Options on Coupon Bonds in the General Gaussian Interest Rate Model." Merrill Lynch Capital Markets, March 1989.

Jamshidian, Farshid. "The Continuous-Time Limit of the Ho-Lee Model." Technical notes, Merrill Lynch Capital Markets, 1987.

Khang, C. "Bond Immunization When Short-Term Interest Rates Fluctuate More Than Long-Term Rates." *Journal of Financial and Quantitative Analysis*, Vol. 14 (1979), pp. 1085–1090.

Kopprasch, R. O. "Understanding Duration and Volatility." Salomon Brothers, September 1985.

Latainer, Gary D., and David P. Jacob. "Modern Techniques for Analyzing Value and Performance of Callable Bonds." Morgan Stanley, October 1985.

Litterman, R., and T. Iben. "Corporation Bond Valuation and the Term Structure of Credit Spread." Goldman, Sachs, November 1988.

Litterman, Robert, and José Scheinkman. "Common Factors Affecting Bond Returns." Goldman, Sachs Financial Strategies Group, September 1988.

Litterman, Robert, José Scheinkman, and Laurence Weiss. "Volatility and the Yield Curve." Goldman, Sachs, August 1988.

Macaulay, Frederick R. *Some Theoretical Problems Suggested by the Movements of Interest Rates, Bond Yields and Stock Prices in the United States since 1856.* New York: Natural Bureau of Economic Research, 1938.

McCulloch, J. H. "The Tax Adjusted Yield Curve." *Journal of Finance*, Vol. 30 (June 1975), pp. 811–829.

McCulloch, J. H. "Measuring the Term Structure of Interest Rates." *Journal of Business*, Vol. 44 (January 1971), pp. 19–31.

Queen, Maggie, and Richard Roll. "Firm Mortality: Using Market Indicators to Predict Survival." *Financial Analysts Journal* (May–June 1987), pp. 9–26.

Roll, R. "Managing Risk in Thrift Institutions: Beyond the Duration Gap." Working Paper 913–88, John B. Anderson Graduate School of Management, UCLA, October 1987.

Rudd, A. "Duration, Convexity, and Multiple-Factor Models." *Investment Management Review*, September/October 1988, pp. 58–64.

Schaefer, S. M. "On Measuring the Term Structure of Interest Rates." Discussion paper no. IFA-2-74, London Business School Institute of Finance and Accounting, 1973.

Schaefer, Stephen, and Eduardo Schwartz. "Time-Dependent Variance and the Pricing of Bond Options." University of British Columbia Working Paper, 1986.

Shea, G. "Interest Rate Term Structure Estimation with Exponential Splines: A Note." *Journal of Finance*, Vol. 40 (1985), pp. 319–325.

Steeley, James. "Estimating the Gilt-Edged Term Structure: Basis Splines and Confidence Intervals." Financial Options Research Centre, University of Warwick, January 1989.

Toevs, Alden L., and Lawrence Dyer. "The Term Structure of Interest Rates and Its Use in Asset and Liability Management." Morgan Stanley, October 1986.

Vasicek, O. A. "An Equilibrium Characterization of the Term Structure." *Jouranl of Financial Economics*, Vol. 5 (November 1977), pp. 177–188.

Vasicek, O. A., and H. G. Fong. "Term Structure Modeling Using Exponential Spliens." *Jouranl of Finance*, Vol. 37 (1982), pp. 339–356.

INDEX